Understanding the market

an introduction to microeconomics

third edition

Andrew Dunnett

FINANCIAL TIMES

Prentice Hall

An imprint of **Pearson Education**

Harlow, England · London · New York · Reading, Massachusetts · San Francisco
Toronto · Don Mills, Ontario · Sydney · Tokyo · Singapore · Hong Kong · Seoul
Taipei · Cape Town · Madrid · Mexico City · Amsterdam · Munich · Paris · Milan

Pearson Education Limited
Edinburgh Gate
Harlow
Essex CM20 2JE
England

and Associated Companies throughout the world

Visit us on the World Wide Web at:
http://www.pearsoneduc.com

First edition published 1987
Second edition published 1992
Third edition published 1998

ISBN 0 582 32506 4

British Library Cataloguing-in-Publication Data

A catalogue record for this book is available from the British
Library

Library of Congress Cataloging-in-Publication Data

10 9 8 7 6 5 4
06 05 04 03 02

Set by 42 in 10/12pt Baskerville

Produced by Pearson Education Asia Pte Ltd
Printed in Singapore (COS)

Contents

CHAPTER 8
Objectives of the firm 92

CHAPTER 9
Behaviour in oligopolistic markets 101

CHAPTER 10
Trade 128

CHAPTER 11
Multinationals 145

Textbooks don't have prefaces any more. They have *vision statements*. Though this may sound like a prescription from the optician, it is in fact an answer to the question 'Why did I write this book?' The preface to the first edition expressed the answer thus:

> The approach of this book reflects the belief that the teaching of microeconomic theory cannot be divorced from the real world to which that theory can and should be applied. It is thus a mixture of theory and application. Although the microeconomic theory presented is the bare minimum which the student needs to assimilate to appreciate the applied material, it remains an unpalatable fact that this material is often difficult for students to grasp. In writing this book there were two possible strategies I could have adopted. Either I could 'fudge' the issues and spare the reader the mental effort involved in trying to fathom out exactly what was meant by long-run equilibrium, a Pareto optimal allocation of resources, and so on. Or I could do it 'properly' with a degree of rigour appropriate to the discipline of economics, sweetening the bitter pill where possible and rewarding the reader with applied material when the necessary theory had been covered. I took the second option. Notwithstanding this, however, the balance between theory and application in this book is heavily biased towards application, reflecting, I believe, the needs of students and teachers alike.
>
> (Extract from preface to the first edition)

Ten years later, with this third edition, the vision remains essentially the same, though I would hope to express it in a rather less pompous fashion.

Over the last decade the 'massification' of higher education has meant that the task of the teacher of economics has become even more difficult. Many of the students embarking on courses in introductory economics are apprehensive of what they rightly perceive to be the analytical rigour that is required. They need to be persuaded that economics is a discipline that can be mastered. Other reluctant students see economics as an alien world of theory, remote from their experience. They need to be cajoled into accepting that economics is relevant to them. And both groups need to be convinced that the insights that the discipline of economics provides will help them make sense of the world in which they live.

In this new edition there are a large number of detailed but important changes which has meant that inevitably the third edition is slightly longer than that which it replaces. Almost every chapter has a significant amount of new applied material and in some chapters I have re-written the theoretical sections with the aim of increasing clarity and understanding. There is a new chapter on the environment. Chapter 9 on behaviour in oligopolistic markets has been shortened (*sic*) and is much better focused with new case study material.

There are also a number of new devices which are designed to make the book more accessible to the reader – to make it more 'user-friendly'. Key terms are highlighted and repeated at the end of each chapter with page references; there are chapter previews and chapter summaries; and the review questions at the end of each chapter have been much extended and now contain comprehensive answers at the end of the book.

Introduction

Preview

This short introductory chapter gives an overview of the subject matter of microeconomics. It introduces certain key terms and concepts essential for a broad appreciation of the issues. Subsequent chapters in the book develop these ideas in greater detail.

1.1 What economics is about

Definitions are for dictionaries (or, more correctly, dictionaries are for definitions) but some definitions are so abstract and so conceptual that to the uninitiated reader they convey very little meaning. Economics as a discipline covers a broad spectrum of enquiry and hence its subject matter can only be defined in very broad terms. Using such broad terms, we could say that *economics is about making decisions*. The **economic problem** or **choice problem** consists, in its widest sense, of two elements. First, there must be a scarcity of resources – money, labour, time, land and so on. Secondly, because of the scarcity of resources, choices have to be made about how they are used. Defined in this way, of course, the scope of economics appears vast but this is no accident as the scope of economics *is* vast – it is the 'science of choice' and as such its subject matter covers almost every aspect of human activity.

The purpose of this present work is somewhat more modest. It concerns itself with how decisions are made but confines itself to a narrower range of decisions – they are the economic decisions taken by three principal agents, the producer, the consumer and the state. Taken together these decisions shape the sort of society in which we live. The producer decides what will be produced, in what quantities and by what methods, responding to a lesser or greater degree to the wishes of consumers on these same issues. The extent to which the consumer is sovereign, in the sense that ultimately producers merely respond to his or her wishes, will be an important theme in this book. The

1

second key theme concerns the role of the state, the third member of the triumvirate. The state acts as both producer and consumer but, in addition, it determines the legal and institutional framework within which producers interact with other producers and with consumers. Thus, the role of the state is crucial in determining ultimately how society's resources shall be allocated.

Economics is conventionally divided into **macroeconomics** and **microeconomics**. Microeconomics concerns itself with individual decisions – the individual firm, the individual consumer and individual prices. In contrast, in macroeconomics the subject of enquiry is the economy as a whole – thus problems of inflation, unemployment, the balance of payments and economic growth are studied. The reader will appreciate, however, that the study of macroeconomics is predicated upon a particular analysis of how the microeconomy works. This book provides such an analysis.

1.2 Some key terms

One of the difficulties experienced by the student of economics is that certain key terms used by the economist have a meaning and significance peculiar to economics itself and different from the everyday usage of the terms. In this section we introduce some of these key terms while at the same time sketching out how these concepts relate to the wider whole. The aim is to provide the reader with some sort of perspective – a large-scale map of the landscape of this book.

The word **market** refers to the totality of buyers and sellers (both actual and potential) of a particular **good** or commodity or service. Thus, for example, one can talk about the market for shoes, the housing market, the market for foreign exchange and the market for professional footballers. A few markets have a physical existence (for example, before deregulation the Stock Exchange was a place where buyers and sellers came together to trade shares) but most markets do not. When talking about a particular market it should be delineated with care. For example, in air travel the market for scheduled services is distinct from the market for inclusive package tours.

In any market there are those who wish to sell and those who wish to buy. The buyers constitute the **demand** side of the market, the sellers the **supply** side. The demand for shoes therefore means the total number of pairs of shoes people would be prepared to buy at a given price. Note that one can talk about an individual's demand for shoes (normally a few pairs per year) or the market demand for shoes (several million pairs per year in Britain). The concept of demand implies both willingness and ability to pay for a particular good – thus it is different from **need**. A poor man may need a new pair of shoes but unless he has the money to pay for them there will be no demand in the market.

The supply of shoes similarly implies willingness to sell at a particular price. Note that both demand and supply are dependent upon price. The price is the money or other consideration given when goods or services are exchanged. Note also that **price** rather than **value** is used since price is an objective datum whereas value is a subjective assessment of intrinsic worth. (In this respect we are in a world of cynics. Oscar Wilde, remember, defined a cynic as a man who knows the price of everything and the value of nothing.)

The prices paid by buyers and received by sellers can be considered to be **market prices**, that is, determined in some way by the **market forces** of demand and supply. In some situations, however, the price at which a particular good or service is sold is more or less set by the seller, for example, postal charges are set by the Post Office. In such a case, where there is little interaction between demand and supply – or in other words where market forces are very weak – it is more realistic to talk about **administered prices**, rather than market prices.

The former Soviet Union and its satellites were organised as **command economies**. In this system of **central planning** most prices were in fact administered prices, set by the state. The term **mixed economy** refers to an economy such as that of the UK, where some productive decisions are taken centrally by the state (for example, in the sphere of the National Health Service and defence) while other productive decisions are left to the market. Thus, some prices are administered while others are 'market prices'. It is important to note, however, that, even where there is no state intervention, many prices can be thought of as being administered rather than determined by market forces. This is because the supply side of the market is often dominated by a few large firms. Such firms set (or administer) prices. These prices can be considered as market prices only in the very general sense that demand conditions will ultimately determine whether the prices set are sustainable.

Markets that are dominated by a few large firms are known as **oligopolies** or oligopolistic markets. In some cases one firm, called a **monopoly**, supplies the whole market for a particular good or service. For example, Thames Water is a monopoly supplier of water and sewerage services to consumers in London. Markets can in fact be classified according to the **degree of concentration** that they exhibit on the supply side. Markets which are **highly concentrated** on the supply side (monopoly, oligopoly) will typically exhibit different behaviour patterns from those low-concentration or **competitive markets** where market forces or the **forces of competition** hold greater sway. That is, the **structure** of a market will determine to some extent the **conduct** and **performance** of the firms within it. A market structure of extremely low concentration where there are many buyers and sellers, no one of whom is large enough to affect the market price, is known as **perfect competition**. Such market structures are seldom encountered in the real world, except perhaps for some agricultural products, and even here prices are often affected by state intervention.

The foregoing definitions are designed merely to prevent the confusion that might otherwise arise when the terms are encountered for the first time. Short definitions cannot hope to convey the full meanings of some of the terms since many of them carry deep philosophical and ideological connotations, the full import of which will become apparent only as the reader proceeds through the book.

Hopefully, this rather perfunctory introduction has served to dispel some of the more common areas of confusion. Economics is no different from any other discipline in that it needs its own jargon for its practitioners to function effectively and to communicate with one another. All too often, however, in economic discourse words are used in a confusing way, as when Humpty Dumpty in *Through the Looking Glass* said: 'When I use a word, I use it to mean what I choose it to mean'. Small wonder Alice was confused.

Key terms

The following key terms have been introduced in this chapter. They are listed here in the order in which they first appear and the page number where they appear is also given. You will find these key terms in **bold** in the text. Each chapter contains a list of key terms and you may find these particularly useful for revision purposes.

2 Market demand

Preview

In this chapter we analyse the factors which influence the demand for a good or service. You are introduced to the concept of elasticity, which is a measure of the extent to which demand responds to price changes. The factors which influence price elasticity are examined. Demand will also be sensitive to changes in income (this is known as income elasticity) and to changes in the price of other goods (which is measured by cross-price elasticity). Economists can obtain empirical estimates of these elasticities by the statistical techniques of econometrics.

2.1 Determinants of demand

This chapter discusses those factors which determine the demand for a good or service. In order to make the discussion somewhat less abstract we shall consider the demand for a particular good, say, lager. The market demand for lager (which we can measure as so many million barrels per month) will be affected by a number of different factors, including:

• The price of lager. Other things being equal, the higher the price of lager, the less will be demanded.

- The price of **substitutes**, such as other beers, spirits, soft drinks, and so on. Other things being equal, if the price of substitutes goes up while the price of lager remains fixed, then there will be a tendency for people to switch to lager. That is, they will consume more lager and less of the higher-priced substitutes.
- The price of **complementary goods**. Again, other things being equal, a rise in the price of a complementary good may affect the demand for lager. A rise in the price of crisps, for example, will tend to reduce the demand for lager. If we usually consume lager with crisps and we buy fewer crisps because the price has risen, this may result in our buying less lager. In practice of course only a very substantial increase in the price of crisps would produce a discernible impact on beer consumption. *A priori*, however, we could argue that if there is any effect at all we could predict the direction of that effect. That is, an increase in the price of crisps will tend to reduce (rather than increase) beer consumption.
- Income. This may affect lager sales but we cannot predict *a priori* the direction of causation. That is, we cannot say for certain whether an increase in income will increase or decrease (or leave unchanged) the consumption of lager. Normally, however, we would expect higher incomes to increase the demand for most goods including lager.
- **Tastes**. This term tends to be used in economics to represent all the other factors which influence demand other than those specifically mentioned above. In the context of our example there are many influences on tastes. Successful advertising, for example, will increase the demand for lager. The weather may also have some effect (more is consumed in hot sunny weather) and changing social habits (for example, the emergence of wine bars, stricter drink/drive laws and increasing home consumption of alcohol) may also have some long-term influence on lager consumption.

We can summarize what we have said so far in symbols as follows:

$$q_d = \mathrm{f}(P, P_s, P_c, Y, T) \qquad\qquad [2.1]$$

This is simply a shorthand way of saying that the quantity of lager demanded (q_d) depends on, or is a **function** (f) of the set of variables within the brackets, namely, the price of a lager (P), the price of substitutes (P_s), the price of complementary goods (P_c), income (Y), and tastes (T). Equation [2.1] can of course be used to analyse the demand for any good or service – the demand for cars, foreign holidays, two-bedroom rented apartments, cinema tickets, double glazing, economics textbooks, and so on. It is a completely general **model** which is universally applicable. All we have to do is to specify what good or service we are considering and equation [2.1] will provide us with a framework (though nothing more) for determining what factors will influence demand. We must be careful, however, to specify exactly what good is being considered. For example, the demand for one particular brand of lager will be different from the demand for lager generally.

For the time being we shall study the relationship between the demand for lager and the price of lager. That is, we shall assume that all the other factors which influence the demand for lager are held constant. This is known as the **ceteris paribus** assumption, and it is a simplifying assumption which we need to make at this stage.

Ceteris paribus ('other things being equal') demand varies inversely with price – that is, when the price goes up the quantity demanded goes down. An example of this is shown in Fig. 2.1. This figure illustrates a hypothetical **demand schedule**, or **demand function**, or **demand curve** (which may often be a straight line). The units of measurement of the axes are for illustrative purposes only. At a price of 100 pence a pint, market demand will be 1 million barrels per month. At a lower price of 70p, the quantity demanded will increase to 2.5 million barrels. Thus, the demand function shows the relationship between the quantity demanded and price. It is important to emphasize, however, that the demand curve such as that shown in Fig. 2.1 is drawn on the assumption that all the other factors influencing demand are held constant (the *ceteris paribus* assumption). If these other factors are not constant (*ceteris non paribus*) then the demand curve will shift. For example, consider the probable effect of an increase in the price of whisky. Since whisky, in some situations, is a substitute for lager, this will cause some people to increase their demand for lager while reducing their demand for whisky. This is illustrated in Fig. 2.2.

The whole curve shifts to the right, indicating that, at each price, more will be demanded than previously. For example, at a price of 100 pence per pint, market demand increases from 1 million to 1.5 million barrels. Note that in Fig. 2.2 demand has increased because the whole curve has shifted. Thus we can see that the phrase 'an increase in demand' can mean one of two things depending on the context. Either:

1   a **movement along a given demand curve** as a result of a drop in price
    or
2   a **shift of the demand curve** to the right as a result of a change in one of the non-price factors.

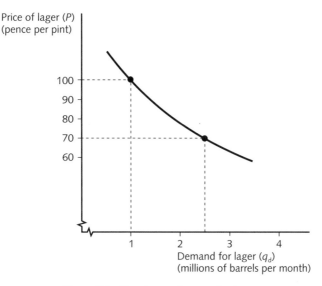

Figure 2.1 The demand curve for lager

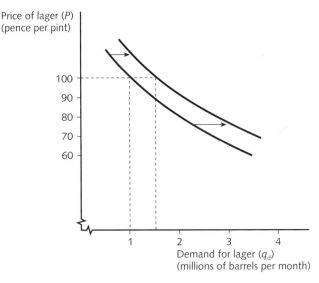

Figure 2.2 A shift in the demand curve

For example, we mentioned earlier the probable effect of an increase in the price of whisky. This, we argued, would cause a drop in the demand for whisky (movement along the demand curve for whisky) which, in turn, would cause an increase in the demand for lager (demand curve for lager shifts to the right). You therefore need to be alert whenever you hear the phrase 'an increase (decrease) in demand'. Either of these two very different meanings may be implied.

Joke
A man went into a shop which sold plumbing accessories and addressed the sales assistant.
'Excuse me', he said. 'Do you happen to stock those little brass keys that you use for getting air out of radiators?'
'Look', said the sales assistant in a rather irritated manner. 'I don't stock them. And you're the third person today to ask me that. I keep telling people – there's no *demand* for them'.

2.2 Demand and elasticity

The knowledge that the demand for lager will fall if the price goes up is not in itself particularly useful. However, it might be quite useful to know the *extent* of any fall in demand consequent upon a price increase. Economists use the term **elasticity** to describe the degree of sensitivity of demand to price changes.

Elastic demand

If a small increase in price causes a large fall in the quantity demanded, then demand is said to be sensitive to price changes or **elastic**. Similarly, if demand is elastic a small drop in price will result in a large increase in demand.

Inelastic demand

If the quantity demanded changes very little as a result of a change in price, then demand is said to be **inelastic** or insensitive to price changes.

Unit elasticity

If a given percentage fall in price leads to an equal percentage increase in demand then demand is said to be of **unit elasticity**. For example, if the demand for a particular commodity is of unit elasticity this implies that a 3 per cent rise in price will lead to a 3 per cent fall in demand.

Elasticity can be defined as:

$$e = \frac{\text{percentage change in quantity demanded}}{\text{percentage change in price}}$$

Its value (ignoring the sign, which will always be negative) varies between zero and infinity, as Table 2.1 illustrates.

The concept of elasticity is an essential part of the economist's analytical apparatus – his bag of tools, as it were. The measure of elasticity we have just defined is only one of a number of elasticities. More broadly the concept of elasticity simply refers to the degree of sensitivity of one variable to another – in this case the degree of sensitivity of demand to price. In order to distinguish this elasticity from others, it is normally known as the **own-price elasticity of demand**.

Table 2.1 Elasticity definitions

Value of e	Description	Meaning
Less than one	Inelastic	Demand fairly insensitive to price changes
One	Unit elasticity	Demand changes by the same percentage as the change in price
Greater than one	Elastic	Demand sensitive to price changes

2.3 Factors influencing the elasticity of demand

The elasticity of demand for any particular good depends primarily on the **availability of substitutes**. If close substitutes are readily available then demand will be elastic, implying that a small increase in price will cause many consumers to switch to the substitutes, resulting in a large fall in demand. If on the other hand there are no close substitutes then demand will be much less elastic. That is, it will be much less sensitive to price changes.

This implies, in terms of the example we considered earlier, that the demand for a particular type of lager will be more elastic than the demand for lager in general. We can illustrate this diagrammatically in Fig. 2.3. The **slope of the demand curve** gives an approximate indication of its elasticity. (This is not strictly true because the scale used for the axes will affect the slope and, as we shall see later on, the elasticity varies at each point on a straight-line demand curve; but it will serve our purposes for the present.) For the moment assume that a steep demand curve indicates inelastic demand (as in Fig. 2.3a) whereas a less steep curve indicates that demand is more elastic (Fig. 2.3b). We shall, for the purpose of this example, invent a new brand of lager. Any Scandinavian or Bavarian sounding name will do, so we shall call it 'Kronerbrau'. Hence we compare in Fig. 2.3 the effect of a price increase on the demand for Kronerbrau and the demand for lager generally.

For the purposes of comparison we have indicated the same percentage price increase in both parts of Fig. 2.3.

The demand for Kronerbrau is much more elastic than the demand for lager generally, since other brands are very close substitutes for Kronerbrau. Hence, if the price of Kronerbrau goes up while the price of other brands remains constant (remember, the demand curve is drawn on the *ceteris paribus* assumption), demand for Kronerbrau will drop sharply (Fig. 2.3b). The same percentage price increase applied to all lagers, however, will produce a much smaller percentage drop in demand since there are no close substitutes available.

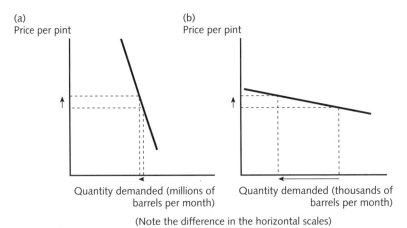

(Note the difference in the horizontal scales)

Figure 2.3 (a) Demand for all lagers (b) Demand for Kronerbrau

2.4 Empirical estimates of price elasticities

Econometrics is the name given to the statistical estimation of economic relationships, such as demand parameters and elasticities. Econometrics involves rather complicated technical procedures – in fact the process of estimating demand elasticities is even more difficult than we suggest in the Technical Appendix to this chapter since there are additional statistical problems which have to be overcome. Econometric techniques have however been developed which allow estimates of demand elasticities to be generated, though these estimates should always be treated with care and used with caution.

One area in which copious amounts of data on consumption levels and prices have been collected is that of food. Table 2.2 shows estimates of the price elasticity of demand for certain foods. As one would expect, the demand for foods for which there is no close substitute – bread, milk, sugar – is rather inelastic. For example, a 10 per cent increase in the price of bread would reduce consumption by less than 1 per cent according to this estimate. Consumers are rather more price sensitive, however, when it comes to things such as cheese and meat, both of which have price elasticities in excess of unity, indicating that in the case of cheese, for example, a 10 per cent increase in price will reduce demand by 12 per cent. As with the demand for any commodity the elasticity depends on the availability of substitutes. There are lots of things other than cheese you can put in your sandwiches.

Note also that the demand for convenience products, such as frozen peas, is relatively elastic. Cheaper substitutes exist and price sensitive consumers can be expected to

Table 2.2 Estimates of the price elasticity of demand for certain foods
(figures in brackets are standard errors – see text)

Bread	−0.09 (0.18)
Milk	−0.19 (0.19)
Sugar	−0.09 (0.18)
Fresh potatoes	−0.21 (0.07)
Other fresh vegetables	−0.27 (0.15)
Processed vegetables	−0.54 (0.19)
of which:	
frozen peas	−1.12 (0.30)
Fruit juices	−0.80 (0.27)
Cheese	−1.20 (0.43)
Carcass meat	−1.37 (0.24)
Other meat and meat products	−0.49 (0.27)
of which:	
bacon and ham	−0.70 (0.29)
chicken (not free range)	−0.13 (0.27)
other poultry	−0.85 (0.29)
frozen convenience meat	
and meat products	−0.94 (0.20)

Source: Annual report of the National Food Survey Committee, MAFF, 1989, Table 5.2.

switch to these substitutes when prices rise – and of course to switch back when prices fall. Note finally that not all meat exhibits price-sensitive demand characteristics. The demand for chicken, for example, is rather inelastic. Chicken perhaps now represents a rather cheap staple source of protein (e = –0.13) in contrast to other poultry (duck, pheasant) which is seen as an expensive luxury (e = –0.85).

The figures in parentheses in Table 2.2 are the **standard errors** of the parameters. They give an indication of how reliable the estimates are. If the ratio of the parameter estimate to its standard error is more than 1.96 (say, roughly 2) then we can be reasonably confident in the estimate. Thus some of the estimates shown in Table 2.2 appear to be rather unreliable, though others appear fairly stable.

2.5 The problem of defining a market: goods and characteristics

Up to now we have glossed over the problems of delineating the market we are studying. The demand for a particular brand of lager is, of course, part of the demand for lager generally, which, in turn, is part of the overall demand for beer. This much is reasonably obvious. What is less obvious is that lager is sold in two quite distinct situations – first in pubs for consumption on the premises and secondly in supermarkets and off-licences for home consumption. These two segments of the lager market are sufficiently distinct for us to be justified in treating them as if they were two separate markets. Ostensibly the product being sold is the same in both situations but this overlooks the point that when people buy things they are expressing a demand for certain **characteristics** which that good possesses. (This was the insight into consumer behaviour provided by the economist K. Lancaster.) People drink lager in pubs as part of a wider social experience – in other words they go to pubs not just to drink but also to meet their friends, to make new contacts, and so on. When they buy drinks in a pub they are purchasing all these attributes or characteristics. When they buy lager in a supermarket they are purchasing different characteristics since the product will be consumed in a different set of circumstances, even though the product itself may be much the same wherever it is purchased.

This has important implications. We could argue for example that the elasticity of demand for lager sold in pubs may be different – probably lower – than the elasticity of demand for lager sold in supermarkets. In other words, people are more aware of, and more responsive to prices when those prices are prominently displayed, as in a supermarket. This in itself might tend to increase the elasticity of demand for supermarket lager above that of pub lager. However, the decision to buy drinks in a pub may be taken when one has already 'had a few' which may itself influence the consumption decision. In the cold light of the supermarket shelves you might see things in quite a different way. The fundamental point, however, is that when you go to a pub you are expressing a demand for certain characteristics – company, conversation, pleasant surroundings, a chance to make new friends and influence people. These are, in effect, included in the price of the drinks. One's demand for these things (these characteristics) may be much less elastic than the demand for the thirst-quenching properties of beer.

2.6 Characteristics: the demand for ice-cream

A further example of the way in which characteristics may delineate distinct market segments is provided by the market for ice-cream. It is possible to identify two market segments. The first is the 'impulse' purchase, where the consumers (often children) buy ice-cream for immediate consumption, usually outside the home. The second is the 'take-home' purchase, where consumers (often parents!) buy ice-cream in bulk from supermarkets to take home and put in their freezer for consumption at some later date. The product being purchased is more or less the same once it reaches the mouth of the consumer but the circumstances surrounding its purchase – and ultimate consumption – are very different. Prices are much lower for take-home products, reflecting the fact that the elasticity of demand is much lower in that sector than in the impulse sector.

The market shares of the various manufacturers are quite different in the two sectors. As Table 2.3 shows, the impulse sector is dominated by Wall's who have a market share approaching two-thirds, with two other manufacturers, Mars and Nestlé Lyons Maid, each having a substantial slice. In contrast, Table 2.4 shows that the largest slice of the take-home market is supplied by the own-label brands of the various supermarkets, although the largest single brand is still Walls.

A notable feature of the ice-cream market, particularly in the last decade, has been the transformation of the product being sold. What was at one time a relatively homogeneous product (that is, vanilla flavoured ice-cream) has now been developed into a multiplicity of product lines with bizarre names, as Table 2.5 illustrates. The entry of Mars into the market (selling Mars Bar flavoured ice-cream) was a major shake-up to the market which in turn provoked a response from the existing suppliers (Nestlé responded with KitKat flavoured ice-cream and so on). However, Wall's had no confectionery brands of its own, until in 1993 it reached an agreement with Cadbury Schweppes to market their brands (Dairy Milk ice cream etc.).

Table 2.3 Manufacturers' shares in the impulse ice-cream market, 1995

	£m	*%*
Wall's	242	63
Mars	61	16
Nestlé Lyons Maid	44	11
Others	38	10
Total	385	100

Source: Mintel.

Table 2.4 Manufacturers' shares in the take-home ice-cream market (1996 estimates)

	£m	%
Own label	206	43
Wall's	158	33
Mars	22	5
Nestlé	34	7
Häagen-Daz	29	6
Other brands	31	6
Total	480	100

Source: Mintel.

Table 2.5 Brands produced by the major impulse ice-cream manufacturers, 1996

	Wall's	Nestlé	Mars
Chocolate bars	Cadbury's Crunchie, Chunky Choc Ice Dairy Milk	KitKat, Lion Bar, Aero	Mars, Twix, Milky Way Star, Galaxy, Caramel Swirl
Cones	Cornetto	Mega Cone, Extreme	
Adult stick	Magnum, Feast	Toffee Crumble	Galaxy Dove, Bounty
Adult refreshment	Solero, Orange Frutie, Strawberry Split, Bizz	Mivvi, Orange Maid	Opal Fruits, Bounty Tropical
Children's	Mini Milks, Kick Off, Mini Juices, Sparkles, Twister, Spiderman, Zig and Zag Zog Pop, Dennis the Menace, Cool Bits, Mister Long Donkey Kong Country	Mr Men Dairy Milk, Mr Men Real Fruit, Zoom, Fab, Donald, Nobbly Bobbly, Rowntree's Fruit Pastil-Lolly, Hunch Back of Notre Dame, Nerds	Spangles, Skittles, Kermit the Frog ice cream
Tubs	Blue Ribbon Vanilla Bar, Cream of Cornish	Vanilla Cup, Creme de Creme	

Footnote: Wall's is a subsidiary of Unilever. Lyons Maid, which in the 1980s was the second largest ice-cream manufacturer in the UK, was formerly owned by Allied-Lyons, but was then acquired by Clarke Foods who were then themselves acquired by the Swiss food conglomerate Nestlé.

2.7 Income elasticity of demand

Up to now our discussion has been conducted within the *ceteris paribus* assumption – that is, we have assumed that the other factors which influence demand have been held constant. We now turn to a consideration of the non-price factors which influence demand.

The responsiveness of demand to changes in income is known as the **income elasticity of demand**. The formula is:

$$e_Y = \frac{\text{percentage change in quantity demanded}}{\text{percentage change in income}}$$

The value of the income elasticity of demand (e_y) can be either positive or negative or zero. If a rise in income results in a fall in the quantity demanded (e_y negative) then the good in question is termed an **inferior good**. Classic textbook examples of inferior goods are such things as black-and-white television sets, white bread and holidays in Southend. Actually there is nothing wrong with Southend (apart from the fact that the tide goes out rather a long way) but the argument runs that the result of an increase in income will be to make people buy fewer rather than more holidays in Southend as their increased affluence allows them to switch to higher-priced substitutes (for example, holidays in Spain). Most goods are non-inferior (or **normal**) – that is, the income elasticity of demand is positive, implying that an increase in income leads to an increase in demand.

Table 2.6 gives some empirical estimates of the income elasticity of demand for a number of different foods. Some foods are inferior in the sense that, as income rises, consumers switch to a superior product. All the staple foods – milk, fats, potatoes, sugar and so on – exhibit this characteristic. Similarly, processed cheese is inferior but natural cheese is not. As income rises consumers buy less of the cheaper processed cheese and more of the superior, more expensive natural cheese.

Note that the demand for bread has a negative income elasticity but the demand for cakes is normal, in the sense that its income elasticity is positive. This points up how out of touch Marie Antoinette was when told that the poor people of Paris had no bread. She replied: 'Qu' ils mangent de la brioche'. (Let them eat cake) – a somewhat insensitive remark.

Note, finally, that more affluent middle-class households tend to consume more 'healthy' foods like yoghurt and fresh vegetables whereas lower income households, like

Table 2.6 Estimates of the income elasticity of demand for certain foods (1989)

Milk	−0.40	(0.05)
Margarine	−0.25	(0.03)
Potatoes	−0.48	(0.07)
Sugar and preserves	−0.54	(0.08)
Bread	−0.25	(0.03)
Cakes and biscuits	0.02	(0.5)
Tea	−0.56	(0.09)
Instant coffee	0.23	(0.09)
Cheese	0.19	(0.06)
of which:		
natural	0.22	(0.06)
processed	−0.12	(0.15)
Fruit juices	0.94	(0.08)
Yoghurt	0.58	(0.08)
Fresh vegetables	0.35	(0.04)

Source: as for Table 2.2. Figures in brackets are standard errors.

the poor people of Paris, fill their bellies with bread and margarine and chips, washed down with a mug of tea, while the middle classes sip their cup of Nescafé.

It is important to note that the *income* elasticities shown in Table 2.6 measure something quite different from the *price* elasticities of Table 2.2. Price elasticities show the responsiveness of demand to changes in price. Income elasticities show the responsiveness to changes in income. Price elasticities are always negative. Income elasticities can be positive, negative or zero.

2.8 Cross-price elasticity of demand

The demand for some goods is sensitive to changes in the price of other goods. For example, the price of holidays in Spain will affect the demand for holidays in Greece, Italy and the UK. Such goods are clearly substitutes. The **cross-price elasticity of demand** measures the responsiveness of demand to changes in the price of other goods. The formula is:

$$e_X = \frac{\text{percentage change in the quantity of good A demanded}}{\text{percentage change in the price of good B}}$$

Goods which are substitutes have a *positive* cross-price elasticity of demand. As one would expect, and as can be seen from Table 2.7, the demand for beef is sensitive to changes in the price of other meats – if the price of mutton rises by 10 per cent then the demand for beef will rise by about 1 per cent.

Some other pairs of goods have a cross-price elasticity of demand which is negative. Such goods are termed complements or **complementary goods**. Examples of complementary goods are video recorders and video tapes (if the price of video recorders goes down the demand for video tapes will go up) and, as can be seen from Table 2.7, bread and butter.

Table 2.7 Estimates of cross-price elasticities of demand

Cross-price elasticity of demand for	With respect to the price of		
Beef and veal	Mutton and lamb	0.13	(0.10)
Beef and veal	Pork	0.03	(0.10)
Apples	Pears	0.01	(0.06)
Pears	Apples	0.08	(0.34)
Butter	Bread	−0.22	(0.10)

Source: as for Table 2.2 except for the estimate relating to bread and butter which is taken from the 1980 Report. Estimates for later years have failed to find statistically significant estimates of the coefficients both for substitutes and complements. All the 1989 estimates shown in this table are statistically not significant, as judged by the standard errors shown in brackets.

2.9 Technical Appendix: Estimating the elasticity of demand

Economics cannot proceed very far unless it can make *quantitative* predictions based on empirical estimates of parameters such as demand elasticities. For example, it is not very useful to be told that if the price of milk goes up then the demand will go down. However, a prediction that the demand for milk will drop by, say, 5 per cent following a 10 per cent increase in price is a very useful piece of information, always provided of course that it is more or less correct.

To make such a prediction, however, it is necessary to have an (accurate) estimate of the price elasticity of demand for milk, derived from data which records consumers' responses to changes in the price of milk in the past. Obtaining reliable estimates of such elasticities is by no means a straightforward task. What we shall do here is to illustrate how such estimates could, in principle, be derived, glossing over some of the more intractable problems which are beyond the scope of this book.

As the reader will by now be aware, the elasticity of demand is dependent on the slope of the demand function. Hence we shall discuss initially the way in which the demand function is estimated. Suppose you wish to estimate the elasticity of demand for Kronerbrau, and that you have available information from previous months on the sales of Kronerbrau (q_d) which were achieved at a number of different prices (P). This information is given in Table 2.8 and the same information plotted in Fig. 2.4. As you can see, there is a clear tendency for demand to increase as price falls, that is, there is an inverse relationship between price and quantity demanded.

We argued above that the quantity demanded will depend on price plus a number of other factors. That is:

$$q_d = f(P, P_s, P_c, Y, T) \qquad\qquad [2.1]$$

We will therefore have to assume that all these other factors were constant during the period to which our data relate if we are to estimate the relationship between demand and price. The simplest form of such a relationship is a straight-line demand 'curve' of the form

$$q = a - bP \qquad\qquad [2.2]$$

Table 2.8 Price and quantity of Kronerbrau

Price per pint (P)	Quantity demanded (q_d) (thousands of barrels per month)
65	120
55	150
51	200
45	210

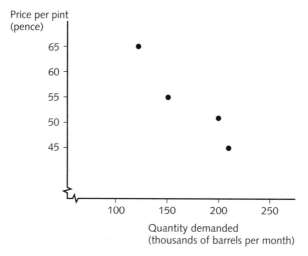

Figure 2.4 Price of Kronerbrau and quantity sold

where *a* and *b* are known as the **parameters** of the equation. It would be nice if we could straightforwardly translate equation [2.2] into a line on a graph in Fig. 2.4. To do this, however, it is preferable to rotate Fig. 2.4 through 90° so that price is now plotted on the horizontal axis and quantity on the vertical axis, as in Fig. 2.5.

The reason for this is that when we plot functional relationships it is a convention in mathematics that the *dependent* variable should be measured on the vertical axis and the *independent* variable on the horizontal axis. The quantity demanded depends on (or is a

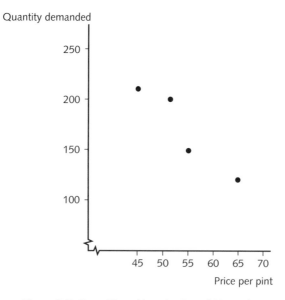

Figure 2.5 Quantity sold and price of Kronerbrau

function of) the price – hence quantity is the dependent variable and price is the independent variable. It is merely a convention – like driving on the left-hand side of the road in Britain – but Alfred Marshall (1842-1924), one of the founding fathers of modern economics, appears not to have known this. Hence he drew his diagrams the 'wrong' way round as in Fig. 2.4, and since then everyone in economics has followed suit. To be consistent with the way that mathematicians plot functional relationships, however, we shall – in this section only – adopt the mathematical convention as in Fig. 2.5. Thereafter we revert to the normal Marshallian treatment.

To the scatter of points in Fig. 2.5 we can fit a line such as that in Fig. 2.6. The technique used to fit such a line – which we shall not discuss here – is known as **regression analysis**.

The slope of the estimated demand curve shown in Fig. 2.6 gives us an indication of the elasticity of demand. Consider Fig. 2.7.

The slope of the demand curve q/P shows the ratio of the change in quantity q to the change in price P. This is not quite the same as the elasticity which shows the ratio of the *proportional* change in quantity to the *proportional* change in price. Because of this it turns out that elasticity is in one way a rather inconvenient measure, because the value of the elasticity is different at each point on a straight-line demand curve.

This is illustrated in Fig. 2.8 (where we have reverted to the standard Marshallian treatment). The fall in price from P_1 to P_2 is the same in absolute terms as the fall from P_3 to P_4 and it produces the same absolute increase in quantity demanded. However, when price falls from P_1 to P_2 the *proportional* fall in price is quite small but it produces a large proportional increase in demand – hence the elasticity of demand is high.

Conversely, the fall in price from P_3 to P_4 represents a large proportional drop in price but it produces a small proportional increase in demand, hence elasticity here is

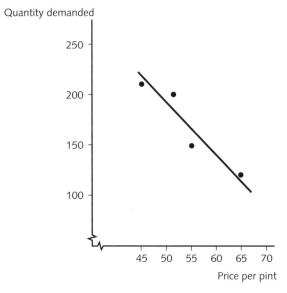

Figure 2.6 An estimated demand curve

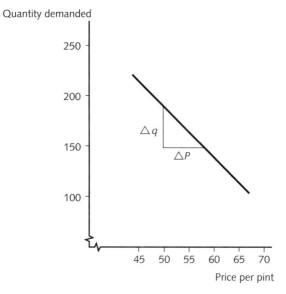

Figure 2.7 Measuring the slope

low. Thus, given a straight-line demand curve, elasticity is high (that is, more than 1) at the 'top' (that is, at high prices) and elasticity is low (that is, less than 1) at the 'bottom' (that is, at low prices). Since the value of the elasticity coefficient falls as we move 'down' the demand curve, it follows that there must come a point, roughly in the middle of the curve, where the value of the coefficient is equal to unity.

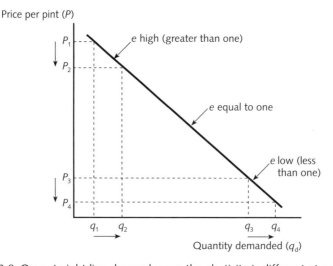

Figure 2.8 On a straight line demand curve the elasticity is different at each point

The fact that the value of the elasticity coefficient is different at different points on the straight-line demand curve is, as we said before, an inconvenient feature. Clearly we would prefer to have a single value for the elasticity coefficient rather than an infinite number of such values. The way that this problem is normally overcome is to model the relationship between demand and price not by a linear demand function such as that in equation [2.2], but by an exponential demand function such as:

$$q_d = aP^b \qquad\qquad [2.3]$$

This looks intractable (and indeed it may look incomprehensible to readers without some mathematical knowledge) but it turns out that such an equation can be estimated almost as easily as the linear equation [2.2]. Moreover, such an equation has a constant elasticity.[1] This is the way in which the estimates of elasticity in section 2.6 have been derived. We have of course glossed over the problems of estimation. In practice these problems are considerable, so the reader is warned to treat any such estimates with caution.

Summary

The demand for any good depends upon the price of that good and upon other factors. We can analyse the relationship between demand and price by assuming that all those other factors are held constant (the *ceteris paribus* assumption). The elasticity coefficient measures the extent to which demand is sensitive or insensitive to price changes. The market for a particular good can often be sub-divided into distinct segments according to certain characteristics. Some market segments will be more price sensitive than others.

Demand is also affected by the income of consumers. The degree to which a change in income leads to a change in demand is measured by the income elasticity of demand. Some goods are inferior – which means that rising incomes cause consumers to buy *less* of the good in question and switch to superior substitutes.

Cross-price elasticity is a measure of the responsiveness of the demand for one good to changes in the price of another. Goods which are substitutes – such as margarine and butter – will have a positive cross-price elasticity of demand. Complementary goods which are consumed together will have a negative cross-price elasticity of demand.

Notes

1   The equation is 'transformed' by taking logarithms of both sides, thus:

$\log qd = \log a + b \log P$

so that linear regression techniques can still be applied. Equation [2.3] has a constant elasticity since

$$e = -\frac{dq}{dp}\frac{p}{q} = -abp^{b-1}\left(\frac{P}{ap^b}\right) = -b$$

2   Lancaster, K. (1974) *Introduction to Modern Microeconomics*, Rand McNally.

Key terms

Review questions

2.1 In terms of elasticity how would an economist describe the following:
  (a) Quantity demanded fell very little as a result of a substantial rise in price.
  (b) A large increase in demand resulted from a small reduction in price.
  (c) Quantity demanded fell by the same percentage as the rise in price.
2.2 If the demand for a certain product is said to be *inelastic* it means:
  (a) A small increase in price will lead to a big drop in the amount demanded.
  (b) A small increase in price will lead to a small rise in the amount demanded.
  (c) Consumers are rather insensitive to price changes.
  (d) Large changes in price have only a small effect on demand.
2.3 What are the most important factors affecting the elasticity of demand for a product?
2.4 Do you expect the demand for Cadbury's Fruit'n Nut to be more elastic or less elastic than the demand for chocolate generally? Explain your reasoning.
2.5 During the oil crisis of the mid-1970s motorists queued at garages for petrol. Milton Friedman, an economist, remarked at the time that in a few years' time we would have oil 'coming out of our ears' – a prediction which proved to be correct since in the mid 1980s world oil prices slumped because of a glut. Why is it that the elasticity of demand for oil (or petrol if you like) seems to be more elastic in the long run than in the short run?
2.6 State whether you would expect the cross-price elasticity of demand between the following goods to be positive, negative or zero, and explain why.
  (a) margarine and butter

(b) petrol and motor vehicles

(c) coffee and cocoa

(d) motor cycles and motor cycle helmets

(e) CD players and CDs

(f) coal and gas

(g) holidays in Ireland and holidays in Scotland.

2.7 What in economics is meant by an 'inferior good'?

State which of the following goods you would expect to be normal and which inferior: (a) standard white loaves (b) croissants (c) remould tyres (d) Earl Grey tea (e) colour television (f) coffee (g) rice (h) monochrome television (i) package holidays to Spain (j) Armani suits.

2.8 The following statements relate to the term 'inferior good' as used in economics. Choose the *two* which are correct.

(a) If your income goes up you will buy less of the good in question.

(b) The term 'inferior good' is a subjective term. It means the person speaking doesn't like the good in question.

(c) An inferior good is a good of low quality.

(d) If the good in question has a negative income elasticity of demand it is termed inferior.

(e) The good in question will have a negative price elasticity of demand.

2.9 Recently sales of natural gas have risen despite an increase in its price. Does this mean that the demand curve for natural gas is upward sloping? How else could you explain the phenomenon?

2.10 On the Friday of each week a petrol filling station cuts the price of petrol from 60p to 57p per litre. Sales on Fridays rise to 12 000 litres per day, which compares with an average of 10 000 litres per day during the rest of the week. Use this information to calculate the price elasticity of demand facing the filling station. Give two reasons why this estimate may not be valid.

2.11 After Easter most Easter-eggs remaining unsold in the shops tend to be marked down in price. This is not generally true of Cadbury's Creme Eggs (the small chocolate eggs filled with a sweet glutinous mass which sell for about 20p). Can Lancaster's 'characteristics' approach to demand theory help explain this?

2.12 Why do shops have January sales?

2.13 Suppose the price elasticity of demand for petrol is estimated to be –0.1 and the income elasticity is estimated to be +1.2.

State whether the following statements are true or false:

(a) A tax on petrol will not have much effect on consumption.

(b) A tax on petrol will raise lots of revenue because demand is inelastic.

(c) A rise in incomes of 10 per cent will lead to an increase in the amount of petrol bought of more than 10 percent.

(d) The price and quality of public transport, and the presence or absence of cycleways, will affect the elasticity of demand for petrol.

2.14 What factors will determine the price charged to users of the Channel Tunnel?

2.15 Consider the estimates of price elasticity of demand for certain foods shown in Table 2.2. Explain why the demand for fruit juice is more elastic than that for milk. How do you explain the difference between the elasticity of demand for chicken and that for other poultry?

2.16 Why are some of the estimates of income elasticity in Table 2.6 shown to be negative? What does this imply?

3 Market supply

Preview

This chapter looks at the four main models of market structure – perfect competition, imperfect competition, oligopoly and monopoly. The main distinguishing feature is the degree of concentration – the number of firms that supply the market, but other aspects of market structure are also important.

3.1 Market structures

In the previous chapter we considered the demand side of the market. We now turn to a consideration of the factors influencing the supply of a particular good or service, the so-called supply side of the market.

In a particular market the degree of concentration on the supply side – that is, the number of firms who together make up the market supply – will be an important influence on the behaviour we can expect to find in the market. Consider two extreme cases, on the one hand atomistic or perfect competition and, on the other, monopoly.

3.2 Atomistic competition

The term **atomistic competition**, or **perfect competition**, refers to a situation in which the market is supplied by many small firms, no one of which is large enough to have any influence on prices. That is, each individual firm constitutes such a small proportion of total market supply that it cannot affect the price it receives for the product being sold. If the firm were to substantially increase or decrease the amount it produces, the effect on total market supply would still be negligible because each firm is but a tiny part – a tiny atom – of the overall market supply. Such a firm is known as a **price taker** because it has no influence on market price but must accept that price as a given datum. Such a firm, in effect, faces a demand curve for its product which is perfectly elastic, as in Fig. 3.1.

The firm can sell as much as it likes at the market price, P_m, but any attempt to charge a higher price will result in all the firm's customers switching to a rival supplier. It is important to note that atomistic competition can only exist in markets where the good or service is **homogeneous** – that is, the output of one seller is indistinguishable from that of other sellers. This condition is more or less satisfied in the market for some agricultural products. If the requirement that there should be a large number of sellers is also satisfied then we are justified in describing such markets as being atomistically competitive. A better example, however, is the foreign exchange market where the commodity being traded is foreign currency. This is completely homogeneous – Belgian francs being sold by individual A are indistinguishable from those being sold by individual B. Moreover, the multiplicity of traders ensures that none of them can have an appreciable impact on market supply (nor an appreciable impact on market demand since in this case there are also lots of buyers).

The terms perfect competition and atomistic competition are here used interchangeably. The use of the word 'perfect' is not meant to imply that there is anything particularly meritorious about this form of market structure. It does imply, however, that this represents an extreme case – or polar case. Perfect competition, then, is the most unconcentrated form of market structure that can be imagined. At the opposite extreme, the most highly concentrated form of market is one in which a single firm supplies the entire market for a particular good or service – a monopoly.

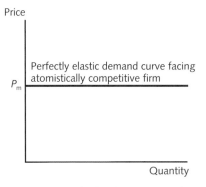

Figure 3.1 Perfectly elastic demand curve

3.3 Monopoly

Monopoly literally means 'single seller'. Since such a firm is the sole supplier of a particular good the demand curve facing that firm is the market demand curve. The degree of elasticity of this demand curve depends among other things on the extent to which substitutes are available even though, by definition, there are no close substitutes. Thus, for example, London Underground is a monopoly seller of underground train services in the capital, but substitutes do exist in the form of transport by private car, bus, taxi, bicycle, and so on. The degree to which one or more of these alternative modes of transport is an acceptable alternative – that is, a close substitute – will determine the elasticity of the demand curve facing London Underground.

Unlike the perfectly competitive firm which is compelled to accept the ruling price as a given datum, a monopolist is a **price maker**. Such a firm is free to charge whatever price it likes though it cannot, of course, force consumers to buy at these prices – the higher the price charged the less will be the market demand – and in determining what price to charge the monopolistic firm will have regard to the elasticity of demand for its product.

The model of perfect competition and that of monopoly may be seen as representing two ends of a spectrum. They are polar cases. Although there are markets in the real world which approximate closely to one or other of these polar cases, most markets exhibit a degree of concentration which would place them somewhere in between these two extremes. Such market forms are known as *imperfect competition* (or monopolistic competition) and *oligopoly*.

3.4 Imperfect competition

An imperfectly competitive market is similar to a perfectly competitive one in that the market is supplied by a large number of sellers. However, unlike the perfectly competitive market where the product is homogeneous, in an imperfectly competitive market the output of each firm is differentiated in some way from that of other firms – the product is **heterogeneous**. This is achieved mainly through **branding** which emphasizes in the mind of the consumer the distinguishing characteristics of each firm's product. Thus, for example, soap was at one time sold by weight. It was a homogeneous product in much the same way as salt or sugar are now. In the post-war period, however, soap manufacturers began to differentiate their product from that of rivals by marketing techniques which included distinctive packaging, colour and scent, and extensive advertising expenditure designed to accentuate the special characteristics of their product and to promote its brand image. This **product differentiation** is partly real and partly imaginary. There may be some real differences between the various brands of soap but these differences are not as great as the advertisers would have us believe. Often, however, the advertising does not emphasize any real distinguishing attribute of the firm's product, since these are minimal anyway. Rather, it seeks to establish in the mind of the consumer a favourable product image by associating it with vitality, luxury or sexual success. 'Use Acme soap and famous film stars will lust after your body.'

Extensive advertising expenditure is a feature of imperfectly competitive markets. It is one of the most important forms of **non-price competition**. Competition by price becomes less of a feature since the product has been rendered non-homogeneous and the fact that it is not sold in standard weights or standard sizes makes it more difficult for the consumer to compare the value for money he is getting from the various brands.

Imperfectly competitive firms are price makers though the amount of discretion they have in setting prices is not as great as that of the pure monopolist. The demand curve for their product is, however, downward sloping and the elasticity of demand for their product will depend upon how successful they have been in differentiating their product from that of rivals. A successful advertising campaign which convinces consumers that Acme soap (and no other brand) brings vitality, luxury and sexual success will render the demand for Acme soap inelastic since other brands (substitutes) do not have these desirable attributes – at least, not in the mind of the consumer. The important implication of this, of course, is that, if Acme Soap plc can establish a brand loyalty for its product and thereby render the demand inelastic, it can increase prices without suffering a large drop in demand and can thereby increase its sales revenue and profits.

Such product differentiation through advertising is an important form of non-price competition since it allows firms who are selling what is essentially a homogeneous product to enjoy the same quasi-monopolistic market conditions as those firms selling a heterogenous product. Examples of successful attempts at product differentiation abound but there are also examples of unsuccessful attempts, one such being in the retailing of petrol. In the early 1960s each of the oil companies attempted to differentiate its product from that of rivals by extensive advertising suggesting that their brand was superior in terms of power generated and miles per gallon delivered. The introduction in the mid-1960s of the star octane rating system (by which petrol was graded by a star system corresponding to its octane rating) made it more difficult for the oil companies to pursue these claims so that they abandoned the attempts at product differentiation. Thereafter oil company advertising was designed merely to promote the overall image of the company rather than directly to promote its particular brand of petrol. This lasted until the mid-1990s when a petrol price war broke out. Oil companies were forced to acknowledge what consumers had long suspected – that petrol is a homogeneous commodity. With such a commodity consumers buy from the cheapest supplier.

3.5 Oligopoly

In imperfectly competitive markets firms sell similar but differentiated products. Strictly speaking, a market can be classified as imperfectly competitive only if the number of supplying firms is large. An oligopolistic market, in contrast, is one in which the number of supplying firms is small. (Oligopoly means literally 'a few sellers'.) Thus it is a market form in which a few firms supply the entire market for a particular good or service. An extreme form of oligopoly is known as **duopoly** – that is, just two firms supply the entire market or, at least, the vast bulk of the market. Of necessity oligopolistic firms are large, sometimes very large. These highly concentrated markets are common, so much so that oligopoly can be thought of as representing the dominant mode of organisation in many sectors of the economy.

Some indication of the degree of concentration in a particular market is given by the **market shares** of the leading firms. For example, as Table 3.1 shows, the market for mobile phones is dominated by two service providers who jointly have almost 90 per cent of the market.

The combined shares of the leading firms in a particular market can be summarised by the so-called **concentration ratio**. The five-firm concentration ratio, C_5, shows the proportion of the market supplied by the five largest firms in the industry. Table 3.2 shows such concentration ratios for seven product groups in Europe. Note that some industries, such as motor vehicles, are highly concentrated – and you could probably make an inspired guess about the names of the top five European motor manufacturers. In other industries, such as clothing manufacture, there are lots of small firms, and you should ask yourself why this should be the case.

Before proceeding, we note a number of difficulties associated with the estimation and use of concentration ratios. First, data on *sales* are generally not available in the form in which the researcher would like. As a result it may be necessary to use data on *employment* (which are more readily available) as a proxy for sales data, and the resulting estimates are known as **employment concentration ratios**. Whether employment or sales are used as the basis for calculation, the choice of the top five firms, rather than three or seven, is essentially arbitrary. The five-firm ratio is, however, the most widely used. The second problem with concentration ratios is that they relate to sales of *home-produced* goods only. Some of these home-produced goods will be exported. More importantly, domestic markets are often supplied partly by importing firms. If an attempt is made to take account of such imports, the measured degree of concentration would fall for most industries. It has been argued, however, that to do so would produce an unrealistic picture of the extent of competition. The reasons for this are that, first, many imports are inputs into domestic production. For example, Ford makes extensive use of imported components in its 'UK produced' cars. Secondly, many imports which are nominally competitive are, in fact, complementary since they are resold by major domestic firms under their own brand name. For example, Vauxhall (a subsidiary of the American firm General Motors) imports cars produced in Germany

Table 3.1 Market shares of UK cellular subscribers by system, May 1995 (percentage of volume)

	Market share
Vodaphone	45.8
Cellnet[1]	43.7
Mercury One 2 One	6.7
Orange	3.8
Total	100.0

Note: 1. Cellnet is 60% owned by BT.
Source: EIU *Retail Business*, No.451, September 1995.

Table 3.2 Concentration ratios (C_5) in the European Community (1986)

	%
Office equipment	65.3
Machine tools	12.5
Electricity	40.4
Motor vehicles	51.0
Textiles, leather, clothing	3.7
Chemicals	41.5
Tobacco	43.7

Source: 'Horizontal Mergers and Competition Policy in the EC' in *European Economy*, No.40, May 1989.

and Belgium and sells them under the Vauxhall name. These are both features of the activities of multinational companies, a major theme which will be taken up again in a later chapter.

The final caveat that one should note in connection with concentration ratios is that **firm concentration ratios** are not the same as **plant concentration ratios**. For example, a given firm, even though it dominates the market for a particular product, may be supplying that market from a number of small plants rather than from one large one. Consider, for example the market for eggs. In as much as there are over 30 000 egg production establishments in Great Britain one might suppose that this was an example of a more or less perfectly competitive market. However, most of these production facilities are owned by one of the four main firms who dominate the market in the UK – Thames Valley Eggs, Stonegate Farmers, Deans Farm, and Daylay. The market is in fact highly concentrated.[1] There may be considerable economies (for example, savings in transport costs) to be gained from **multi-plant operation**. However, the existence of such multi-plant operations significantly weakens the case for the social benefits that are claimed to flow from the existence of large firms with market power.

3.6 Oligopolistic behaviour

Oligopolistic firms enjoy a protected position in much the same way – though not to the same extent – as monopolistic firms. This protection is afforded by barriers to the entry of new firms (commonly called simply **barriers to entry**) which prevent newcomers entering the industry taking for themselves part of the profits enjoyed by oligopolists by virtue of their protected market position. Such entry barriers take a variety of forms. There may be legal barriers – the Post Office, for example, enjoys a monopoly position in the delivery of letters which is protected by law. Alternatively, the barriers may be technical or conferred by ownership – BSkyB can prevent other companies from competing in the market for satellite TV. It has an effective monopoly because it owns the satellite systems which transmit the broadcasts. Often entry barriers result from sheer size alone – the oil companies, for example, make large profits which are undoubtedly the envy of other firms. These other firms find it difficult to break into the oil business, however, because of the difficulty of starting in a small way in the oil business. Large amounts of capital and expertise are needed to compete on equal terms with the existing major oil companies.

In oil exploration and exploitation the nature of the entry barrier is essentially technical: the technology involved is such that only very large-scale operations can be profitable since the set-up costs involved are high. In other industries, however, low unit costs can be achieved at quite small levels of output. Oligopolistic firms in such industries are potentially vulnerable to attack from outsiders, but such firms have evolved a number of defensive strategies designed to exclude interlopers by the erection of **artificial entry barriers**. Advertising expenditure is one such barrier to the entry of new firms since any potential entrant cannot penetrate the market unless he is prepared to spend large sums on advertising. Thus, even though there are no technical reasons on the production side to deter new entrants, they are prevented from entering the industry by the high cost of advertising necessary to gain a foothold in the market.

A particularly effective entry barrier is provided by the marketing strategy known as **brand proliferation**. This is practised with particular effectiveness by the tobacco industry. This industry is virtually a duopoly in the sense that just two firms dominate the market – Imperial Group (part of Hanson Trust) and Gallagher (part of American Brands). These two firms account for about 75 per cent of the cigarette market, with Rothmans and PJ Reynolds taking a further 16 per cent between them, though they do not manufacture in the UK. There is, however, a multiplicity of brands, as can be seen in Table 3.3.

These brands are heavily advertised and promoted through sports sponsorship. Given the multiplicity of brands, a new entrant into the cigarette industry can hope to pick up only a small fraction of brand switchers at any one time, and then only if his new brand is heavily promoted. Thus new entrants are deterred from attempting to break into the industry.

Table 3.3 Major cigarette brand shares, 1993

Brand	Supplier	Billion sticks	%
Benson & Hedges Special	Gallagher	14.0	16
Silk Cut	Gallagher	8.8	10
Superkings	Imperial	8.7	10
Berkeley	Gallagher	7.9	9
Regal King Size	Imperial	5.7	7
Lambert & Butler	Imperial	5.2	6
Rothmans Royals	Rothmans	3.5	4
John Player Special	Imperial	3.4	4
Embassy No.1	Imperial	3.4	4
Rothmans King Size	Rothmans	2.6	3
Embassy	Imperial	1.8	2
Raffles 100s	Rothmans	1.8	2
Others (inc. own label)		22.1	25
Total		88.9	100

Source: Mintel, 1995.

Chocolate

The UK chocolate market is and always has been dominated by three major manufacturers – Cadbury, Mars and Nestlé Rowntree (following Nestlé's takeover of Rowntree). These three firms jointly have about three-quarters of the total market, but they also have a large number of brands, each of them heavily supported by advertising. Table 3.4 shows the top five brands in each of the five sectors of the market, and the owner of that brand.

Table 3.4 The leading chocolate confectionery brands by sector, 1992

Rank	Brand	Supplier
Countlines		
1	KitKat	Nestlé
2	Mars Bar	Mars
3	Twix	Mars
4	Snickers	Mars
5	Bounty	Mars
Blocks		
1	Dairy Milk	Cadbury
2	Galaxy	Mars
3	Fruit 'n Nut	Cadbury
4	Wholenut	Cadbury
5	Yorkie	Nestlé
Boxed		
1	Roses	Cadbury
2	Quality Street	Nestlé
3	Milk Tray	Cadbury
4	After Eight	Nestlé
5	Ferrero Rocher	Ferrero
Bite size		
1	Maltesers	Mars
2	Smarties	Nestlé
3	Rolo	Nestlé
4	M&Ms	Mars
5	Chocolate Buttons	Cadbury
Seasonal		
1	Creme Eggs	Cadbury
2	Mini Eggs	Cadbury
3	Chocolate Button Eggs	Cadbury
4	Smarties Eggs	Nestlé
5	Mars Bar Eggs	Mars

Source: EIU *Retail Business*, No.426, August 1993.

3.7 Summary: aspects of market structure

We have in this chapter considered a number of different aspects of market structure which are summarised in Table 3.5.

The most obvious aspect of market structure is the degree of concentration, but the presence or absence of entry barriers and the degree of product differentiation are also important. These things, then, determine the structure of the industry. The conduct of the firms within the industry will be determined to a large extent by this structure. Thus, for example, in industries of high concentration we would expect to find significant amounts of advertising and other forms of non-price competition. Price competition, if it does occur, will tend to be in industries where the product is homogeneous.

It is important to emphasize at this point that what we have provided are four different **models of market structure** – atomistic competition, monopolistic competition, oligopoly and monopoly. In analysing any particular market situation one should be careful to select the appropriate model with which to analyse the situation. If one considers the market for petrol, for example, then the choice of the appropriate model of market structure will depend upon what aspect of that market we are considering. The major oil companies, once called the Seven Sisters, are clearly oligopolistic. At the retail level, however, since there are many retail outlets – lots of individual filling stations and garages – the market is clearly an imperfectly competitive one. Moreover, we could even argue that, since the product being sold is perceived as being homogeneous then the degree of imperfection is slight, that is, the market is almost perfectly competitive. The implication of this is that price competition between garages will tend to result in them all charging the same price, since each garage in effect faces a perfectly elastic demand curve. On the other hand, certain garages may enjoy an element of monopoly by virtue of their geographical location – a garage which is the only one within a fifty miles radius is unlikely to engage in price competition to attract custom.

Table 3.5 Degree of concentration, market structure and characteristics

Perfect (atomistic) competition	Imperfect competition	Oligopoly	Monopoly
Many sellers	Several sellers	A few sellers	One seller
Example Agricultural produce	Estate agents, road haulage	Vehicle manufacture, publishing	London Transport, the Royal Mail (letters only)
Features Homogeneous product	Product differentiated by branding	Differentiated product	Only supplier of this product
No entry barriers	No entry barriers	Entry barriers	Entry barriers
Price taker	Price maker	Price maker	Price maker
	Advertising	Advertising	Advertising
	Other non-price competition	Other non-price competition	Other non-price competition

Summary

Perfect competition is the name given to a situation in which the market for a particular good is supplied by a large number of small firms, each one of which is too small to have any influence on market price. The product being supplied is homogeneous – the output of one firm is indistinguishable from that of another. Such firms are price takers.

Imperfectly competitive firms differentiate their product from that of rivals by branding. They are price makers in the sense that they can choose the price that they charge their customers, but because they face a downward sloping demand curve the higher the price they charge the less they will sell.

In an oligopoly a few large firms supply the whole market. This therefore is a highly concentrated market, the extreme form of which is a duopoly where the market is dominated by just two firms.

In a monopoly one firm supplies the whole market. Barriers to entry prevent other firms coming into the market.

Notes

1   See EIU *Retail Business*, No. 432, February 1994.

Key terms

atomistic competition	24	market shares	28
perfect competition	24	concentration ratio	28
price taker	25	employment concentration ratios	28
homogeneous good	25	firm concentration ratios	29
price maker	26	plant concentration ratios	29
heterogeneous	26	multi-plant operation	29
branding	26	barriers to entry	29
product differentiation	26	artificial entry barriers	30
non-price competition	27	brand proliferation	30
duopoly	27	models of market structure	32

Review questions

3.1 The following features relate to various aspects of market structure. State whether each is a feature of a perfectly competitive market, an imperfectly competitive market, an oligopoly or a monopoly. Note: Some features will exist in more than one type of market structure.
(a) The products being sold by different firms are more or less the same, i.e., they are homogeneous.
(b) There are barriers to the entry of new firms.
(c) A few firms supply the whole market.
(d) There is extensive non-price competition.

(e) Firms are price takers.

(f) Firms are price makers.

(g) There are lots of suppliers with similar products which are only differentiated by branding.

(h) It is easy for new firms to enter the market (and to leave it).

(i) Existing firms enjoy cost advantages over new firms by virtue of their size.

(j) There are lots of traders and none can affect the price.

3.2 Economists tend to analyse markets in terms of models which correspond to certain ideal types – perfect competition, monopoly, oligopoly and imperfect competition. Which of these models would you choose to analyse the following markets in the UK? You may need to qualify your answers.

(a) minicabs in London

(b) instant coffee

(c) painters and decorators

(d) potatoes

(e) confectionery (e.g., chocolate bars)

(f) water and sewerage services in London

(g) food retailing

(h) the foreign exchange market for sterling

(i) the 'rag trade'

(j) tobacco and tobacco products

(k) postal deliveries

(l) mobile phone services (i.e., not the handsets themselves)

(m) the domestic supply of mains gas

(n) hairdressers

(o) milk production

(p) motor cycles

(q) home delivery pizza restaurants

(r) household detergents.

3.3 Thinking in terms of the four main models of market structure (perfect competition, imperfect competition, oligopoly and monopoly) explain:

(a) why perfectly competitive firms are unlikely to advertise in Yellow Pages;

(b) what sorts of firms are likely to advertise in the national press or on television;

(c) what sorts or firms are likely to advertise in the local press or in newsagents' windows.

3.4 State which of the following firms are price takers and which are price makers.

(a) a perfectly competitive firm

(b) a monopolist

(c) an oligopolist

(d) an imperfectly competitive firm.

3.5 Coca Cola and Pepsi Cola jointly have about 40 per cent of the soft-drinks market. They both spend large amounts on advertising. What form does this advertising take? Why do they not engage in price competition? What is the intended effect (on the elasticity of demand for Coke) of slogans such as 'It's the real thing' and 'Coke is it'?

3.6 Why did the EC seek to introduce common standards for items such as cauliflowers, apples and sausages?

3.7 An oligopolistic firm suspects that if it cuts prices its rivals will follow suit. How will this action on the part of the rivals affect the elasticity of the demand curve facing the firm?

(a) It will make the firm's demand curve more elastic.

(b) It will make the firm's demand curve less elastic.

(c) It will not affect the elasticity of the firm's demand curve.

3.8 Refer to the estimates of concentration shown in Table 3.2. Explain what these estimates mean. Why is the estimate for the clothing industry so low in comparison with that for motor vehicles?

4 The market price

Preview

This chapter looks at the way in which market prices are determined in competitive markets by the forces of demand and supply. Economists use demand and supply diagrams to analyse the effects which non-price factors will have on the equilibrium market price and quantity traded. This analysis is really only applicable to markets of low concentration where firms are price takers. In highly concentrated markets prices are manipulated by sellers, but in a more fundamental sense it is still true that 'prices are determined by demand and supply'.

4.1 The determination of market price

Chapter 2 looked at the demand side of the market. Chapter 3 considered the supply side of the market by looking at those factors affecting the structure of the market for a particular good or service. In this chapter we bring these two things together to study how prices are determined in competitive markets.

It is possible to conceive of an **industry supply curve** or **market supply curve** – in many ways analogous to the market demand curve – such as that in Fig. 4.1.

Like the market demand curve it is drawn on the *ceteris paribus* assumption and its upward slope illustrates the general proposition that more will be supplied (that is, offered for sale) at higher prices than at lower prices. This makes sense because the higher the price per unit, the easier it will be for firms to make a profit and more firms will be

36

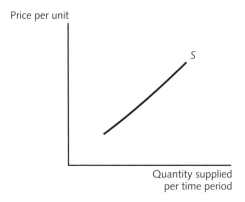

Figure 4.1 The market supply curve

attracted into the industry, thereby expanding industry supply. Note, however, that supply conditions in any particular market will depend to a large extent on the *structure* of that market. In perfectly competitive markets there are no barriers to the entry of new firms and no single firm is large enough to influence market supply significantly. Therefore prices are determined by the market forces of demand and supply and each individual firm is a price taker rather than a price maker. The determination of this market price is illustrated in Fig. 4.2. In the figure *S* denotes the supply curve and *D* the demand curve.

Price P_e is an **equilibrium price**. At this price the amount being offered for sale is exactly equal to the amount consumers are prepared to purchase. This is the **market clearing price** at which there is neither excess demand nor excess supply. In Fig. 4.3, however, at price P_h there is **excess supply** since the quantity which firms would like to sell (q_s) is greater than the amount consumers are prepared to buy. The existence of this excess supply will tend to depress prices, driving them down towards the market clearing level P_e. Note that there is an automatic tendency for this to happen; that is, in the absence of any factors to prevent it, price will tend to move towards the equilibrium level. Similarly, if there is an **excess demand** as in Fig. 4.4, the efforts of buyers to secure for themselves the available supply will push prices up towards the

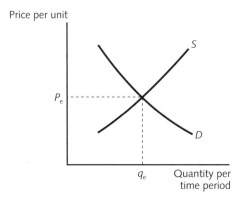

Figure 4.2 The determination of market price

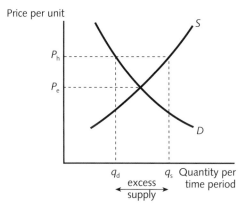

Figure 4.3 If price is above the equilibrium there is excess supply

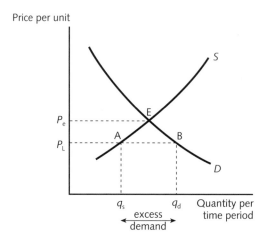

Figure 4.4 If price is below the equilibrium there is excess demand

equilibrium level where both buyers and sellers are satisfied. Note that as the price increases from P_L to P_e two things happen. First, the increase in price encourages firms to supply more; that is, there is a movement along the supply curve from point A to point E. Secondly, the increase in price discourages consumers. In effect, some purchasers who would have bought at the lower price P_L are not prepared to buy at the higher price P_e. Thus there is a movement along the demand curve from point B to point E.

4.2 Shifts in supply

Provided we continue to think in terms of perfectly competitive markets we can analyse the effect on market price of shifts in the supply curve. As will be shown in Chapter 5, the industry supply curve will depend upon the costs (both production and selling costs)

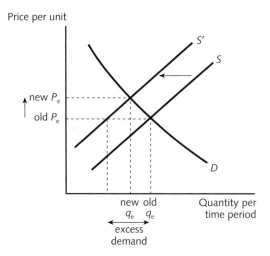

Figure 4.5 An increase in costs shifts the supply curve to the left

of the firms in the industry. A reduction in costs will cause the industry supply curve to shift to the *right*, indicating that more will be supplied than previously at each price. Similarly, an increase in costs causes the supply curve to shift to the left. This increase in costs is illustrated in Fig. 4.5 as a shift from curve S to curve S'. As a result of the shift in the supply curve, excess demand will emerge at the old equilibrium price and the existence of this excess demand will drive up the price to a new equilibrium.

The quantity traded also falls. Thus the market moves from one equilibrium position (old P_e, old q_e) to a new equilibrium (new P_e, new q_e).

The effect of shifts in demand can be analysed in a similar manner. For example, an increase in the price of a substitute will make the demand curve shift to the right. As Fig. 4.6 shows, this will result in an increase in market price and an increase in the quantity traded.

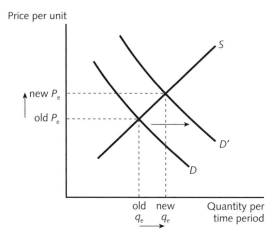

Figure 4.6 An increase in demand raises the equilibrium price

4.3 Elasticity of supply

In section 2.2 we introduced the concept of elasticity – the responsiveness of one variable to changes in another. The **own-price elasticity of supply** is defined as:

$$e_S = \frac{\text{percentage change in quantity supplied}}{\text{percentage change in price}}$$

If supply is elastic, therefore, this means that a relatively small change in price will result in a relatively large change in the quantity supplied. On the other hand, if supply is inelastic it will be relatively unresponsive to price changes. Obviously, supply elasticities are positive, an increase in price leading to an increase in supply and a fall in price leading to a fall in supply.

4.4 Price in non-competitive markets

Strictly speaking, industry supply curves such as those shown in Figs 4.1 to 4.6 only make sense in the context of perfectly competitive markets where firms are price takers. In markets where individual firms can choose the price they charge (that is, in all markets other than perfectly competitive ones) we can no longer talk about market price since prices are set by sellers. We shall use the term *administered price* to distinguish this situation from the competitive situation for which we reserve the term market prices. Administered pricing will be analysed in detail in Chapter 9.

There is, however, a less rigorous and more general sense in which to interpret Figs 4.2 to 4.6. This interpretation is that in *all* markets, regardless of market structure, the price of a particular good or service will depend upon relative scarcity, that is, how much buyers are prepared to pay relative to how much sellers are prepared to accept. In other words, there exists a market clearing equilibrium price which is determined by demand and supply. This proposition is correct in a fundamental sense, but it may be too general and non-specific to take us very far in analysing real-world situations. Moreover, it tends to obscure certain important features. For example, if prices are administered (as they are in non-competitive markets), excess demand or supply is often eliminated by *quantity* adjustments rather than price adjustments.

We have also ignored the possibility of trading taking place at prices other than equilibrium prices, a possibility we explore in the following section.

4.5 The stability of equilibrium

We have assumed up to this point that equilibrium prices are **stable equilibria** in the sense that the actual market price automatically tends to move towards the equilibrium price. In certain markets, however, for reasons explained below, prices tend to be rather unstable, oscillating from a high price to a low price but never converging on an

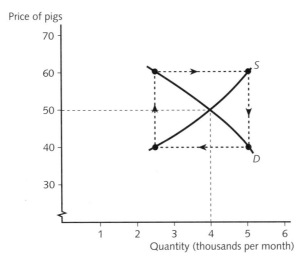

Figure 4.7 Cycles in pig prices and output

equilibrium. The markets for certain agricultural products exhibit this tendency, the market for pig meat being a well-documented example.

The market for pigs is fairly competitive on the supply side, though becoming less so as factory-farming methods become increasingly more common with the decline in the number of producers and the increase in the average size of a pig unit. In pig production there is a biologically determined production period of a more or less fixed length which means that supply reacts to price changes only after a time lag. In addition, farmers have historically responded to price information in a rather naive way, not realising that high prices which encourage lots of farmers to move into pig production will, after a certain time lag, lead to a glut of pig meat and hence a slump in pig prices. These two factors can produce **cycles** in pig prices such as that illustrated in Fig. 4.7.

Suppose the initial equilibrium price of £50 is disturbed by some random shock – perhaps an outbreak of foot-and-mouth disease – which causes the quantity supplied to fall from 4000 to 2500. The price immediately jumps to £60 per pig and this encourages more farmers to move into pig production. After a time lag, supply therefore expands to 5000 but the market will only absorb this amount if prices drop to £40 per pig. This causes some producers to switch away from pig production, and after a time lag output therefore drops to 2500, and the cycle starts all over again.

4.6 Market prices and administered prices

In competitive markets, where price is determined by the market forces of demand and supply, prices often fluctuate much more than they do in those markets where prices are administered by firms. That is, markets where firms are price makers will exhibit more price stability than markets where firms are price takers.

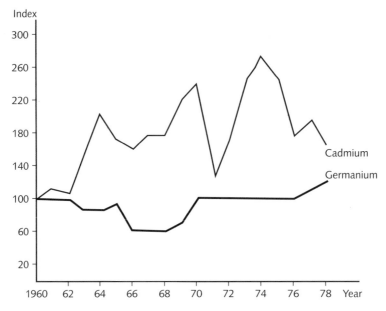

Figure 4.8 Price-relative index for cadmium and germanium (*Source*: T. Wilkinson, 'The economics of mineral byproducts and co-products' in *Economics*, Journal of the Economics Association, Vol. XIX, Part 3, No. 83, Autumn 1983 p. 85)

Compare, for example, the market for cadmium with that for germanium. Both metals are in fact produced as by-products in the production of other metals but supply conditions are very different in the two cases. Cadmium is a by-product of zinc production which is fairly widely diffused among a number of firms. Hence the supply of zinc is fairly competitive, with no single producer or group of manufacturers being in a position to control the market. It follows therefore that the market for cadmium is also competitive with each firm being a price taker.

In contrast, the market for germanium is a producer-controlled oligopoly. In the period to which the figure relates there were only thirteen producers worldwide, five of whom produced 78 per cent of total world output in 1977–78. The producers of germanium would therefore be in a much better position to control germanium prices than the cadmium producers who would have to accept passively the market prices. Figure 4.8 shows this to be the case. In the competitive industry (cadmium) prices fluctuated in response to changes in demand brought about by changes in worldwide economic activity. In the oligopolistic market (germanium) producers achieved a much greater degree of price stability over the period.

4.7 When is a market not a market?

Why should there be greater price stability in producer-controlled markets than in competitive markets? There are two possible explanations. The first is that in producer-controlled markets equilibrium is restored to the market by movements in quantity rather than by movements in price. That is, producers affect and control the market price by restricting supply when prices are tending to fall and by expanding supply when prices are tending to rise. The second explanation is rather different. This is that in producer-controlled markets there is no such thing as a market price, that is, an equilibrium price determined by the forces of demand supply. The price is simply that determined by the producer. This is clearly the case in monopolistic markets, but the same may also be true for oligopolistic markets, particularly where one producer is a dominant firm within the oligopoly. This possibility is explored in Chapter 9.

Summary

The equilibrium market price and quantity are determined by the intersection of the demand curve and the supply curve. At this equilibrium the market clears in the sense that the amount which buyers wish to purchase is exactly the same as the amount sellers wish to supply. In a competitive market there are forces which arise automatically to push the market towards this equilibrium point. Anything which causes the demand curve or the supply curve to shift will result in a change to the equilibrium market price and quantity.

In concentrated markets (oligopoly, monopoly) firms have much more influence on the prices charged and the output produced and in such markets prices tend to be more stable than they are in competitive markets.

Key terms

industry supply curve	36	excess demand	37
market supply curve	36	own-price elasticity of supply	40
equilibrium price	37	stable equilibrium	40
market clearing price	37	cycles in prices	41
excess supply	37		

Review questions

4.1 Consider the market for cocoa beans. What will be the probable effect on equilibrium price and quantity of the following?
  (a) a successful advertising campaign for Cadbury's Drinking Chocolate;
  (b) a drought in the cocoa-producing areas;
  (c) an increase in the price of coffee and the introduction of a new high-yield strain of cocoa bean.
4.2 For a particular week in June, three families – Smith, Jones and Brown – have the demand schedule for strawberries shown in Table 4.1. Assuming these three families comprise the whole market, calculate the market demand for strawberries and plot it on a graph. On the same graph plot the supply function using the data in column A. What are the equilibrium price and equilibrium quantity?

Table 4.1 Strawberries

Price per punnet (p)	Quantity demanded			Market demand	Quantity supplied	
	Smith	Jones	Brown		A	B
35	3	5	5		8	11
40	3	5	4		9	12
45	2	4	4		10	13
50	1	4	3		15	18
55	0	3	2		20	23

Now suppose that favourable weather conditions produce a bumper crop. Growers will now be willing to sell more at each of the old prices. This causes a shift of the whole supply function. Plot this new supply function from the data in column B. What are the new equilibrium price and quantity?

4.3 Table 4.2 shows production levels and prices for oilseed rape (used in the production of margarine, etc.).

Table 4.2 Price and output of oilseed rape

	Quantity harvested	Price
1973	31	79
1974	55	172
1975	61	128
1976	111	136
1977	142	162
1978	155	182
1979	198	215
1980	300	230
1981	325	255
1982	581	270
1983	563	310

Source: *Annual Abstract of Statistics 1985*, Tables 9.4 and 18.10.

Consider the validity of the following statements, amending or deleting where necessary.

(a) Over the period the percentage increase in output was much more than the percentage increase in price. Therefore the supply of this commodity is shown to be very inelastic/elastic.

(b) The easier it is to switch from growing one crop to growing another, the more elastic/inelastic will be the supply.

(c) Any estimate of the elasticity of supply is valid only if we are prepared to accept the assumption of *caveat emptor/ceteris paribus/per ardua ad astra*. In practice, other things may not remain the same. For example, the price of cereals and vegetable crops may also have increased.

(d) Switching from wheat production to rape production depends on relative prices/absolute prices – that is, the price of rape relative to the price of wheat.

4.4 House prices in Ealing, West London, as elsewhere, are determined by market forces. What will be the probable effect on house prices of the following? (Assume *ceteris paribus* throughout and explain your answer.)

(a) The Building Societies adopt a more generous attitude to borrowers when granting loans for house purchase.
(b) Mortgage interest tax relief is abolished.
(c) A new motorway is built linking Ealing with Central London.
(d) The local authority relaxes planning restrictions on new housing development.
(e) House prices in Acton (near Ealing) rise.
(f) The cost of building new houses increases.
(g) Banks start to give mortgages for house purchase.

4.5 The principal source of diamonds is the South African mines, all of which are controlled by the De Beers company. Evidence suggests that De Beers could supply many more diamonds than it chooses to do. In other words diamonds are not as scarce in the earth's crust as might be supposed. Why do you think the De Beers company acts in this way?

4.6 The following shows the output of an agricultural commodity over a ten-year period together with the price:

	Output	Price (£/tonne)
1980	100	16
1990	300	32

Which of the following statements are true?
(a) The supply of this commodity seems to be inelastic.
(b) The percentage increase in output is more than the percentage increase in price. Therefore supply is said to be elastic.
(c) We would expect supply to be elastic since it is easier for farmers to switch from growing one crop to another than it is for industry to switch from producing one manufactured product to another.
(d) In deciding what to grow a farmer will ignore the price of other crops. That is, he will base his decision on *absolute prices* rather than *relative prices*.

4.7 Consider the market for bauxite, the raw material from which aluminium is made. This is a competitive market in which price is determined by demand and supply. What will be the effect of each of the following (assume *ceteris paribus* throughout and illustrate your answer with demand and supply diagrams)?
(a) an increase in recycling of scrap metals by local authorities;
(b) a decision by the Coca Cola company to discontinue the use of aluminium cans to package its product, and simultaneously an increase in productivity in bauxite production.

4.8 Consider the market for veal in France. What effect will the following have on the price and the amount bought (assume *ceteris paribus* and sketch demand and supply diagrams to illustrate your answers)?
(a) a fall in the price of pork;
(b) the publication of a report showing that vegetarians are less susceptible to heart disease and cancer;
(c) a government ban on live animal exports from the UK.

This chapter explores a number of different cost concepts. Our calculation of the cost of performing a particular activity will depend upon whether certain factors of production are considered to be fixed or variable. In the so-called *long run*, when all factors are considered to be variable, economies of scale normally cause unit costs to fall as output increases. Sometimes, however, large-scale operations result in higher unit costs – so-called diseconomies of scale.

5.1 Cost concepts

'Costs', as one of my colleagues once remarked, 'is difficult'. Despite the seemingly ungrammatical nature of this remark, it illustrates that what is apparently an unambiguous and straightforward concept turns out to be much less straightforward on closer examination. To take a simple example: say one wished to know the cost of driving from London to Birmingham in order to make a comparison with the cost of doing the same journey by train. The total cost of car ownership can be broken down into three main headings:

1 **Variable costs**: that is, those costs which are directly related to distance travelled, in this case petrol and oil.

2 **Fixed costs**: those costs which are incurred whether the car is used or not, in this case insurance premiums, road tax and the depreciation in the value of the car that occurs solely on account of its ageing.
3 **Semi-fixed costs** (or semi-variable costs): the depreciation that occurs in the value of the car by virtue of use rather than ageing, for example, tyre and brake pad wear, engine wear and general mechanical deterioration.

In practice it may be quite difficult to measure what we have called semi-fixed costs and to distinguish these from truly fixed costs since the market value (that is, the second-hand value) of a car is determined almost exclusively by age rather than by distance travelled.

What then is the cost of driving from London to Birmingham? If we assume that you already have a car and a current driving licence, there are essentially two ways of looking at the cost of such a journey. One could argue in this context that the only cost that should be taken into consideration is the variable cost, that is, the cost of petrol, since the other costs (fixed costs) would be borne anyway whether or not you drove to Birmingham. The extra cost that is incurred as a result of the trip (that is, the cost of 4 gallons of petrol, or whatever) is called the **marginal cost** of making the trip. It is the increase in the total costs of car ownership which results from making the journey.

On the other hand, one could argue that the real cost of driving from London to Birmingham is seriously underestimated if one only takes into account the marginal cost of the journey. If, for example, one is contemplating buying a car in order to make this journey every week for a year, and one wishes to compare the annual cost of travelling by car with the annual cost of doing the same number of journeys by train, then, for a valid comparison to be made, the cost of travelling by car should include some, if not all, of the fixed costs. Since these fixed costs constitute a substantial part of the total cost of car ownership this will clearly materially affect the assessment of the relative cost of travelling by car as opposed to rail. In this context the relevant cost is not the marginal cost but rather the **average cost** of doing the journey, that is, the total annual cost divided by the number of journeys.

Clearly, therefore, the context in which one is assessing the costs will determine what should be included and what should be excluded. The first example we considered – in which the fixed costs would be borne irrespective of whether the car was used for the trip or not – we will term the **short-run context**. The short run, in economics, is defined as a situation in which there are fixed factors. In this case, the car is a **fixed factor**. On the other hand, the second example we considered in which one was contemplating the purchase of a car in order to make repeated journeys, we will call the **long-run context** because here there are no fixed factors.

It is important to note that the terms 'long run' and 'short run' do not refer to time periods. They refer only to the fixity or non-fixity of factors. The long run can, in fact, be extremely short in terms of time. Consider the situation where you are contemplating making a single trip to Birmingham but you do not own a car. The cost of driving to Birmingham then is the cost of petrol plus the cost of hiring a car for a day. Is this a short-run or a long-run context? Well, in terms of our definition (which is the standard definition), this is a long-run context because there are no fixed factors. In this long-run context, however, the marginal cost of the trip will be much higher than it would have been if you already owned a car – that is, the **long-run marginal cost** will be much higher than the **short-run marginal cost**.

The concept of marginal cost (along with similar concepts such as marginal revenue) is central to traditional neo-classical analysis, yet, initially it can be a difficult concept to grasp. Marginal cost is the increase in total cost which results from the additional activity being considered. It is not the same as variable cost (though it is similar). Nor is it the same as short-run cost because the short run is a *context* within which various cost concepts are considered. We shall go on in section 5.2 to explain the concept more formally. Table 5.1 may also help to summarize what has been said so far.

Note that for the sake of completeness we have included in Table 5.1 yet another context in which we could assess costs. This we call the **very long run**. Here there are no fixed factors but more importantly *technology* is also variable. 'Technology' here means the skill with which you use those factors. Without straining the analogy too much it could, for example, correspond to a situation in which one has neither car nor driving licence, yet one is contemplating the cost of repeated trips by car as opposed to rail. A valid comparison would therefore have to take into account the additional cost

Table 5.1 Cost concepts

Context	Example	Relevant cost	Features
Short run	Single trip to Birmingham (already owns car)	Extra cost incurred, i.e., marginal cost. Short-run marginal cost is cost of petrol	Fixed factor, i.e., the car
Long run	Weekly trip to Birmingham for one year	Average cost over 12 months, i.e., total cost divided by number of trips	No fixed factors, i.e., can decide whether or not to buy car and, if so, what type
Long run	Single trip to Birmingham (but has to hire car)	Extra cost incurred, i.e., marginal cost. LRMC more than SRMC	Defined as being a long-run situation because there are no fixed factors
Very long run	Repeated trips to Birmingham (but has to learn to drive first)	Average cost	All factors variable including 'technology' (i.e., the skill with which you use those factors). When you have done it once it becomes easier to repeat it. 'Learning effect'

of acquiring a driving licence. Once this has been acquired, however, we move from a very long-run context to a different context. This is known as a **learning effect**.

In sections 5.2 and 5.3 we look at costs in a short-run context. In section 5.4 we move to the long run and in section 5.6 we consider learning effects.

5.2 The variation of costs with output in the short run: the special case

Initially we shall describe a special case to illustrate how unit costs (average costs) can vary as output varies in the short run. In the following section we explain the technical relationship between the various cost concepts and finally, in section 5.4, consider a more usual example of how unit costs vary with output in the long run.

The special case is taken from the shipping industry and the context we shall consider is a short-run context in which the only variable factor is the amount of fuel used by the ship. The rate at which fuel is burnt – the amount of the variable factor used – is determined by how fast the ship steams. All other factors – depreciation of the vessel, insurance, crew's wages, and so on – are fixed. These fixed costs remain the same regardless of the speed at which the ship steams. The faster the ship steams, therefore, the more these fixed costs can be spread. The 'output' being produced in this example is a service – transportation of cargo. Output is measured in tonne-kilometres transported and one unit of output is one tonne of cargo transported one kilometre. If the ship steams faster it will therefore be increasing output since it will cover a greater distance in a given time. Since this allows the fixed costs to be spread more thinly, we can say that **average total costs** (or **unit costs**) are falling as output increases. This explains the downward sloping part of the average total cost curve, shown in Fig. 5.1.

However, Fig. 5.1 shows that average total costs do not decline continuously as output increases. Rather, they begin to level off after a certain while and then start to increase. That is, in this special case, the short-run average total cost curve is U-shaped. The reason why average costs start to increase beyond a certain point is because the

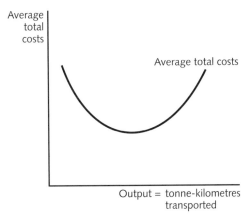

Figure 5.1 Average costs vary with output

speed of the ship is not linearly related to the amount of fuel used. For example, steaming at 14 knots requires more than twice as much fuel as steaming at 7 knots. In fact, there is a sort of 'cube law' governing the relationship between speed and fuel used: the fuel used is proportional to the cube of the speed:

$$F = kS^3$$

A similar physical law applies to the speed at which a car is driven and the amount of fuel used: driving at 80 mph takes more than twice as much petrol as driving at 40 mph, and the reasons are similar in both cases. Water resistance (in the case of the ship) and wind resistance (in the case of the car) are related to speed in a non-linear fashion.

This explains why, beyond a certain point, average costs start to increase as shown in Fig. 5.1. At fairly slow speeds the increased fuel cost resulting from faster steaming is more than offset by the cost reduction resulting from spreading the fixed costs more thinly. Thus, as output increases, average total cost falls. However, because of the 'cube law' alluded to above, at higher speeds the increased fuel costs resulting from faster steaming more than outweigh the benefits derived from spreading the fixed costs. The resultant short-run average total cost curve is U-shaped.

5.3 The variation of costs with output in the short run: the normal case

In the previous section we explained why the short-run average cost curve is U-shaped. However, this was a special case. A more normal short-run situation is one in which average costs stay constant over a range of output before eventually starting to increase. This is illustrated in Fig. 5.2.

Given the mathematical relationship between average cost and marginal cost (which is explained in the Technical Appendix to this chapter) it follows that if average cost is constant then it will equal marginal cost, that is, between output levels A and B marginal cost and average cost are the same, as illustrated in Fig. 5.2.

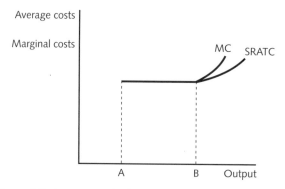

Figure 5.2 Average costs stay constant over a range of output

At output levels beyond B, average costs are shown to rise. This is because we are illustrating a short-run situation, that is, one in which there are fixed factors of production. If more and more units of the variable factor are applied in a situation in which other factors are fixed then, eventually, the returns to this variable factor will start to diminish. Take, for example, the manufacture of a particular product, where the fixed factors can be considered as the floor space in the factory and the machines within it, and the variable factor can be considered to be the amount of labour employed. If the amount of labour employed increases there is some scope for increasing output without increasing unit costs. Beyond a certain level of output, however, average costs will start to rise because the combination of factors (labour, machines, floor space) is non-optimal. In practice, the range of output over which short-run average costs are constant may be quite small because many production processes are characterized by **fixed factor proportions**. For example, suppose a drilling machine requires a single operator. The employment of a second operator to take over when the first has a break would probably raise output a little but would add a lot to the costs. Thus average costs would rise sharply. Obviously, with a given technology, in this situation only one combination of factors is sensible (one operative to each machine).

The short-run situation is in fact a very restricted context. In general, the long-run context in which the number and type of machines, the number of people and even the size and number of factories can be varied is a more valid and interesting context in which to investigate the variation of costs with output. This is discussed in the following section.

5.4 The variation of cost with output in the long run

When we allow all the factors to be variable there is no reason to suppose that an increase in output will produce an increase in average costs. Thus the long-run average cost (LRAC) curve in most industries would be downward sloping or horizontal, as in Fig. 5.3.

If increased output results in lower unit costs, we say that there are **economies of scale**, otherwise known as **scale economies** or **returns to scale**. These are almost

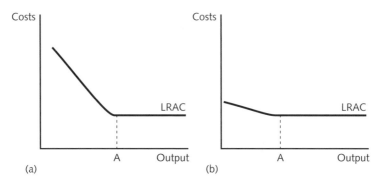

Figure 5.3 (a) and (b) Long-run average cost curves

universally present. For example, to build a double garage is not twice as expensive as building a single garage. Running a double-decker bus is cheaper than running two single deckers. Two can live as cheaply as one (almost). It may be, however, that beyond a certain level of output all the benefits of economies of scale have been reaped. Beyond this point the long-run average cost curve becomes horizontal. Fig. 5.3 illustrates a situation in which there are economies of scale up to the points labelled A. Beyond these points there are constant returns to scale.

The levels of output labelled A in Fig. 5.3 would be called the **minimum efficient scale** (MES) or **minimum efficient plant size** (MEPS). This is because firms or plants operating below this level of output are too small to reap all the benefits of economies of scale. However, one should be careful to distinguish between *firm size* and *plant size*, since a large firm may, for example, operate a number of small production units. Firm size in itself may confer benefits but these tend to be **financial economies of scale** rather than **technical economies of scale**. For example, by virtue of its size, the large firm may be able to borrow more cheaply or buy raw materials more cheaply because its buying power enables it to exert influence over suppliers. Unlike technical economies, which benefit society as a whole, these financial economies benefit the firm at the expense of other sections of society. Whereas technical economies of scale may provide a valid justification for the existence of large firms, often with monopoly power, financial economies do not.

Estimates of the MEPS were gathered together by Pratten in the late 1980s. Though these estimates were mostly drawn from an earlier period and are hence rather dated they are nevertheless interesting and are shown in Table 5.2. These are so-called 'engineering type' estimates since they attempt to estimate costs which could be achieved in plants of various sizes using the best technology currently available. Note from Table 5.2 that in some industries, for example bricks, the MEPS is quite small, or rather it is a relatively small proportion of the total UK produced sales (only 1 per cent of UK sales). In other industries, however, the MEPS is a large proportion of UK produced sales. In steelmaking for example, the MEPS represented over 70 per cent of total UK produced sales.

This is a collection of estimates brought together by Pratten. Some of the estimates can be regarded as more reliable than others.

In assessing the benefits of large size, one must take into account not only the estimated MEPS but also the cost penalty incurred from operating below it. For example, any firm operating in an industry with the cost conditions illustrated in Fig. 5.3a would be at a clear disadvantage if its plant size were less than a plant which produced at output level A. In Fig. 5.3b however, although the MEPS is the same, the cost penalty for operating below it is minimal.

Table 5.2 also gives an estimate of the cost penalty suffered by a firm operating below the MEPS. In some cases this cost penalty is small (for example in cigarette manufacture). In other cases it is much larger (for example, in the manufacture of cement).

There may be some instances in which MES is so large that it may be difficult to operate at such a scale. An example of this is provided by the tanker industry. Other things being equal, the larger the tanker, the lower the unit costs of transporting crude oil. This is illustrated in Fig. 5.4, where the dotted line shows the LRAC curve of

Table 5.2 Minimum efficient plant size

Industry	MEPS as % of UK output	MEPS as % of EC output	% Increase in costs at one-third of MEPS
Oil refining	14	2.6	4
Integrated steel plants	72	9.8	>10
Bricks	1	0.2	25
Cement	10	1.0	26
Petrochemicals	23	2.8	19
Paint	7	2	4.4
Nylon/acrylic	4	1	9.5 to 12
Ball-bearings	20	2	8 to 10
Cylinder blocks	3	0.3	10
TV sets	40	9	–
Washing machines	57	10	7.5
Marine diesels	30	5	8
Beer	12	3	5
Cigarettes	24	6	2.2

Note: the last column, the percentage increase in costs, shows the cost penalty suffered by a plant whose size is only one-third of the MEPS (except for bricks, nylon, cylinder blocks and diesels where the size of the hypothetical plant is one-half of the MEPS).
Source: C.F. Pratten, *Costs of Non-Europe*, Vol. 2, 1989.

conventional tankers. Unfortunately, when conventional tankers become very large their increased draught prevents them from entering shallow ports and this tends to restrict their usefulness.

As can be seen from Fig. 5.4, a compromise solution is the ultra-shallow draft vessel (USDV) which is as large as a conventional supertanker but, being much wider, has a

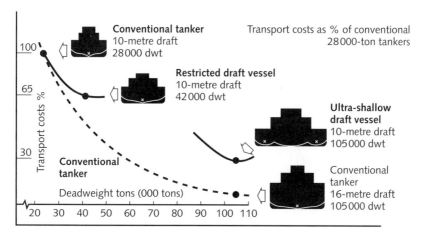

Figure 5.4 Transport costs as percentage of conventional 28 000 ton tankers (*Source: The Economist*, 20 February 1982)

smaller draught. The costs per ton of oil transported of such a vessel would be higher than those of a conventional supertanker but much lower than for conventional small tankers, and it would be able to enter ports previously restricted to small vessels.

5.5 Diseconomies of scale: Chiefs and Indians

Most of the empirical evidence supports the proposition that unit costs fall as output rises. However, it is popularly believed by people who work in organisations that the number of administrators responsible for running the organisation seems to increase at a much faster rate than the number of people actually carrying out the tasks for which the organisation was established. That is, there is a natural law of organisations which states that the larger the organisation the greater the number of Chiefs relative to the number of Indians. If this were indeed the case it would be some sort of evidence for the existence of diseconomies of scale.

Table 5.3 presents some evidence from UK manufacturing industry. What it seems to show is that as firm size increases the number of administrative, technical and clerical employees increases relative to the number of operatives. That is, the firm becomes top heavy.

It is of course possible that there is some alternative explanation for this empirical finding. It could be, for example, that the ratio of managers to operatives depends on

Table 5.3 Number of Chiefs per Indian, by firm size

Firm size (employment)	Managers per operative
1–99	0.39
100–199	0.42
200–299	0.43
300–399	0.44
400–499	0.50
500–749	0.47
750–999	0.51
1000–1499	0.51
1500–1999	0.60
2000–2499	0.59
2500–2999	0.67
3000–3999	0.51
4000–4999	0.56
above 5000	0.62

Note: The ratio 'managers per operative' shows the number of administrative, technical and clerical employees per operative. Firm size relates to firms rather than plants, except that where a business engages in a number of separate manufacturing activities these are treated as separate businesses.
Source: derived from *Business Monitor*, PA 1002, 1988, Table 6. The nomenclature 'operative' is that used in the *Business Monitor*.

the sub-sector of manufacturing that is being considered. However, the evidence from the *Business Monitor* suggests that even within a particular sub-sector the ratio increases as firm size increases.

5.6 Learning effects

Large firms may have significant cost advantages over small firms not just because of the current scale of their activities, but also because of the accumulated experience they have in a particular industry. This experience can only be gained by operating in the industry and it gives rise to what is known as **learning by doing**. Such learning effects produce cost savings, the magnitude of which is well documented in a number of studies. So-called learning curves have been drawn up for a number of different industries and three examples are shown in Figs 5.5, 5.6 and 5.7.

Note that, unlike the LRAC curves of Figs 5.3 and 5.4 which measure the current scale of output on the horizontal axis, the learning curves of Figs 5.6-5.8 relate unit cost to *accumulated* output.

Accumulated experience and scale tend to go hand in hand of course, the one reinforcing the other, so that large firms have a cost advantage by virtue of the large scale of their plants, but the ability to design and run such plants in a cost-effective way only comes with experience. Figure 5.8 shows the combined effects of scale and experience in the manufacture of a plastic resin. The learning effect is embodied in the acquired technology necessary to construct and run larger plants.

Figure 5.8 is very much a hybrid. It illustrates the short-run, the long-run and the very long-run contexts which we considered at the beginning of this chapter. At any particular time, for example in the late 1950s, with a given plant size we are in a short-run situation since we have a fixed factor (the size of the plant). Even with a given plant size, however (for example, the 3125 TPA trains typical in the late 1950s), cost reductions can be achieved by operating the plant at a higher level of capacity utilization (each of the short-run average cost curves is downward sloping). However, for a given

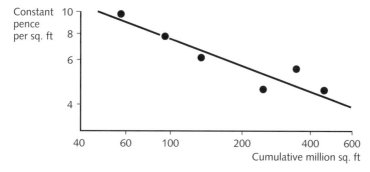

Figure 5.5 Pilkington Brothers float glass (1962–67). Total cost per square foot (*Source: The Monopolies and Mergers Commission Green Paper, 1978, A Review of Monopolies and Mergers Policy*)

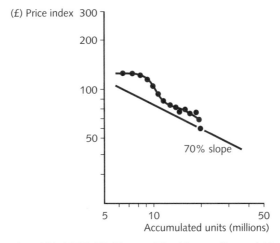

Figure 5.6 Refrigerators UK, 1957–71 (*Source*: The Monopolies and Mergers Commission Green Paper, 1978, *A Review of Monopolies and Mergers Policy*)

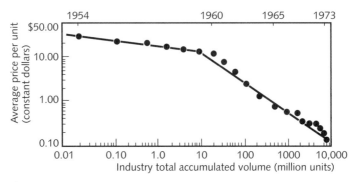

Figure 5.7 US silicon transistors (*Source*: The Monopolies and Mergers Commission Green Paper, 1978, *A Review of Monopolies and Mergers Policy*)

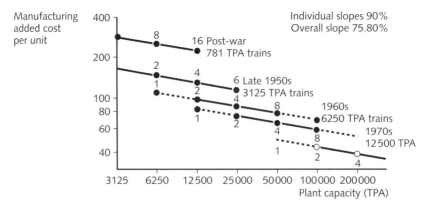

Figure 5.8 Scale evolution over time – A plastic resin (*Source*: The Monopolies and Mergers Commission Green Paper, 1978, *A Review of Monopolies and Mergers Policy*)

plant capacity (measured along the bottom axis), for example, 12 500 TPA, experience enables it to be run more efficiently. For example, the four firms operating plants of this size in the 1950s had average costs of 140p per unit whereas the single firm operating a plant of this size in the 1970s had average costs of 90p per unit. This is the effect of learning. Learning also enables bigger plants to be built, and this is the effect of scale.

5.7 A case study on costs: the motor industry

Some of the cost concepts we have introduced in this chapter will be illustrated in this section in the context of the motor industry, both in Britain and mainland Europe and worldwide. The data are drawn from a variety of sources but the reader should be reminded that data on costs are no more reliable – and in some cases may be less reliable – than data in the social sciences generally. It is not so much the case that, as Disraeli claimed, 'there are lies, damned lies and statistics'; rather the reader should try to develop *respect for the data*, a respect which is only gained by careful consideration of how the data involved could have been collected and what they are intended to show. For example, many studies of minimum efficient plant size cite the pioneering but now somewhat dated work of Pratten whose estimates of the variation of costs with output were of the 'engineering' type. That is, they were not based on the costs of plants actually in existence but, rather, they were based on the estimates of engineers, skilled in their particular field, of the costs of operating plants of various sizes. Moreover, it should be noted that data on costs are often commercially sensitive. Companies will not readily reveal any information about costs because it could be an advantage to their rivals to know it. Economists working in this field therefore have to make inferences about cost structures, piecing together little bits of information here and there. Figure 5.9 comes from a study by Rhys. It shows the cost advantages enjoyed by the larger firms in the motor industry. As can be seen, severe cost penalties would be incurred by firms producing less than 500 000 units per year. A firm producing only 100 000 units, for example, would have average costs some 25 per cent higher than one producing 500 000 units. Beyond this level, however, the advantages of large-scale production are not so marked.

Table 5.4 shows the output levels which were being achieved by the major car makers in the 1980s. As can be seen, the only remaining British volume car manufacturer at that time, Rover, was operating on a scale where it could not achieve the full benefit of large-scale production. It was awkwardly placed between the true volume manufacturers like Ford and Fiat and the luxury car manufacturers like Saab and Rolls Royce whose value-added originated from their exclusivity.

However, the total number of cars produced by a particular manufacturer may be a poor indicator of the potential for scale economies. The number of units of any particular model and the extent to which common components can be fitted to a number

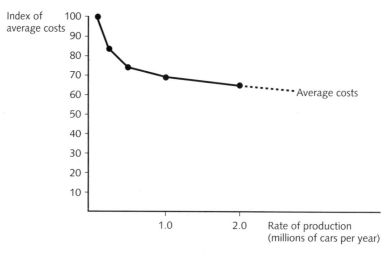

Figure 5.9 (*Sources*: Cost data derived from Pratten's (1971) estimate cited by D. G. Rhys in P. S. Johnson *The Structure of British Industry*. Granada (1980) and Rhys in *Economics*, Winter 1988, Vol. XXIV Part 4, No. 104)

Table 5.4 Worldwide car output of selected manufacturers (Thousands of units per year. Representative figures for the 1980s)

General Motors	4800
Ford	3000
Toyota	2700
Nissan	2100
Renault	2000
Volkswagen-Seat	2400
Peugeot-Citroën	1800
Fiat	1700
Chrysler	1400
Honda	1000
Toyo Kogyo	850
Lada	800
Mitsubishi	600
Daimler Benz	550
BMW	450
Rover	**400**
Volvo	400
Alfa Romeo	200
Saab	110
Jaguar	50
Rolls Royce	3

Source: G. Rhys, 'Economics of the Motor Industry', in *Economics*, Vol. XXIV, Part 4, No. 104, Winter 1988.

Table 5.5 Minimum efficient scale (MES) of different manufacturing operations

Manufacturing operation	MES (units per plant per year, thousands)
Casting of engine block	1000
Casting of various other parts	100–750
Power train (engine, transmission) machining and assembly	600
Pressing of various panels	1000–2000
Paint shop	250
Final assembly	250

Source: as for Table 5.3.

of different models should also be taken into account. This is because the volume required to achieve the potential cost reductions varies considerably from one operation to another, as Table 5.5 illustrates.

Note particularly from Table 5.5 that the MES for some operations is very much larger than it is for others. In final assembly, for example, minimum costs are achieved at an output level of only 250 000 units a year but in the casting of the engine block an output level of four times this amount is required to minimise unit costs – a full one million units per year. This helps to explain why manufacturers choose to use common components (engines, gearboxes) across a range of cars and why manufacturers may buy in major components from other manufacturers.

Note also that the MES in the pressing of body panels seems to be very large indeed – one to two million units per year. This helps explain why even very large manufacturers like Ford of Europe produce only four basic models – Fiesta, Escort, Sierra and Granada, even though there may be numerous variations to trim levels and engine capacities for each of these basic models.

Finally, note that there are non-technical economies of scale in car production. These are to do with *firm* size rather than *plant* size. Estimates are given in Table 5.6. Note in particular that the MES is huge when R&D expenditures are considered – a full five million units. This explains why even large companies like Ford of Europe and Volkswagen choose to engage in joint ventures, sharing the development costs on new models such as the Ford Galaxy/Volkswagen Sharan (the same model apart from the

Table 5.6 Minimum efficient scale. Non-technical economies of scale. Minimum output of the firm required to achieve minimum average costs (thousands of units per year)

Advertising	1000
Sales	2000
Risks	1800
Finance	2500
Research and Development	5000

Source: cited in Rhys (1988).

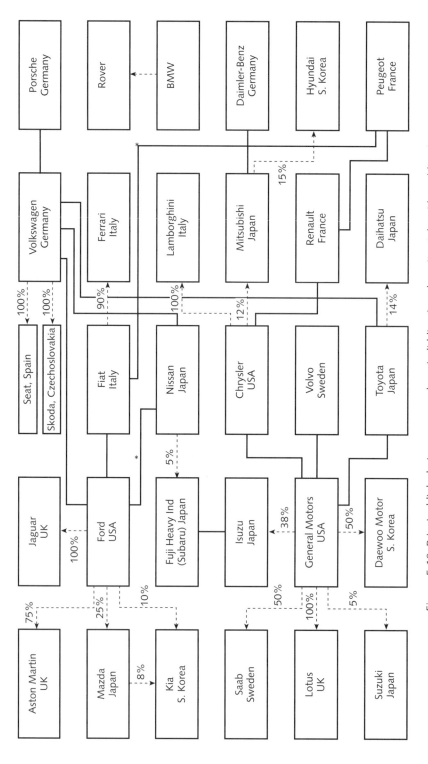

Figure 5.10 Principal links between car makers (solid lines) and equity stakes (dotted lines)
*Commercial vehicles. (*Source:* Adapted from *The Economist*, 24 February 1990, modified by the author)

badge on the bonnet). It also explains why companies like Rover were hugely uncompetitive when it came to developing new models, and why they were forced to embark on joint ventures with companies such as Honda, long before their eventual takeover by BMW. Almost all the world's car makers engage in joint ventures. Some of the more important ones are illustrated in Fig. 5.10. The figure also illustrates the equity holdings which certain car makers have in other car makers.

Costs in the short run

The discussion so far has been about minimum efficient scale. In other words, in terms of the nomenclature introduced earlier, it has been about costs in the long run. However in the short run, costs also vary according to capacity utilisation. Table 5.7 gives estimates of the cost breakdown for the manufacture of an average car at two levels of capacity utilisation, the break-even volume (that is, the minimum volume needed for total revenue to cover total costs) and the 'standard output' level (that is, the average level of capacity utilisation, which is about 80 per cent of the maximum possible).

Notice how fixed costs are spread more thinly as the level of capacity utilisation increases from the break-even level to the standard output level, so that they constitute a smaller fraction of costs as output rises, whereas variable costs like materials constitute a larger fraction of the total.

A peculiar feature of Table 5.7 is the treatment of labour as a fixed cost. It seems that because of the impact of employment protection legalisation in the 1970s and early 1980s labour costs became regarded as fixed in the short run because firms were reluctant to vary the size of their workforce in response to short-term fluctuations in demand. However, Rhys[1] comments that 'as the 1980s unfolded and the necessity of improving efficiency to survive became more pressing, so the use of labour has become increasingly "variable" once again'.

Table 5.7 Unit cost breakdown for an average car (Standard output is a higher level of output than the break-even volume)

	At break-even volume (%)	At standard output (%)
Variable		
Materials	53	62
Warranty costs	2	4
Variable overheads	7	10
Fixed		
Direct labour	12	8
Fixed overheads and capital costs	26	16
	100	100

Source: derived from D.G.Rhys in P.S.Johnson, *The Structure of British Industry*, Granada, 1980 and from Rhys (1988) – see Table 5.3.

5.8 Technical Appendix: the relationship between average cost and marginal cost

This appendix illustrates graphically the relationship between the various cost concepts. Though useful, it is not essential to an understanding of these cost concepts and could be omitted by those readers wishing to avoid the more technical aspects of the subject.

With a U-shaped average cost curve such as that discussed earlier in Fig. 5.1 there exists a technical relationship between total costs, average total costs and marginal costs which owes more to the laws of mathematics than to the laws of economics (if, indeed, there be any). This is illustrated in Figs 5.11a and 5.11b. Note that both figures have the same horizontal scale (output) but the vertical scales are different. We have put an (arbitrary) scale on the vertical axes to emphasize this. Figure 5.11a shows the relationship between average costs (labelled SRATC; short-run average total costs) and

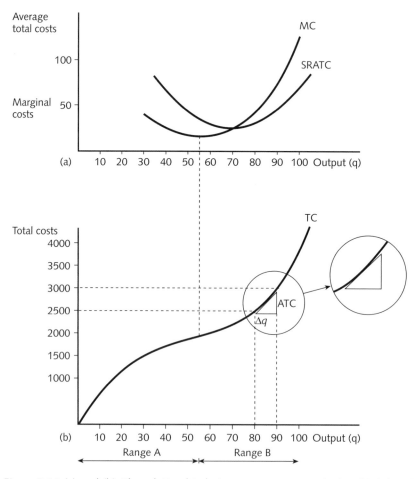

Figure 5.11 (a) and (b) The relationship between average, marginal and total cost

marginal cost (MC). Marginal cost is equal to average cost at only one point, namely where average cost is neither rising nor falling (that is, at the bottom of the U-shaped curve). The marginal cost curve cuts the average cost curve from below at its lowest point.

To appreciate why this should be so, consider an analogous example, namely that of a football team whose average height is six foot. If an extra player comes along (the marginal player) whose height is 6ft 1in. then the average height of the twelve players must rise. Thus if 'marginal' is greater than 'average' then 'average' is rising. Similarly, if the new player is only 5ft 11in. then the average height of the team will fall. Thus, if 'marginal' is less than 'average' then 'average' is falling.

By looking at this in reverse it is clear that if the average is falling then 'marginal' must be less than 'average' and if the average is rising then 'marginal' must be greater then average. As with the football team, so with the cost curves shown in Fig. 5.11a. And, of course, if the height of the extra player is exactly 6ft then the average height of

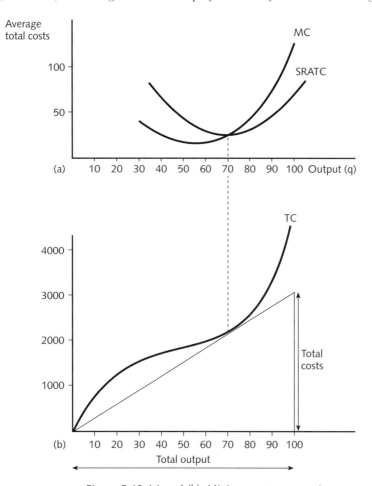

Figure 5.12 (a) and (b) Minimum average cost

the team will not change (that is, marginal and average are equal when the average is not changing).

Figure 5.11b shows how total costs (TC) rise as output rises. The slope of the total cost curve in fact measures marginal cost. To see why this should be so, consider what happens as output rises from 80 to 90 units. (This change in output is marked as ΔQ on the inset diagram.) As can be seen, costs rise by 500 $\Delta TC = 500$. Thus: $\Delta TC = 500$ and $\Delta Q = 10$. This is the change in total costs that results from producing 10 more units of output. Strictly speaking, marginal cost is the change in total costs that results when output increases by a *very small* amount. As the inset in Fig 5.2b emphasizes, $\Delta TC/\Delta Q$ only measures this approximately since with the slope of TC changing the triangle is only tangent to the TC curve at one point. If we make ΔQ small, however (say, one unit), then ΔTC will be 50. That is, at this level of output marginal cost is approximately equal to 50 (as can be seen from Fig. 5.11a).

Figure 5.11 has been drawn so that the slope of TC (that is, MC) falls into two distinct regions. In range A (up to about 55 units of output) total cost is increasing at a decreasing rate (that is, the slope of TC is decreasing). Hence MC is decreasing. In range B the slope of TC is increasing; hence MC is increasing.

Finally consider Figs 5.12a and b. This is identical to the previous figure except that here we highlight the relationship between TC and ATC. Note that the ray from the origin is tangent to the TC curve at an output level of 70 units. This corresponds with the level of output where SRATC is at a minimum. The slope of the ray is of course equal to average cost (TC/Q) as can be seen.

Summary

Our estimate of the cost of performing a particular task will depend upon whether certain factors are considered to be fixed or to be variable. In the short run all of the factors of production except one are fixed and average costs will inevitably rise as more and more units of the variable factor are added to the production mix. However, in the long run, when all factors can be varied so that the optimal factor mix can be employed, there is no reason why average costs should rise as output increases. Indeed the opposite is likely – as output increases average costs will fall as a result of scale economies. The existence of these scale economies explains why large firms have lower costs than small firms. Because small firms cannot compete effectively against the lower costs of their larger rivals they often do not survive. This leads inevitably to greater concentration.

Notes

1   Rhys, G. 'Economics of the Motor Industry', in *Economics*, Vol. XXIV, Part 4, No. 104, Winter 1988.

Key terms

Review questions

5.1 A firm finds that the total cost of producing 1000 units is £400. The cost of producing 1001 units is £405. Therefore marginal cost at this level of output is:
(a) £1 (b) £5 (c) £405 (d) £1000.

5.2 If British Rail is running half-empty trains, what is the marginal cost of carrying extra passengers?

5.3 Which of the diagrams in Fig. 5.13 are logically incorrect?

5.4 Give examples of the following types of scale economy:
(a) technical
(b) financial
(c) managerial
(d) marketing and research and development
(e) risk bearing.
Which of the above do not represent real savings of resources from society's point of view?

5.5 A seaside hotel has fixed costs of £1000 per month. During the winter it makes a loss since in addition to its fixed costs it has variable costs (heating, lighting, staffing, food) of £5000 per month, whereas its revenue from guests is only £5100 per month. Should the hotel close during the winter?

5.6 The cost data below relate to a British Airways scheduled flight by Boeing 747 between London and New York. (£ per flight)

Flight crew, salaries and expenses to include captain, first officer, engineer, chief steward, three pursers and 13 stewards	9250
Aircraft fuel and oil	11 882
Landing fees and navigation charges	9920
Passengers' services to include catering (two meals for the 8-hour flight), free gifts of comfort pack and drinks	15 870
Ground service to include aircraft maintenance for the flight, aircraft cleaning, baggage handling, check-in and other airport facilities	17 200
Contribution to airline overheads, including general administration, advertising and promotion, depreciation, ticket sales, aircraft overhauls, insurance	68 350

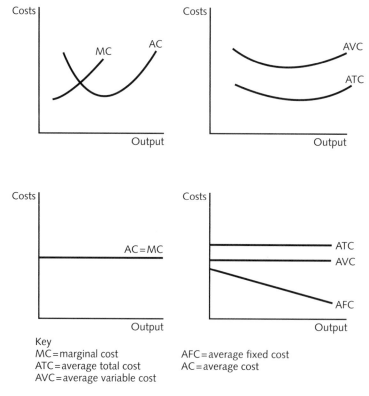

Key
MC = marginal cost
ATC = average total cost
AVC = average variable cost

AFC = average fixed cost
AC = average cost

Figure 5.13 Some cost curves don't make sense

(*Source*: data from a question in a GCE A-level Economics paper quoted in *Economic Review*, Vol.14, No.3, February 1997)

Using examples from these data distinguish between the fixed costs and the variable costs of a transatlantic flight.

5.7 In 1996 BP and Mobil agreed to merge their European refining and marketing activities. What was the reason for this?

5.8 The manufacture of training shoes is not characterized by large technical scale economies. It is a relatively labour intensive activity, and for this reason is often carried out in the Far East where labour costs are lower. Nevertheless the market for trainers is highly concentrated with a few large firms such as Nike and Reebok dominating the market. How do you explain this? (Useful concept: advertising as an artificial barrier to entry)

5.9 In 1994 British Gas estimated that if it were to link the prices charged to customers more closely to the costs of supplying gas this would result in small users paying up to 80 per cent more for their gas while large users could pay almost 20 per cent less. Fig. 5.14 illustrates the changes that would result. What does this graph tell you about the LRAC curve of British Gas?

Source: 'A balancing act that means small users will pay more', *The Guardian*, 13 July 1994.

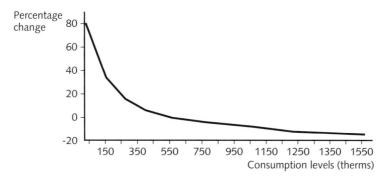

Figure 5.14 The effect of true cost pricing for gas

6 Revenue, cost and profit

Preview

This chapter examines the technical relationship between the elasticity of the demand curve facing the firm and the impact which a change in price will have on its revenue. A condition for revenue maximization is developed. An alternative objective, profit maximization, is then considered and the technical conditions which must be satisfied for this to be achieved are derived.

The chapter then explains that the search for profit is the driving force which causes firms to enter or leave a particular sector. Firms will be encouraged to enter a sector where large profits are being made. The expansion of supply which this brings about will reduce the profits of all the firms in the sector, eventually driving them down to a more normal level.

6.1 Elasticity and revenue

The Gotham City Transport Executive was worried. A meeting had been called to discuss the future of the city bus service which was in crisis again, as it had been every year for the past few years. The number of people using its services was dwindling and it was again unable to meet its operating costs.

Two opposing views were emerging in the Transport Executive. One view advocated an increase in fares, possibly accompanied by the excising of the unprofitable routes from the system. The other view was diametrically opposed to this.

'What we need to do', said one advocate of the opposing view, 'is to *cut* fares, not increase them. Then more people will use the City buses and our total revenue will go up. If you raise fares again it will only make matters worse. More people will switch to using their private cars and the net result will be that our fare receipts will go down. It's a cut in fares we need, not an increase.'

'With the greatest respect, Mr Chairman,' said one of the other members of the Executive, 'that is complete and utter nonsense. If we cut fares the numbers of extra passengers we shall attract on to the system will be minimal. Since all the existing passengers will be paying less than before the net result will be a fall in our revenue. Anyway, people like using their cars. It's more convenient so that even if the bus were cheaper they would still use their cars.'

'Rubbish', said the first speaker. 'For most journeys the bus is a perfectly acceptable substitute. I say cut fares and increase revenue.'

At that very moment Batman and Robin arrived in the nick of time to prevent the members of the executive coming to blows.

'Well, Caped Crusader,' said the chairman of the executive, 'What's the answer? If we want to increase our revenue should we cut fares or increase them?'

'It depends,' said Batman, 'on the elasticity of demand.' If demand for bus services is inelastic, he went on to explain, this means that it is insensitive to price changes so that an increase in fares will result in only a small drop in demand. Hence total fare receipts will rise. If, on the other hand, demand is elastic, an increase in fares will cause lots of people to switch to their cars and total fare receipts will fall.

This can be illustrated with a numerical example. Table 6.1 shows the number of passengers (Q) who would be prepared to travel at each of the flat fares (P). The data from Table 6.1 are plotted in Fig. 6.1. As can be seen, if the bus service was free ($P = 0$) then the number of passengers who would use it would be 10 (that is, ten thousand passengers per day). At the other extreme, a flat fare of 40 pence (P = 40) chokes off demand completely ($Q = 0$). From the data given in columns 1 and 2 of Table 6.1 we can work out the total fare receipts (total revenue) which will accrue at each price. This is shown in column 3. As can be seen, revenue is maximised at a price of 20 pence, where the number of passengers will be 5000 per day. This corresponds, not coincidentally, to a point half-way down the demand curve shown in Fig. 6.1 where elasticity is equal to unity.

This can be further illustrated by considering the **marginal revenue** that results when output is increased. Marginal revenue is a concept similar to the concept of marginal cost introduced in section 5.1. It measures the change in total revenue when output is increased by a small amount (in our example this small amount is one unit of one thousand passengers). As can be seen, marginal revenue declines as output increases but as long as marginal revenue is *positive* the increase in output increases total revenue. As soon as marginal revenue becomes negative, however, the increased output results in a reduction of total revenue. The data in column 4 of Table 6.1 are also plotted in Fig. 6.1 and trace out the **marginal revenue curve**. As can be seen, the marginal revenue curve cuts the 'quantity' axis at $Q = 5$. Here marginal revenue is zero. This point on the marginal revenue curve corresponds to a point on the demand curve where price is equal to 20. This, as we saw before, is the price at which revenue is maximized.

Table 6.1 Variation of revenue with price

Q	P	TR	MR
0	40	0	
			36
1	36	36	
			28
2	32	64	
			20
3	28	84	
			12
4	24	96	
			4
5	20	100	
			−4
6	16	96	
			−12
7	12	84	
			−20
8	8	64	
			−28
9	4	36	
			−36
10	0	0	

Q = quantity, P = price, TR = Total revenue,
MR = marginal revenue.

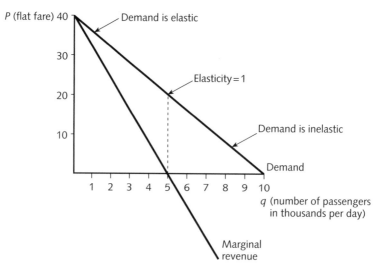

Figure 6.1 The marginal revenue curve

It is worth noting a few technical details illustrated by our numerical example. First, marginal revenue measures the change in revenue when output changes by a small amount. Hence, for example, we have shown marginal revenue to be equal to 36 when output increases from 0 to 1 and this can be read off from the graph (MR = 36 when output = 1/2). Secondly, note that the marginal revenue curve cuts the quantity axis half-way along from where the demand curve cuts the axis. This is not an accidental occurrence but results from the mathematical relationship between the two curves.

Summarising the main points:

- If marginal revenue is *positive* this implies that demand is *elastic* and that therefore a cut in price will lead to a more-than-proportional increase in demand, thus increasing total revenue.
- If marginal revenue is negative this implies that demand is inelastic and that therefore a cut in price will lead to a less than proportional increase in demand, thus decreasing total revenue.
- Where marginal revenue is zero, elasticity is equal to unity. At this point revenue is maximized since a change in price will lead to an equal proportionate change in demand.

Thus, a firm wishing to increase, or maximize, its sales revenue has only to estimate the elasticity of demand for its product and then apply the simple rules set out above. Unfortunately, when we leave Gotham City and return to the real world we have to recognise that the problem of estimating the elasticity of demand may be inordinately difficult, for reasons sketched out in section 2.9. Often an indication of the elasticity of demand can only be obtained by trial-and-error experimentation. This yields an estimate after the event which, had it been available before the event, would probably have led the firm not to undertake the experiment. For example, in 1981 London Transport (without the benefit of advice from the Caped Crusader) cut fares on its bus and underground services by 30 per cent, anticipating that this would lead to a sizeable increase in traffic (measured by passenger-miles). However, traffic increased by only 11.5 per cent, leading to the eventual abandonment of the policy.[1]

In practice, of course, the demand curve would not be defined over its entire range as it is in Fig. 6.1. Rather, an estimate of the demand curve (and hence of its elasticity) may be available for only a small range of price/output combinations near to the existing price/output combination.

6.2 Elasticity in the short run and the long run

It is worth noting that the elasticity of demand in the short run may be less than that in the long run. Note that here we are using the terms 'short run' and 'long run' to refer to periods of time rather than to situations in which there are fixed factors (short run) or in which all factors are variable (long run). In a sense, however, the two definitions run together, that is, the elasticity of demand for a particular good tends to be low in the short run (time period) because of the existence of fixed factors; and higher in the long run

Table 6.2 Elasticities of demand for petrol in the EEC

Short run	Price	−0.23
(1 year)	Income	0.53
Long run	Price	−0.75
	Income	1.73

Source: G. J. Kouris, 'Price sensitivity of petrol consumption and some policy implications', *Energy Policy*, Vol. 6, No. 3, September 1978.

(time period) because there are no fixed factors. Consider, for example, the elasticity of demand for petrol. An increase in price will lead to only a small drop in demand initially (that is, the elasticity of demand is low in the short run) because people's consumption patterns are to a large extent determined by their own particular circumstances. For example, if they live a long distance from their work and no public transport is available they will have no alternative but to drive to work, at least in the short run, because of the existence of the fixed factors – location of home and job and type of car. In the long run, however, they could get another job nearer their home, or move nearer to their work, or buy a smaller, more fuel-efficient car. In the still longer run, of course, the increased demand for fuel economy in cars will result in manufacturers developing more fuel-efficient vehicles, thereby further reducing the demand for petrol. Thus, in the long run, the elasticity of demand for petrol is higher than in the short run.

Estimates of such elasticities are of course difficult to obtain in practice because *ceteris non paribus*, that is, other factors have a nasty habit of not remaining constant. The demand for petrol will obviously be affected by income so that, over time, if incomes rise this will induce a rise in the demand for petrol which will partially or totally offset the effect of the price increase. Statistical techniques are, however, available which can separate out the effects of a price change from the effects of an income change. Thus, estimates of both price and income elasticities for both the short run and long run can be obtained. One such set of estimates is shown in Table 6.2.

Because this is such an important area it has been the subject of a considerable number of independent empirical studies. The values of the elasticities obtained from 120 such studies were averaged by Goodwin[2] (1992) to obtain the estimates shown in Table 6.3. Note that these estimates are consistent with the estimates shown in the earlier Table 6.2.

Table 6.3 Estimates of the price elasticity of demand for petrol; results obtained by averaging 120 independent studies

	Time-series estimates	*Cross-section estimates*
Short term	−0.27	−0.28
Long term	−0.71	−0.84

Note: Time-series estimates are obtained from aggregate data covering a period of years. Cross-section estimates take a snapshot at a particular point in time by comparing the expenditure on petrol of different income groups.
Source: P.B. Goodwin, 'A review of new demand elasticities with special reference to short and long run effects of price changes', *Journal of Transport Economics and Policy*, Vol. 26, No.2, pp. 155-69, 1992.

What we can see from these estimates is that, as one might expect, the demand for petrol is very unresponsive to price changes in the short run – a 10 per cent increase in price leads to a fall in demand of less than 3 per cent. Demand is more responsive in the long run but even then demand is still price inelastic – an increase in price will lead to a less than proportional fall in demand. Goodwin's estimates suggest that a 10 per cent increase in price will lead to a drop in demand of around 8 per cent.

6.3 Profit maximization

In section 6.1 we showed how a firm would maximize its sales revenue. However, most firms take account not only of the *revenue* to be gained from a certain level of output but also of the *costs* of producing that output. Therefore, profit – which is revenue minus costs – will be an important consideration. In this section we shall illustrate the rule that should be applied by the firm wishing to maximize profits.

In Fig. 6.2 we take the example of a firm facing a downward-sloping demand curve for its product (that is, any firm other than a perfectly competitive one). The associated marginal revenue curve is also shown (the relationship between the demand curve and the marginal revenue curve was explained in section 6.1). In this example we assume that the cost conditions facing the firm are such that average costs remain constant over a wide range of output. Thus the average cost curve is shown as being horizontal over the relevant output levels. It is important to note that this implies that marginal cost will also be constant and equal to average cost over this same range (for reasons explained in section 5.3).

A firm facing these demand and cost conditions has to decide two things – how much to produce and what price to charge, but the two decisions are not independent. Once the level of output has been determined, the maximum price the market will be prepared to pay to take up this level of output will be determined by demand conditions, as summarized in the demand curve facing the firm.

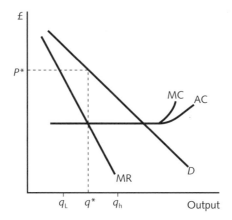

Figure 6.2 The profit maximizing level of output

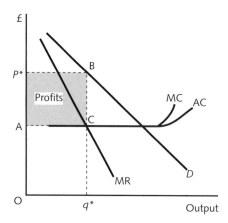

Figure 6.3 Total revenue minus total costs equals profits

First the firm decides on the **profit-maximizing level of output**. This is q^* in Fig. 6.2. This is the level of output at which **marginal cost equals marginal revenue**. The reason why this level of output should yield maximum profit can be demonstrated by considering other possible output levels – a lower level of output (q_L) and a higher level of output (q_h). At q_L marginal revenue is greater than marginal cost (the MR curve is above the MC curve). This means that, if one considers a small increase in output, the resultant increase in revenue (MR) will be more than the resultant increase in cost (MC). Since revenue is increasing more than costs, profit must also be increasing. The same must be true for all levels of output below q^* – an increase in output adds more to revenue than to costs, hence increasing profits. For similar reasons, at levels of output greater than q^*, such as q_h, the opposite is true. MC is above MR, hence a *reduction* in output reduces costs more than it reduces revenue, and hence profits increase. Thus q^* is the profit-maximizing level of output.

Having decided on the level of output, the profit-maximizing firm then charges the maximum price per unit that the market will bear. This is given by the demand curve and is labelled P^*.

Figure 6.3 illustrates the amount of profits achieved by such a firm. Profits are the difference between total revenue and total costs. The rectangle OP^*Bq^* represents total revenue since it is the price per unit (OP^*) multiplied by the number of units sold (Oq^*). Total costs are represented by the rectangle $OACq^*$ since this is the average cost per unit (OA) multiplied by the number of units sold (Oq^*). The difference between the two – the shaded rectangle AP^*BC – thus represents profits.

6.4 Profit maximization in perfect competition (short run)

Unlike the monopolist and the monopolistically competitive firm, the perfectly competitive firm faces a demand curve for its product which is perfectly elastic – that is, a horizontal line. The perfectly competitive firm is a **price taker**. It can sell as much as it likes at the prevailing market price. This means it can sell additional units without

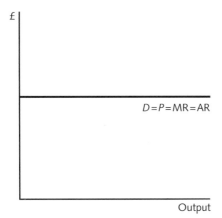

Figure 6.4 The demand curve facing the competitive firm

reducing the price on *all* units sold. Thus marginal revenue and price are the same thing. In Fig. 6.4 therefore we show the demand curve facing the competitive firm and label it to indicate that it is equal to price, marginal revenue and, also, average revenue.

The profit-maximizing level of output for the perfectly competitive firm, like any firm, is where marginal cost and marginal revenue are equated. This level of output is only defined therefore if the marginal cost curve is upward sloping since a horizontal marginal cost curve such as that in Figs 6.2 and 6.3 would have no point of intersection with the marginal revenue curve (or an infinite number of points if MC and MR happened to coincide).

In order to arrive at a solution value for the profit-maximizing level of output for the perfectly competitive firm we will therefore have to assume that the marginal cost curve is upward sloping. In effect, therefore, we are considering a short-run (fixed factor) context such as that of section 5.2. In such a context a U-shaped short-run average total cost curve implies that marginal cost will eventually start to rise as in Fig. 6.5. The profit-maximising level of output – the level of output where marginal cost equals marginal revenue – is again labelled q^*. As before, the level of profits is AP^*BC since this is the difference between total revenue (OP^*Bq^*) and total costs ($OACq^*$). (Re-read the relevant parts of section 6.3 if you are unsure of the reasoning behind this.)

6.5 Super-normal profits and the entry of new firms

In Fig. 6.5 the level of output labelled q^* is an equilibrium level in the sense that there will be no tendency for it to change. It is important to emphasize, however, that it is short-run equilibrium in two senses of the term 'short run'. First, it is short-run in the sense that there are fixed factors of production. Secondly, it is short-run in the sense that the existence of these 'profits' can only be a transient phenomenon. The reason for this is because these 'profits' are above average, that is, they are **super-normal profits**. This, in turn, is due to the fact that the costs we have been talking about include a normal return to capital. In other words, part of the legitimate costs of the firm, from the

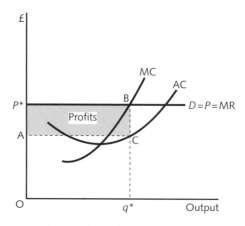

Figure 6.5 Profits in the short run

economist's point of view, is the return which the capital tied up in the firm could earn in an alternative use. Economists call this the **opportunity cost of capital** or **transfer price of capital**. For example, if the amount of capital tied up in the firm is, say, £10 000, then any evaluation of the firm's costs should include the interest that could be gained by investing this sum of money in some alternative way – for example, by purchasing government securities or other securities which yield a relatively riskless return.

In this respect the economist's treatment of costs may differ from that of the accountant. For example, if a firm is owned by an individual who has invested his own capital in the firm there will be no *monetary* cost attached to the use of that capital. He will not, for example, have to pay interest on money borrowed since there is no loan involved. This is the way that accountants treat cost. For the economist, however, even though there is no monetary cost involved in the use of the capital, there is an opportunity cost – the return which this capital could have earned in the best alternative use.

Therefore, since economic costs include the opportunity cost of capital, the profits shown in Figs 6.3 and 6.5 should be regarded as super-normal profits – that is, profits in excess of those that can currently be earned elsewhere, in industries with a similar risk. In a perfectly competitive market these super-normal profits can only be short-lived because their existence will encourage other firms to enter the industry. This will cause an expansion of market supply, and the market price will drop. This process, in theory, will continue until all the super-normal profits have been eliminated by the entry of new firms. This is illustrated in Fig. 6.6. Industry supply increases from S to S' with the entry of new firms, and equilibrium market price thus falls from P_1 to P_2. Each firm in perfect competition takes the market price as a given datum and equates marginal cost to marginal revenue in order to maximize profits (or minimize losses). When market price has been driven down to P_2 an individual firm's most profitable level of output will be q_2^* in Fig. 6.6b.

The shaded area in Fig. 6.6b represents both total costs and total revenue: thus there are no super-normal profits. Fig. 6.6b therefore shows a competitive firm in equilibrium when all super-normal profits have been eliminated. This is sometimes called a **post-entry equilibrium**, that is, the equilibrium that results after new firms have entered

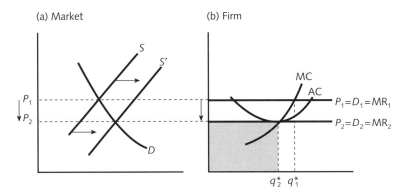

Figure 6.6 (a) and (b) New entrants eliminate super-normal profits

Table 6.3 Summary – short run and long run

As applied to	Short run	Long run
Time period	Less than 1 year or whatever arbitrary cut-off point is chosen	More than 1 year
Costs	Fixed factors of production	All factors variable
Equilibrium	Presence of SNP (also called 'pre-entry' equilibrium)	Absence of SNP (also called 'post-entry' equilibrium)

SNP = super-normal profits.

the market to earn for themselves some of the super-normal profits. It could also be termed a **long-run equilibrium** where the term 'long run' refers to the absence of super-normal profits. Thus we have yet another interpretation of the terms 'long run' and 'short run'. We now have three different definitions of these terms, which are summarized in Table 6.3.

6.6 The elusive long-run equilibrium

To recap, the profit-maximizing level of output, q^*, shown in Fig. 6.5, is a short-run equilibrium level of output both in the sense that it exists in a short-run (fixed factor) cost context and also in the sense that it gives rise to super-normal profits, the existence of which triggers off responses from other firms which will eventually undermine this equilibrium, that is, change it from an equilibrium to a disequilibrium position. What of the long-run equilibrium position? Well, like the pot of gold at the end of the rainbow, the long-run equilibrium position does not exist. From a certain spot you can see the rainbow but you can never reach the crock of gold. The reason for this is not because of the ephemeral nature of the rainbow but because it only exists when viewed from afar. Close to, it vanishes. The same applies to the 'long run' in economics. From a particular short-run perspective you can contemplate the long run, but when you arrive at what you thought was the long run you find you are in another short-run position. You are always in the short run in the sense that the factors you are using are fixed at that particular point in time. You can change these factors but in so doing you do not move to the long run; you merely move to another short-run position.

Consider the example of a farmer producing, say, oil-seed rape, the raw material of margarine and other foods. If he is a profit maximizer he will expand production up to the point where the cost of the last tonne produced equals the market price. With a given area under cultivation (that is, in the short run) this is a profit-maximizing equilibrium level of output. If the demand for margarine and hence for oil-seed rape is high this may result in super-normal profits being earned and, if it does, then next season other farmers may switch into rape production, expanding supply, depressing market price and eroding the profitability of rape production – a process which will continue until all the super-normal profits have been eliminated. Each individual farmer, however, always operates in a short-run context, aspiring to a short-run (profit maximizing) equilibrium position. The concept of long-run equilibrium therefore should be seen as a description of a process (involving the entry and exit of other firms) rather than as a static point of equilibrium. Figure 6.6 therefore should be seen as a description of this process.

6.7 The industry supply curve in perfect competition

We talked in section 4.1 about how price is determined in perfectly competitive markets by the intersection of the demand curve and the supply curve, and we showed in Fig. 6.6 the interaction between the market and the individual perfectly competitive firm. We are now in a position to describe formally how that market supply curve is formed. This is merely an extension of the process described in Fig. 6.6. Suppose the industry is composed of just two firms, as in Fig. 6.7 – clearly a contradiction in terms since we assumed that in perfect competition there are many small firms, but an expedient assumption that we must make for purposes of exposition.

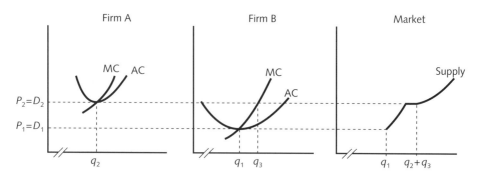

Figure 6.7 How the industry supply curve is derived

At a price of P_1, firm A will produce nothing since it has a higher cost structure than firm B and, at this price, it cannot produce at a profit. Only firm B will supply, at an output level of q_1, and this therefore is the market supply at this price. At a higher price of P_2, however, firm A will also find it profitable to produce (at output level q_2) and firm B will expand its output to q_3. Thus market supply at price P_2 is equal to the sum of firm A's production plus firm B's production $(q_2 + q_3)$.

In a similar way, by considering other prices we can trace out a market supply curve. This market supply curve is the horizontal summation of each individual firm's marginal cost curves – or, more specifically, that portion of the marginal cost curve which is above the average cost curve.

It is worth emphasising two points. The first is that each firm is in a position of short-run equilibrium. Thus, the industry supply curve should properly be interpreted within a short-run context – that is, we have derived a short-run market supply curve. The second point which should be reiterated is that an industry supply curve is only defined in the context of a perfectly competitive market structure. In other market structures the 'supply curve' – if it exists at all – is the firm's marginal cost curve.

Summary

If demand is inelastic, total revenue will be increased if prices are increased. In contrast, if demand is elastic, revenue is increased when prices are cut. It follows therefore that revenue is maximized at that point on the firm's demand curve corresponding to unit elasticity.

To maximize profits firms take account not just of revenue but also of costs. Anything which adds more to revenue than it does to costs will increase profits. Since an expansion of output will increase both revenue and costs a firm wishing to maximize profits should continue to increase output as long as the increase in revenue (marginal revenue) is more than the increase in costs (marginal costs). The profit maximizing point will be reached when output has been expanded up to the point where marginal revenue equals marginal cost.

If some firms earn exceptionally high profits this will act as a signal to other firms persuading them to move into the sector in question to obtain some of these high profits for themselves. The entry of these new firms will expand supply in that sector and drive profits down to a more normal level. This will happen only in a competitive market. In a monopoly there are barriers to the entry of new firms which prevent this happening.

Notes

1   London Transport Executive, Annual Reports.
2   Goodwin, P.B. (1992) 'A review of new demand elasticities with special reference to short and long run effects of price changes', *Journal of Transport Economics and Policy* 26 (2): 155-69.

Key terms

Review questions

6.1 A monopolistic firm can affect the price at which it sells. If it wishes to increase total revenue and it believes that the demand for its product is elastic should it raise, lower or leave unchanged the price at which it sells?

6.2 If a price-making firm wants to maximize its sales revenue it should:
(a) set the highest price it can get;
(b) set the lowest price which covers its costs;
(c) choose a selling price at which the elasticity of demand for its product is unity;
(d) choose a selling price where the extra revenue received from the last unit sold exceeds the extra cost of making that unit.

6.3 'London Transport should cut fares to increase its revenue.' Do you agree? What effect might an increase in demand have on London Transport's costs?

6.4 How does the concept of opportunity cost help to evaluate the cost of a training scheme which uses skilled workers to train apprentices?

6.5 In January 1997 lone yachtsman Tony Bullimore was rescued from his upturned craft in the Southern Ocean by the Australian navy. Critics complained about the resources that had been used to rescue Mr Bullimore (a figure of £2 million was mentioned). How does the concept of opportunity cost help to shed light on the cost of the rescue operation?

6.6 Table 6.4 contains information on six firms, all of whom are monopolists who wish to maximize profit. Complete the table and advise in each case whether the firm should:
(a) increase price (and reduce quantity produced and sold);
(b) reduce price (and increase quantity produced and sold);
(c) remain at present position;
(d) none of the above: the figures supplied cannot be correct.

Table 6.4 Profitability of six firms

	Price (£/p)	Marginal revenue (£/p)	Output	Total revenue (£)	Total cost (£)	Profit	Average costs (£/p)	Marginal cost (£/p)
A	1.00	0.80	3000	3000	2500			0.75
B	1.50	1.20	5000				1.50	1.20
C		0.90	5000			Zero SNP	1.00	0.90
D	1.20	1.50	4000					1.50
E	1.00		4000	4000	2500		62.5	1.00
F	0.90	0.75	4000	3600	2000		At a minimum	

 Case Studies in pricing

Preview

Economics is all around us. You have only to open your eyes to see it, provided of course that it's part of your perceptive set. In this chapter we look at a number of examples that illustrate a fundamental point: the elasticity of demand for a product is an important influence on the price charged.

7.1 Price discrimination

Walk into your local travel agent and pick up a few brochures. They usually have lots to spare. Then take them home and study how the prices for a particular package holiday or a particular trip vary according to the time of year it is taken. Table 7.1 shows a standard return fare on the DFDS ferry sailing from Harwich to Esbjerg in Denmark, though we could of course have given literally thousands of similar examples. As one might expect the highest fare is charged in the peak holiday season, between 14 July and 18 August. This peak fare of £216 is almost twice as much as the fare of £112 charged during the low-season period. Note, however, that the ferry company does not simply divide the year into high season (or on-peak) and low season (or off-peak) segments. Rather it divides the market in a more complex way, identifying three levels of demand – low, mid and high. The customer may well be confused by the complexity of this and holiday brochures often make use of colour coding in the brochure so that the customer can identify which fare applies.

The cheapest price of £112 applies from 5 January after the Christmas and New Year period has (mercifully) ended and runs through until 26 March when people start

Table 7.1 Standard return fare for ferry
to Denmark (£)

'Low season'	
5 January – 26 March	
1 October – 19 December	
24–26 December	£112
'Mid season'	
1–4 January	
27 March – 13 July	
19 August – 30 September	
20–23 and 27–31 December	£166
'High season'	
14 July – 18 August	£216

Source: DFDS (Scandinavian Seaways) brochure 1997.
The price shown is per person in a standard 4-berth cabin.

to think about an Easter holiday. From 27 March a 'mid-season' price of £166 applies and this lasts until 14 July, the start of the 'high season' when the price is £216. On 19 August we revert to a mid-season price (summer ends early in Scandinavia!) and on 30 September we are back to the low-season rate again. Note, however, that the ferry company puts the price up again at Christmas so that people travelling just before Christmas or just before New Year have to pay the mid-season fare.

It is very important to note that the variations in the price set by the ferry company have nothing to do with variations in cost. The cost to the company of running a ferry between England and Denmark is the same on 5 January as it is on 5 August – yet in August they charge almost twice as much. The price differentials reflect differences in the level of demand – or more precisely the *elasticity of demand* at different times of the year. This is an example of what economists call **price discrimination**. The price charged depends upon the elasticity of demand – the more inelastic the demand the higher the price and *vice versa*.

We should perhaps pause and ask ourselves what determines the elasticity of demand for ferry trips between England and Denmark and to answer this we need to look at consumer motivation. Ferry trips to Denmark are mostly taken because people *want* to do them rather than *need* to do them. They are for most people a leisure activity, a holiday. Economic theory tells us that the elasticity of demand for any good or service depends upon the availability of substitutes. What we need to look at therefore are the alternative ways in which consumers could spend their surplus income. Most people find the prospect of bobbing about on the North Sea for eighteen hours on a winter's night rather unattractive. Hence other forms of leisure activity, even staying at home and watching television, seem preferable. There are, in short, plenty of other things for consumers to spend their money on – there are plenty of substitutes. In winter therefore the demand for ferry trips to Denmark is elastic – high prices will simply put people off altogether, so the ferry company charges a low price in an attempt to stimulate demand.

Note what happens at Christmas, however. At this time people's desire to travel is stronger so prices go up but prices are not as high as they are in summer. This is because the motivation for taking a ferry trip at Christmas is different from that in the summer.

In the summer people enjoy the trip itself. Sitting out on deck breathing lungfuls of sea air is a pleasurable experience. But at Christmas time people may feel they *need* to travel to be reunited with their families. The primary motivation is to get there – the trip itself is probably rather irksome. And of course if the motivation is primarily to arrive, then better substitutes are available in the form of air travel which is considerably faster and no more expensive. The fact that these substitutes are available will make demand more elastic.

Consumer motivation is complex and the underlying reasons why consumers choose a particular service rather than spending their money on something else may be unknown to the ferry company and may indeed be unknowable. Nevertheless, knowledge of the elasticity of demand will be important in the company's pricing decisions. Even though the ferry company may never even have heard of the concept of elasticity they will know by long experience that they can charge higher prices in the summer than in the winter. Years of experience with various sets of prices will have told them that consumers are less price sensitive in the summer than they are in the winter.

7.2 Price discrimination and profit maximization

We should perhaps ask ourselves why DFDS chooses to discriminate. The answer quite simply is that by so doing they make larger profits than they would if they charged the same price all year round. Figure 7.1 illustrates this.

In Fig. 7.1 we assume that unit costs are constant and that there are just two market segments, summer and winter. In summer, there is more demand than in winter and demand is more inelastic – consumers are not discouraged by higher prices. We have chosen to illustrate this by drawing summer demand as a steeper curve than that for winter (see technical note at the end of this section). Total demand will be the sum of these two. In our diagram this will be the horizontal summation of the two curves. If the same price were charged all year round the profit maximizing price would be P_T and the profit accruing to the company is represented by the shaded area. If, on the other hand, the company separates the two market segments, equating marginal cost to marginal revenue in each of the sub-markets, the price charged in winter will be P_w while

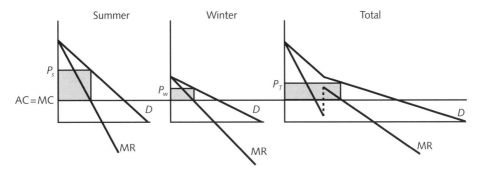

Figure 7.1 Price discrimination: you pay more in summer

that in summer will be P_s. The total profit will then be the sum of the shaded 'winter' area and the shaded 'summer' area which is greater than the shaded 'total' area. Thus discrimination increases the overall profitability of the company.

The key point to note relates to what the economist calls **equi-marginal returns**. To maximize its profit the firm must ensure that its marginal returns – in this case its marginal revenue – are the same in each market segment. Figure 7.1 shows this to be the case since at a price of P_s in summer marginal revenue is the same as that in winter when the price is only P_w (that is, marginal revenue is the same in summer and winter, even though price is different). If the same price were charged in summer and in winter marginal revenue would be different, given the difference in demands. This is illustrated in Fig. 7.2.

This is a very fundamental, though not very obvious, conclusion. To understand why equi-marginal returns are necessary in order to maximize profit, consider the case where marginal returns are *not* equal. Suppose for example the same price were charged in summer as in winter (shown as 'common price' in Fig. 7.2). This would result in marginal revenue being higher in winter than in summer – that is, the last ticket sold in winter yields more revenue than the last ticket sold in summer. If there were some way in which the company could transfer this demand from summer to winter, it would increase its overall profitability because the reduction in revenue resulting from the loss of the last ticket sold in summer would be more than offset by the increase in revenue resulting from the extra ticket sold in winter (because MR in the winter exceeds MR in the summer). Thus the company should try to persuade passengers to switch their demand from summer to winter as long as this holds true. But of course as the number of units sold in winter increases so the MR declines (there is a movement down the MR curve), and as the number of units sold in summer decreases so the MR increases (there is a movement up the MR curve). Thus the company should continue its persuasion by adjusting prices – until MR in summer equals that in winter, as in Fig. 7.1. This demonstrates that equi-marginal returns are necessary if the firm is to maximize its overall profit.

There are a couple of additional points that need to be made. First, to be able to discriminate, a firm needs market power. A perfectly competitive firm, in contrast, faces a perfectly elastic demand for its product (horizontal demand curve) and therefore by definition cannot identify different market segments and discriminate between them.

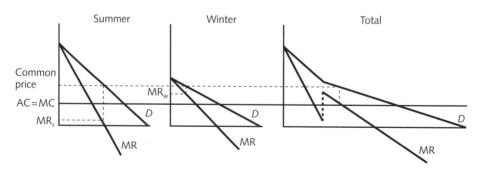

Figure 7.2 If the same price were charged profits would not be maximized

For this reason, some textbooks refer to price discrimination as *monopolistic* price discrimination. What is required, however, is not that the firm is a true monopolist but simply that it faces a downward sloping demand curve. DFDS is incidentally the only company operating the Harwich-Esbjerg route (it is a monopolist) but similar examples of price discrimination can be found on the cross-Channel route, where two firms compete against the Tunnel, and in rail and air services.

Second, successful discrimination requires that consumers cannot switch from one segment to the other. To take a rather far-fetched example, suppose that Fig. 7.1 related not to the demand for trips but to the demand for baked beans. That is, suppose the demand for beans is lower and more price-sensitive in the summer months. If the baked beans manufacturer attempted to charge a higher price in winter than in summer consumers would simply buy beans for the whole year in summer and store them until they required them in winter. In short, beans can be stored, trips cannot and it is this that enables discrimination to take place.

Technical note to Figures 7.1 and 7.2

Students attempting to replicate Figs 7.1 and 7.2 should note that they need to be drawn accurately and the only way to do this satisfactorily is to use graph paper. The 'total' curve must be the horizontal summation of the 'summer' and 'winter' curves and the MR curves must bear the correct relationship to the demand curves to which they relate. Where the demand curve kinks there is a discontinuity so MR is undefined at this point – hence the 'break' in the MR curve.

In Fig. 7.1 the sum of the shaded 'summer' and shaded 'winter' areas exceeds the shaded 'total' area (that is, profits are greater if the firm discriminates) but to satisfy yourself that this is the case you need to measure the shaded areas. In fact, in our diagram, profit is about 50 per cent greater with discrimination than it is without.

Note also that we have assumed that the slope of the demand curve is indicative of its elasticity, a shallow demand curve being more elastic than a steep one. This is only approximately correct since a straight line demand 'curve' exhibits a different elasticity at every point.

7.3 'Special discounts'

In the previous section we saw how the prices set by the ferry company DFDS varied according to the time of year. However, in common with other transport operators DFDS has a complex rate structure which offers among other things:

(a) Cheaper fares (25 per cent discount) to retired people ('Senior Voyagers').
(b) Cheaper fares to students – also 25 per cent discount.
(c) Discounts for travel mid-week.

The rationale for the cheaper fares available to retirement pensioners and students is straightforward. It is another example of price discrimination. Students, and – to a somewhat lesser extent – retirement pensioners, form a low-income group who would be put off by high prices. However, these concessionary fares are only available for mid-week sailings. But pensioners and students generally have more free time than other people and enjoy greater flexibility about *when* to travel and therefore can more easily be persuaded by the cheaper fares to take the mid-week sailings. In short, the ferry company has identified a **market segment** – pensioners and students – whose demand for trips is more elastic than that of ordinary passengers and it sets its prices accordingly.

Note also that no matter what time of year the trip is taken discounts are available for travelling mid-week. Airlines often refer to these as 'Apex' fares and DFDS calls them 'Seapex' discounts. The ferry company here offers 40 per cent off the standard fare provided the departure is between Sunday and Thursday (and the trip must be booked at least 21 days in advance). It is tempting to try to explain this as an example of monopolistic price discrimination between two market segments characterized by a difference in the elasticity of demand. To some extent this is legitimate but for a full understanding we also need an additional concept – that of peak load pricing, to which we now turn.

7.4 Peak-load pricing

BT (British Telecom) is the dominant supplier of telephone services in the UK though it now faces competition (particularly in the provision of long-distance calls) from companies such as Mercury Communications, Ionica and some cable companies. In common with all telephone companies its cost structure is rather unusual in that its fixed costs are high and its variable costs are very low. In other words once the capital equipment – the cables, the exchanges, the satellites and so on – have been installed the cost of using that equipment is very low indeed. Marginal costs, that is, are very low provided there is sufficient capacity in the system to deal with the demands placed on it at any one time. Therein lies the problem. The demand for telephone services varies according to the time of day. Demand is at its highest during the working day but in the evening and at night, and particularly at weekends, the level of demand is much lower. In economists' terminology this is a classic **peak-load problem**.

As we shall see, however, the peak-load problem facing BT has many of the same features as the problem facing the ferry operator DFDS. Similarly, the way in which BT tackles the problem is to engage in price discrimination.

Consider the key features common to the two examples. For BT, as for DFDS and for the consumers of the services, output is not storable. Demand, however, varies in a predictable way. It is possible to identify different market segments, corresponding in BT's case to different times during the day and different days in the week. These segments are characterized by different levels and elasticities of demand. Because BT is a price-maker rather than a passive price-taker it can discriminate by setting different prices for different times of the day.

These prices are illustrated in Fig. 7.3 which shows the pence per minute for a call. As can be seen, charges depend not only on the distance but also on the time of day and the day of the week in which the call is made. For example, the cost of a local call

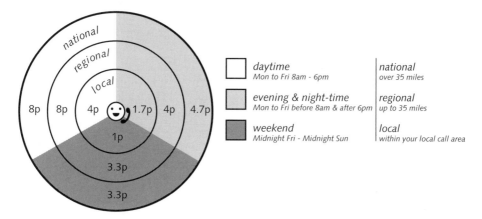

8p   8p   4p   🙂 1.7p   4p   4.7p

1p

3.3p

3.3p

□ **daytime**
Mon to Fri 8am - 6pm

▨ **evening & night-time**
Mon to Fri before 8am & after 6pm

▨ **weekend**
Midnight Fri - Midnight Sun

national
over 35 miles

regional
up to 35 miles

local
within your local call area

Figure 7.3 Pence per minute for a UK call, July 1997 (*Source*: BT Pricing Information Service)

rises from 1 penny per minute at weekends to 1.7 pence per minute during the evening from Monday to Friday and rises again to 4 pence per minute during the working day from Monday to Friday. The peak rate is therefore four times as expensive as the cheap rate.

A number of points need to be re-emphasized. First, for any firm the price charged is influenced by both the *costs* of providing the service and the *demand* for it. BT knows that its marginal costs – the cost of providing an extra unit of output – are very low in the short run provided there is spare capacity. If capacity is fully utilised, however, then in the short run the cost of providing an extra unit of output is infinitely high.

Figure 7.4 represents this diagrammatically. In the short run, that is, with a given amount of capacity, the cost of producing an extra call is only *Oa*. However, once the system becomes fully utilized at its full capacity *Ox* the cost of producing additional calls, given the fixed capacity, becomes infinitely large, so the SRMC curve becomes vertical at that point. The long-run marginal cost curve includes not only the running

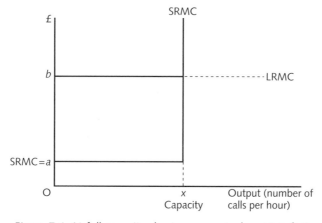

Figure 7.4 At full capacity short-run marginal cost is infinite

costs *Oa* but also the cost of providing additional units of capacity, by installing extra lines, larger switching complexes and so on. This is represented in the diagram by distance *ab* giving an LRMC of *Ob*.

In a sense the prices charged by BT reflect these differences in the costs of providing an extra unit of output. The low price charged to off-peak users reflects the low short-run marginal costs when demand is below capacity. The higher price charged on-peak reflects the higher SRMC when demand pushes up against the capacity constraint.

However, we can also interpret BT's pricing structure as an example of monopolistic price discrimination. Even if costs did not differ between the on-peak and off-peak periods the profit maximizing objective would require a higher price to be charged on-peak where demand is higher and more inelastic. Analytically, that is, the situation is identical to that shown in Fig. 7.1 where the ferry company sets a higher price on-peak even though costs do not vary between high and low season.

BT of course is able to monitor the exact time during the day in which calls are made. It knows that during working hours demand is much more inelastic. The reasons for this are complex but they include *inter alia* the fact that many business calls are made by employees on their employer's behalf. Employees are likely to be much less careful about how they spend their employer's money than they are about how they spend their own.

Prices will, however, affect demand. Although subscribers will probably be unaware of the details of BT's rate structure they will, to a lesser or greater extent, be aware that savings can be made by using the phone off-peak rather than on-peak. This will tend to reduce the peak demand and boost the off-peak demand which is exactly what BT wants. In economists' terminology this is an example of a **shifting peak**.

Pricing and capacity decisions

For a firm faced with a peak-load problem the pricing decision is complex since it will also have implications for the decision about how much capacity to install. In Fig. 7.5 we have superimposed demand curves on to the cost curves we showed earlier in Fig.

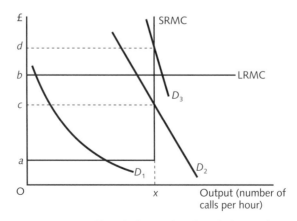

Figure 7.5 Off-peak demand and peak demand

7.4. We have identified, for the purposes of exposition, three levels of demand D_1, D_2 and D_3. The lowest and the most elastic demand is represented by D_1, corresponding to an off-peak demand. A low price of *Oa* will be charged at this time to encourage people to use the phone more. Even at this low price of *Oa*, however, there still remains substantial excess capacity on the system.

At the levels of demand labelled D_2 and D_3, however, the demand for telephone services is pushing up against the limits imposed by the capacity of the system. Demand will always be related to price and a high price will choke off demand so that it can be kept within the capacity of the system. But what price should the firm charge when faced with demands such as D_2 or D_3?

For reasons which will be explained later, economists have traditionally argued that utilities, even if they are monopolies, should be forced to set prices which reflect marginal costs, since this, it is argued, is what competitive firms do. It is unclear, however, which marginal costs – short run or long run – should determine price. Consider the situation that would exist if demand were at D_2. Clearly price must be higher than *Oa* because at this price demand would be far in excess of the capacity of the system. But how high should the price be – *Oc* or *Ob*? At *Oc* the price is just high enough to keep demand within capacity. At a higher price *Ob*, demand would be restricted so that spare capacity would emerge but here the firm is asking consumers to pay the cost of installing additional capacity (LRMC) even though spare capacity already exists (and incidentally violating the $P = SRMC$ rule for price setting).

If demand were D_3 there are again two options for the firm. It can charge a high price of *Od* in order to keep demand within capacity. But this seems a very high price because it exceeds LRMC – in other words it is higher than the cost of providing the service even taking into account the cost of providing the capital equipment in the first place. The alternative is to charge *Ob* and simply let people wait – and play them some soothing music while they hold (usually Vivaldi's *Four Seasons*).

This strategy does, however, produce extreme customer dissatisfaction, and while a monopolist may be able to shrug off customer complaints a competitive firm is likely to lose business to rivals.

There is no easy solution to this problem. The textbook solution (and this is a textbook) is shown in Fig. 7.6 where the firm has expanded its capacity from *Ox* to *Oy* so that, at a price of *Ob*, price is equal to both short-run and long-run marginal cost. In other words the price that a firm charges will be related to the capacity that it has installed. The two decisions – how much to invest in increasing capacity and what price to charge – are thus related.

It must be admitted that the textbook solution is an ideal which is unlikely to be achieved in practice. The reasons for this are that there are time lags involved in the installation of new capacity and that the demand function will not be perfectly predictable and stable.

There is one final but very important point. In Figs 7.4, 7.5 and 7.6 we have sketched out cost curves which, we argued, characterized those facing BT. In fact, they are a rather poor caricature, drawn this way merely for simplicity. In telecommunications there are massive scale economies particularly in satellite communications and other high technology systems. The long-run average cost curve must therefore be

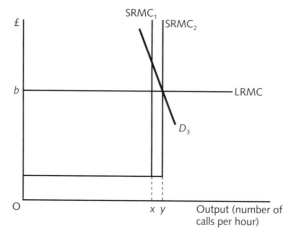

Figure 7.6 Price is related to capacity installed

steeply downward sloping and, for reasons discussed earlier, the long-run marginal cost curve is therefore likely to be downward sloping as well. The implication of this is that extra capacity is likely to *reduce* unit costs – and perhaps prices.

7.5 Down to the sea again: 'Seapex' fares revisited

In section 7.2 we saw how DFDS offered cheaper fares for mid-week travel. These fares are the response of the transport operators to a peak-load problem. No matter what the time of year, the localized peaks in demand occur at weekends, the troughs mid-week. The prices set are designed to encourage passengers to switch their journeys from week-ends to mid-week so as to even out demand.

Summary

It is often possible for firms selling a particular good or service to divide the total market into distinct segments. If demand is more elastic in one segment than in another the firm can increase its overall profitability by charging lower prices where demand is elastic and higher prices where demand is inelastic. Such price discrimination explains why firms such as transport operators and holiday companies charge a higher price on-peak than they do off-peak.

There may also be cost differences to be taken into account. In the short run, when capacity is fixed, marginal costs rise as capacity limitations are reached, implying that higher prices should be charged to reflect these higher costs and to choke off demand. In the long run, when it is possible to vary the amount of capacity installed, pricing and investment decisions are interrelated.

Key terms

Review questions

7.1 'The utilities such as the electricity and telephone companies face a peak-load problem but British Gas does not.' Explain why this is the case.

7.2 Rail operators normally offer cheap return tickets which can only be used for off-peak travel – normally after 10.00 in the morning and at weekends. Explain why.

7.3 Ferry companies tend to charge *more* on Saturdays than they do on Thursdays. But rail operators and airlines tend to charge *less*. What does this tell you about the motivation of the passengers (and who is paying for the ticket)?

7.4 Do you know how much you are paying your phone company for calls at different times of the day? If you are a BT customer you can phone them on 0800 800 891 to find out. This number is almost always busy however. So unless you really want to hear all four of Vivaldi's *Four Seasons* it might be quicker to look at the information available on the Internet at http://www.bt.com/home/.

   Why don't they send you the information with your bill, or send pricing information in advance to all customers?

8. Objectives of the firm

Preview

Neo-classical economics has traditionally assumed that firms have a single objective, that of profit maximization and that they set prices accordingly. But other theories point to the lack of realism of such theories, emphasizing particularly that modern large companies are owned by shareholders but controlled by paid managers who may not benefit directly from the profits the company makes. These managers may therefore pursue different objectives, even though the pursuit of those alternative objectives must be tempered by the requirement to make a reasonable return on assets and thus prevent the company being taken over. The chapter concludes with a look at some recent survey evidence about the objectives which firms pursue and how this influences their pricing decisions.

8.1 Do firms maximize profits?

In Chapter 6 we set out the rules to be followed by the profit-maximizing firm: expand output up to the point where the last unit sold adds as much to revenue as it does to cost – that is, equate marginal revenue (MR) and marginal cost (MC) – and then charge the maximum price the market will be prepared to pay for this level of output. The question which occurs to everyone sooner or later is – do firms actually behave in this way? Do they maximize profit? Do they equate marginal cost and marginal revenue?

The notion that firms maximize profits seems on the face of it to be an overly simplistic view of behaviour. Moreover, it apparently fails to take account of certain important features of firms in the real world. The first of these is the so-called **divorce**

of ownership from control. The dominant form of industrial organization, as we have already noted, is the large firm. Such firms are run by managers who are not themselves the owners of the firm. The owners of the firm are shareholders and it is to this group that profits accrue. Since the shareholders in a public company are normally a widely dispersed group they will find it difficult to exert effective influence on the managers who will therefore be able to pursue whatever objectives they see fit. Therefore, it is said, there is no logical reason to argue that the objectives pursued will be those of profit maximization since profits *per se* do not benefit the individuals who make the pricing and output decisions. Thus the divorce of ownership from control makes the assumption that firms do indeed maximize profits seem less plausible.

Secondly, the process of profit maximization apparently requires firms to equate marginal cost with marginal revenue – two magnitudes which the firm may find it difficult or impossible to measure. In other words, firms will typically not possess the information necessary for them to follow the rules necessary to profit maximization; nor can they acquire such information except, possibly, at prohibitively high cost. We shall investigate the implications of these two points below, in sections 8.2 and 8.3.

8.2 The implications of the divorce between ownership and control

If the managers of large firms are not motivated by the desire to maximize profits – because they themselves do not receive such profits – then what does motivate their behaviour and what are the implications of this for their pricing and output decisions? A number of plausible hypotheses exist. One such is that firms (in the person of the managers who make the decisions in such organizations) attempt to maximize something other than profit. They may for example try to maximize the firm's sales revenue or the long-term growth of the firm. Such hypotheses are associated respectively with Baumol[1] and Marris.[2] Generally speaking, a firm which pursues **sales revenue maximization** as an objective will sell a larger quantity at a lower price than the profit-maximizing firm (the rules for achieving sales maximization are explained in section 6.1). However, their basic objective may need to be tempered by the necessity to attain a certain minimum level of profitability, so that in practice the price and output level may be somewhere between the profit-maximizing level and the sales revenue maximizing level. Note also that sales revenue maximization as an objective is similar – though not identical – to the maximization of market share.

The growth of the firm is the objective pursued by managers in the Marris model. By considering the fortunes of the firm in the longer term, Marris attempts to lift the theory of the firm from its traditional static context into a more dynamic setting. The implications for price and output decisions are by no means clear cut, however. The necessary finance to fund the long-term expansion of the firm can most readily be obtained internally through retained profits. Thus growth maximization is not necessarily inconsistent with profit maximization. It may, however, also be consistent with the Baumol model of sales revenue maximization, since the managers could equate the growth of sales with the growth of the company.

A slightly different approach associated with Williamson[3] is to argue that managers attempt to maximize their **utility**, that is, the intrinsic satisfaction they get from their work. Managers derive utility from a number of different aspects of their job. They may, for example, derive satisfaction from the status that they have within the company and from the company's status within the wider corporate environment (that is, relative to other firms) and in society generally. Their personal status within the company will depend on the number of staff for whom they are responsible – the size of their department within the company – and the number of managerial perks they can acquire – company car, expense account, trips abroad, and so on. Thus one might expect that, if such managers attempt to maximize anything, they would, within the limits of their discretion, attempt to maximize expenditure on staff and **managerial slack** (that is, perks). Their standing in the world outside the company, however, will depend on the image that the company presents. Thus, other things being equal, one would expect the managers to promote not just the growth of the company but, more importantly, to promote those activities designed to enhance its corporate image. Thus sports sponsorship, support for the arts and local community projects, and expenditure on lavish office buildings can be seen as having a dual role. Not only do such expenditures assist the company in marketing its products by promoting a favourable image of the company to the consumer, they also increase the utility of its managers, since the status of the manager depends on the status of the firm. Such expenditures would be termed **discretionary investment**. They are expenditures over and above what is necessary to maximize the firm's profits or its sales revenue.

Williamson formalized his model of managerial behaviour in terms of a utility function. Subject to a minimum profit constraint, managers attempt to maximize their utility (U) which depends on expenditures on staff (S), discretionary investment (ID) and managerial slack (M).

$$U = f (S, ID, M)$$

Because of these expenditures such firms have operating costs in excess of those which are strictly necessary to promote the firm's growth or profitability. In a sense, therefore, such firms are inefficient, but they are deliberately inefficient through choice. The term **X-inefficiency** was coined by Leibenstein[4] to describe such a situation in which a firm suffered from – or enjoyed – a cost structure which had built into it an allowance for these non-necessary expenditures. X-inefficient firms can still be profit maximizers, however, so in this sense the Leibenstein model is rather different from that of Williamson.

Up to now all the models we have discussed have an explicit maximand: profits, sales revenue, growth or utility. Some authors would argue, however, that typically firms do not attempt to maximize anything. These are the so-called **behavioural theories of the firm**. Such theories, associated with a number of writers including Cyert and March,[5] and Simon,[6] analyse or describe the process by which decisions are arrived at in the firm. It is important to recognize, they argue, that the firm is an organization composed of a number of groups with differing and possibly opposing interests. For example, the sales department may be pursuing market share or sales revenue as an objective; the stock control department may be anxious to avoid stock-out situations even if this means the maintenance of uneconomically high levels of stocks; the marketing department may be concerned with product innovation; the director and shareholders with the profitability of the company; and the technical department (if there is one) with the technical excellence of the product. The decisions which emerge from behind the closed doors of the company are the net result of the interplay between these various interest groups, the outcome obviously being influenced by the relative strength of each group.

Managers working within such an organisation, it is argued, may display '**satisficing**' rather than maximizing behaviour. That is, they will aspire to certain target levels of profitability, sales, market share, and so on. If these levels are not attained, managers will both revise downwards their aspirations and seek other ways of attaining them. In summary, the behavioural theories of the firm describe the *process* by which decisions are taken. Clearly, this process does not involve equating marginal cost and marginal revenue or anything remotely like it.

This brings us back to the second feature of firms in the real world that we mentioned in section 8.1: firms are (apparently) prevented from maximizing profit by a lack of the requisite information on marginal cost and marginal revenue. Instead of attempting to maximize profit therefore, they may simply set prices according to some arbitrary mark-up principle – that is, they work out what their costs are, add on a bit for profit, and that is the price they charge. This is known as **cost-plus pricing** and is the subject of the next section.

8.3 Cost-plus pricing

Hall and Hitch,[7] two American economists working in the 1930s, set out to test the empirical validity of the profit-maximizing model of the firm. They did so in a rather naive way by questioning businessmen about how they arrived at their price and output decisions. The businessmen questioned denied strenuously that they equated marginal cost with marginal revenue or that they maximized profit. One is tempted to quote Mandy Rice-Davis's remark when asked by the Press to comment on a denial made in somewhat different circumstances: 'Well, they would say that, wouldn't they?'[8] In other words, it was a naive question to ask. Businessmen will not use the same words to describe their actions as economists do. Thus phrases like 'profit maximization', 'marginal cost' and 'marginal revenue' are not within the businessman's vocabulary. We have already noted that information on marginal cost and revenue is unlikely to be available, and profit maximization, as an objective, is not something to which firms would readily admit. Such an objective does not fit in well with the image of itself that the company would like to promote – that of a socially responsible and caring organization. What Hall and Hitch's enquiries failed to take into account is the fact that the phrase 'profit-maximization' is merely a shorthand way of saying that profitability is the criterion by which firms judge success, and that they seek success. Put in this somewhat less stark way, many firms would agree that this is indeed their objective. However, very few, if any, would agree that the procedure they use to achieve it involved unmeasurable magnitudes like marginal cost and marginal revenue.

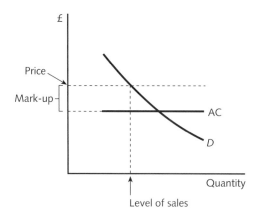

Figure 8.1 Mark-up pricing

Most firms when questioned in fact described a process which has subsequently come to be called cost-plus pricing or **full-cost pricing** or **mark-up pricing**. Such firms first work out their average cost which is reasonably constant over quite a wide range of output, as in Fig. 8.1. They then add on a (possibly arbitrarily determined) mark-up of a certain percentage in order to arrive at the price to charge. They then sell what they can at this price. (Sales will, of course, be determined by the demand curve facing the firm, but firms will typically have no knowledge of this curve).

The major deficiency with this explanation of how firms set prices is that it does not attempt to explain how the magnitude of the mark-up is determined. In practice it may be based on the average rate of return of similar firms in the industry or on some target rate of return. But the theory cannot explain how these average or target rates of return are set. What may well happen in practice is that the size of the mark-up is adjusted and its effect on sales and profitability noted, until by a trial-and-error process the firm arrives at the mark-up, and hence the price, which gives it most profit. In other words, the firm charges the profit-maximizing price, but it arrives at that price via an iterative process rather than by a process which involves equating marginal cost and marginal revenue.

Thus, in common with many of the other behavioural models, full-cost pricing is not necessarily inconsistent with the models of behaviour which take profit maximization to be the objective. The purpose for which the two models are constructed is rather different, however. The cost-plus pricing model is a description of a process: its weakness is that it has little predictive or analytical power. The marginalist (profit-maximizing) model is not meant to be a realistic description. Rather it is an analytical tool and to criticize it for its lack of realism is to misunderstand the purpose behind its construction.

8.4 Pricing and objectives: trainers

Information on prices and on costs can sometimes be used to shed light on the objectives that firms pursue, since one can infer something about the basis on which those prices are set. Unfortunately for the economist, data on costs are seldom available, although data on prices are clearly in the public domain. Occasionally, however, it is possible to make sensible guesses about costs.

Consider the market for shoes, and especially for trainers. Small sizes (up to size 7 in the UK system of measurement) are only suitable for children. These shoes are normally considerably cheaper than larger sizes – often only a half or a third of the price of the larger sizes. Such a large price difference cannot be explained by the fact that only adult shoes are subject to a VAT. Moreover – and this is where the sensible guess comes in – the cost of manufacturing children's shoes is not significantly less than that of adult sizes, since the most important element of the cost is labour, and the amount of labour required to make a shoe will be the same regardless of size. One can therefore infer that the mark-up on adult size trainers must be much greater than that on children's. One presumes that both the manufacturer and the retailer are choosing the mark-up so as to maximize the profits that they get from selling these products, that is, that they are pursuing the objective of profit maximization.

Note also that this is a further example of price discrimination (introduced in the previous chapter). The seller chooses the mark-up according to the perceived elasticity of demand in the segment of the market which he is addressing. In the adult sector of the market, demand is rather price-inelastic, particularly among fashion-conscious teenagers, who are prepared to pay high prices for the fashionable brand. In contrast, children's shoes are bought by their parents who, being older and more boring, will be less swayed by the advertising of the trainer manufacturers, and will also probably have less money to spend on their children's shoes.

Similar price discrimination can be found in the market for cars, a market which has been extensively studied by economists. Prices on the UK market have been significantly higher than prices of identical models sold on the continental European market. Again, this has nothing to do with differences in costs. Rather it reflects differences in the elasticity of demand between Britain and Europe. In Britain the demand for cars is relatively inelastic, partly because such a high percentage of cars are sold to companies rather than individuals (approximately 50 per cent of cars are sold to companies). Thus mark-ups, and therefore prices, are high (though companies can negotiate large discounts on the posted prices). Where demand is more elastic, as in continental Europe, prices tend to be lower. Moreover, within the model range of a particular manufacturer, mark-ups tend to be higher for larger cars. That is, manufacturers make more profit on large cars than on small ones, since large cars are not much more expensive to produce than on small ones. Price differentials within a model range owe much more to differing elasticities than to differences in the cost of production.

8.5 Pricing and objectives: some survey evidence

In principle there are two methods of finding out about firms' objectives. The first is to make inferences from information about prices and costs and this was discussed in the previous section. The second method is simply to ask firms on what basis they set prices, which is a similar methodology to that employed by Hall and Hitch.

Table 8.1 How are prices determined?

	Number of firms	Percentage of firms
Market level	257	39
Competitors' prices	161	25
Direct cost plus variable mark-up	131	20
Direct cost plus fixed mark-up	108	17
Customer set	33	5
Regulatory agency	11	2

Note: the percentage in column 2 sums to more than 100 per cent because companies were able to choose more than one response as their top preference (the total in fact sums to 108 per cent).
Source: 'How do UK companies set prices?' *Bank of England Quarterly Bulletin*, May 1996.

Such an approach was used in a recent survey entitled 'How do UK companies set prices?' in which the Bank of England contacted some 1100 industrial companies, 654 of whom agreed to participate. They were sent questionnaires, the information from which is summarized in Tables 8.1 and 8.2.

When asked how they set prices the largest proportion of respondents (almost 40 per cent) stated that prices were set 'at the highest level the market could bear'. An additional 25 per cent of firms said that they set prices in relation to their competitors. However, a significant minority stated that they based prices on the mark-up principle – 20 per cent of firms applied a variable mark-up and 17 per cent a fixed mark-up.

It is difficult to assess the significance of these results. One reason for this, as we have already noted, is that mark-up pricing is not incompatible with choosing the maximum price the market can bear. The two things can co-exist. For example, the size of the mark-up or the frequency at which it is recalculated may well depend on market conditions – the higher and more inelastic the demand, the higher the mark-up.

Table 8.2 Factors leading to a rise or fall in price

Rise	No.	%	Fall	No.	%
Rise in demand	101	15	Fall in demand	146	20
Rival's price rise	105	15	Rival's price cut	235	32
Higher market share	14	2	Lower market share	69	9
Increase in material costs	421	61	Decrease in material costs	186	25
Increase in interest rates	18	3	Decrease in interest rates	8	1
Fall in productivity	5	1	Rise in productivity	22	3
Prices never rise	26	4	Prices never fall	75	10

Source: derived from 'How do UK companies set prices?' *Bank of England Quarterly Bulletin*, May 1996. Firms were allowed to cite more than one factor as most important, and the percentages shown have been recalculated by the author so that they can be compared.

To try to provide some sort of check on the consistency of the answers given, respondents were also asked what factors were most important in leading to a rise or a fall in prices. There was a marked asymmetry in the answers given. As can be seen from the table, fewer firms stated that a rise in demand would lead to a rise in price than stated that a fall in demand would lead to a price cut. More marked was the fact that many more companies claimed that an increase in costs would lead to an increase in prices than claimed that a fall in costs would lead to a fall in prices.

No clear conclusions can be drawn from this, either as an answer to the question about how prices are set or what this implies about the objectives that firms pursue.

Summary

The divorce between ownership and control calls into question the traditional model of profit-maximizing behaviour. Other models suggest that firms may attempt to maximize sales revenue, market share, the long-term growth of the firm, or the utility of its managers. In addition, the behavioural models stress that the firm may not try to maximize anything – rather the managers may be pursuing their own objectives which may imply some sort of satisficing behaviour.

In general, the behavioural theories seem to provide a more realistic description of the behaviour of firms. But their analytical power is poor, and they are not very useful in examining firms' pricing and output decisions. In contrast, models which assume the objective of profit maximization have strong analytical power despite their seeming lack of realism.

Notes

1 Baumol, W.T. (1967) *Business Behaviour, Value and Growth*, Harcourt, Brace and World Inc.
2 Marris, R.L. (1964) *The Economic Theory of Managerial Capitalism*, Macmillan.
3 Williamson, O. (1964) *The Economics of Discretionary Behaviour: Managerial Objectives in a Theory of the Firm*, Prentice-Hall.
4 Leibenstein, H. (1966) 'Allocative-Efficiency versus X-efficiency', *American Economic Review*.
5 Cyert, R.M. and March, J.G. (1963) *A Behavioural Theory of the Firm*, Prentice-Hall.
6 Simon, H.A. (1969) 'On the Concept of Organisational Goal', reprinted in H.I. Ansoff (ed.) *Business Strategy*, Penguin.
7 Hall, R.L. and Hitch, C.J. (1951) 'Price Theory and Business Behaviour', reprinted in T. Wilson and P.W.S. Andrews (eds), *Oxford Studies in the Price Mechanism*, OUP.
8 For those readers too young to remember or otherwise out of touch with British political scandal in the 1960s, Mandy Rice-Davis was a high-class call-girl who claimed to have had an affair with a cabinet minister, John Profumo. He initially denied the allegation. Miss Rice-Davis, when asked by the Press to comment on his denial, replied 'Well he would say that, wouldn't he?'

Key terms

Review questions

8.1 What do you understand by the following terms?
  (a) divorce between ownership and control
  (b) satisficing behaviour
  (c) utility maximizing behaviour
  (d) managerial slack
  (e) a 'mark-up' model of pricing behaviour
  (f) marginalist theories of the firm.

8.2 (a) Why might the managers of a firm be more interested in growth of the firm than its profitability?
  (b) What constrains these managers in their attempt to maximize growth?
  (c) Why don't firms who base their prices on their full costs of production pay more attention to the demand conditions for their product?

8.3 Is the following statement true or false? Explain why. 'If a firm bases its price on full costs of production it will not be maximizing its profits.'

8.4 Why do economists insist on using models of the firm which assume profit maximization when it is so patently unrealistic?

8.5 News report
In June 1995 4500 British Gas shareholders attended the company's annual general meeting. They voted overwhelmingly for the resignation of Cedric Brown, the Chief Executive, who had recently been awarded a 71 per cent pay increase. Chairman Richard Giordano faced more than five hours of attacks by shareholders on the company's executive pay policy, poor standards of service and other alleged failings. But the demands of those present were quashed by the block votes of major institutional investors who had lined up in support of the Board before the meeting.

British Gas is of course a company characterized by the 'divorce between ownership and control' but does this news report shed any additional light on the issues involved?

Postscript: British Gas was restructured in 1996 and Mr Brown has taken early retirement.

9 Behaviour in oligopolistic markets

Preview

This chapter looks at a number of different aspects of the behaviour of firms in oligopolistic markets. This is often subject to scrutiny by the Monopolies and Mergers Commission which is charged with the responsibility for investigating markets where firms may be abusing their market power. The MMC tends to fix not so much on the degree of concentration currently in existence but on the ease with which firms can enter or leave the market.

The range of strategies pursued by firms in oligopolistic markets is very wide, depending as it does on the competitive position in which they find themselves. This chapter illustrates the types of strategies which are pursued by the use of case studies of different industries.

The chapter also looks at some theoretical models of behaviour in such markets, in particular models developed from Game Theory.

9.1 Concentration and the public interest

A long-standing debate in economics centres around the question of whether highly concentrated market structures (monopoly, oligopoly) are detrimental to the public interest. The idea that competition is good and monopoly is bad is founded on the proposition – based on rather shaky analysis – that price will be higher and output lower under monopoly than they would be under competition. The validity of this proposition can be easily demonstrated, but only if we make two crucial assumptions, one of which is clearly unrealistic. The assumptions are, first, that firms attempt to maximize profits irrespective of the market structure in which they operate and, secondly, that cost structures are the same whether the market for a particular good is supplied by one monopoly seller or by a large number of smaller competing firms. While the first assumption may be a reasonable approximation to reality (readers can judge for themselves, having read Chapter 8), the second is clearly not, since large firms can almost always benefit from scale economies which will give them a cost advantage over smaller firms. If we do make these two assumptions, however, then we can see from Fig. 9.1 the correctness of the proposition that the monopoly price (P_m) is higher than the competitive price (P_c) and monopoly output (q_m) is lower than the competitive output (q_c).

Note that in Fig. 9.1 the industry supply curve (S) is assumed to be equivalent to the monopolist's marginal cost curve (MC). This follows from the assumption we made that cost conditions are the same whether the industry is composed of one firm or is fragmented into a number of small competing firms. In competition, price is determined by the intersection of this supply curve and the demand curve (giving a price of P_c and an output of q_c) whereas the monopolist equates marginal cost to marginal revenue to arrive at an output level of q_m and a price of P_m. In practice, of course, the monopolist would enjoy scale economies which would reduce his costs relative to those of smaller competing firms. If these scale economies were substantial the monopoly price would be less than the competitive price and the monopoly output level higher than the competitive output level. Figure 9.2 illustrates this possibility.

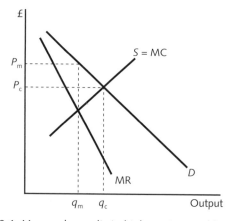

Figure 9.1 Monopoly results in higher prices and lower output

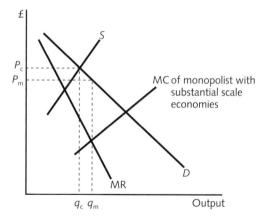

Figure 9.2 But the effect of scale economies can lead to lower prices

Thus the major justification for monopoly – or market concentration generally – rests on the proposition that large firms will enjoy cost advantages over smaller competing firms and that these lower costs will ultimately result in lower prices to consumers. That is, the benefits of lower costs more than outweigh any possible disadvantages which might result from the abuse of monopoly power.

However, we have already noted (in section 3.5) that firm size and plant size are not the same thing. Although large firms with substantial market power may enjoy scale economies as a result of the concentration of production in a few large plants, they often engage in **multiplant operation**, preferring to decentralize their production into a number of smaller plants. The existence of multiplant operation weakens the claim that market concentration is in the public interest. Concentration is only in the public interest if large firms enjoy *technical* cost advantages over smaller firms. Often, however, the advantages they have result from their market power rather than from technical economies of scale.

While bearing this point in mind it is nevertheless true that large firms do benefit from scale economies. This is borne out by the evidence of Chapter 5 and, in particular, Table 5.2 which gives engineering estimates of minimum efficient plant sizes (MEPS) for a number of industries. It would clearly be inefficient and against the public interest to insist that such industries operate below the MEPS merely to ensure a degree of competition in the industry, if significant cost penalties resulted from this.

In Britain the agency charged with the responsibility of investigating industries where firms have substantial market power is the **Monopolies and Mergers Commission (MMC)**. In addition to the merger activity which it is required to investigate (discussed in section 9.7), the MMC is empowered to investigate market situations in which a single firm controls over 25 per cent of the market for a particular product (or where a group of firms, acting together so as to restrict competition, jointly controls over 25 per cent of the market). Thus the terms of reference of the MMC are very much wider than might have been imagined from the definition of a monopoly as a single seller. In fact, the expression 'a monopoly situation' used in this context is merely a convenient shorthand for some rather more cumbersome phrase about 'an oligopoly situation in which the dominant firm's market share exceeds 25 per cent.' The MMC's remit is to consider whether monopoly situations such as these are in the public interest, and in carrying out its remit the MMC has due regard to the evidence on scale economies that it can obtain from the firm under investigation. However, in deciding whether or not a particular monopoly situation is in the public interest there are additional considerations which are taken into account. For example, the MMC investigates the firm's pricing behaviour, aspects of price and non-price competition and any alleged restrictions on competition.

9.2 Traditional and modern views about monopoly

It is possible to discern a shift of emphasis (which some writers[1] have described as a revolution) in the way that economists view the whole question of monopoly and the public interest. The traditional view outlined in section 9.1 has two aspects:

1 A monopoly situation is a market structure which is defined purely in terms of the degree of concentration.
2 Monopolies, so defined, may or may not act against the public interest. This depends on the objectives of the firm, its ability to benefit from scale economies, and so on.

In contrast, the modern view can be characterized as follows:

1 A monopoly situation is a market structure which cannot be defined purely in terms of the degree of concentration. Rather, the ease with which new firms can enter the market (and leave it) should be taken into account.
2 A monopoly situation therefore can be defined as a situation in which a firm has a dominant position and is protected against the entry of new firms by effective barriers.
3 It is highly probable that monopolies, so defined, will act against the public interest so that it is appropriate that anti-monopoly investigations concentrate on the alleged anti-competitive devices employed by a firm (that is, devices designed to bolster the firm's monopolistic position by erection of entry barriers).
4 In addition, the modern view emphasizes that ease of exit is also important. New firms will not commit themselves to high levels of capital expenditure (that is, they will not enter) if that capital equipment cannot subsequently be turned to an alternative use (that is, if they are unable to leave if they wish to do so).

To express these modern views in a slightly different way we can say that if (real) monopoly power exists it will probably be abused, that is, prices and profits will be higher. The existence of these profits will, however, invariably attract other firms into the market to secure some of the profits for themselves, provided that there are no barriers to entry. The threat posed by the potential entry of new firms will cause the existing firms to react in one of two ways. They may moderate their pricing behaviour, limiting themselves to the sort of prices and profits that would be found in a competitive market, thus eliminating the incentive for other firms to enter. Such firms therefore are not true monopolists because any attempt to exercise market power results in its eventual erosion. Alternatively, the threat of new entrants may cause the monopolist to react by indulging in tactics the sole purpose of which is to restrict competition. The erection of entry barriers, which take many different forms, is the most important of these anti-competitive tactics. Only if such anti-competitive tactics are successful in excluding new entrants does a true monopoly situation exist. In this case some government intervention is necessary to limit the power of the monopolist and to prevent it acting against the public interest.

In summary, we can say that the degree of concentration is not the only criterion by which to define monopoly situations. Of equal importance is the degree to which the firm enjoys a position protected from the threat of new entrants. This approach, sometimes labelled the **contestable markets** approach, is thus more dynamic in contrast to the more static traditional approach. It draws attention to the likely future developments which may occur when and if new firms enter the market.

9.3 Case Study: Enter the Mars ice-cream

In section 2.3 we looked at the market for impulse ice-cream which now has three major players – Wall's, Nestlé-Lyons and Mars. However, Mars is a newcomer, having entered the market as late as 1989. Up until that time the market was more or less a duopoly dominated by Wall's and Lyons.

Although Mars found it comparatively easy to penetrate the 'take-home market' (sold through supermarkets) with its new ice-cream Mars, it experienced difficulties in establishing a foothold in the impulse sector. Mars complained to the OFT about certain practices operated by Wall's and Lyons which it claimed acted as barriers to entry designed to prevent new firms getting into the market and to limit competition. The issue was eventually considered by the MMC in a report published in 1994.

One of the key points in Mars' submission to the MMC was that of 'freezer exclusivity'. Both Wall's and Nestlé-Lyons supplied freezer cabinets free of charge to those outlets that stocked their products but only on the condition that the freezer would not be used to stock other company's products. Mars sought to have the exclusivity clause made illegal on the grounds that it constituted a barrier to the entry of new firms.

In delivering its judgement the MMC took into account that in the four years since its entry into the market Mars ice-cream had achieved representation in about 50 per cent of outlets and had gained a market share of about 16 per cent in the impulse sector. It concluded that freezer exclusivity was not a barrier to entry even though it was a *cost* of entry, because Mars was compelled to offer freezer cabinets to outlets to persuade them to stock its product. In this respect it represented a cost to the new entrant similar to other costs such as advertising.

9.4 Pricing strategies in oligopolistic markets

In a monopoly situation, as the reader is now aware, there is an incentive for the monopolist to raise prices above the competitive level and thus earn monopoly profits (super-normal profits). In an oligopoly, particularly a tight-knit oligopoly in which the number of firms with a significant market share is very small, there will be an incentive for the firms to act in concert as if they were a single monopolist, jointly maintaining prices in the industry above the competitive level in an attempt to maximize industry profits. Such behaviour is known as **joint profit maximizing behaviour**. It involves **collusion** since prices in the industry are set and maintained by a tacit agreement among the major suppliers not to indulge in competitive price cutting. Although the incentive to collude is strong there will be an opposing tendency, namely to compete actively by cutting prices in an attempt to steal market share away from the other firms in the industry. However, such action is likely to provoke a response from rival firms. If the rivals match the price cuts brought in by the instigator then the net result will be that prices in the industry will fall. The consumer benefits as prices fall below the joint profit-maximizing level.

Short-term considerations must also be tempered by the desire to maximize profits in the longer run. High super-normal profits will provide an incentive for new firms to enter the industry. The entry of these new firms will weaken the monopolistic position of the existing firms and reduce their ability to earn super-normal profits in the long run. To prevent the possibility of this happening, existing firms may forgo some of the super-normal profits they could earn in the short run, opting instead for lower prices as a way of deterring new entrants. Such a policy is known as **limit pricing** since the prices set are just low enough to discourage other firms from entering the market.

With an eye to the longer term the firm may even attempt to drive its existing rivals out of business by engaging in **predatory pricing**. As the name implies, a market leader who has lower costs by virtue of size may prey on its rivals by forcing prices down. Faced with such an attack, the firm which is being preyed upon has only two defences. It can try to match the price cuts which it will probably be unable to do since its unit costs (including marketing costs) are higher than those of the market leader. Alternatively, it can stick to a higher price, in which case it will lose market share. Whichever of these two options is pursued, it may fall victim to this predatory pricing and be forced out of the market. This leaves the surviving market leader in a stronger monopolistic position where it can raise prices and reap the monopoly profits which are its reward.

Such actively aggressive behaviour is, however, rare, particularly in oligopolies where no clear market leader exists. Even where one firm does have a dominant position in the market, it is likely to tolerate the existence of its smaller rivals. In such situations the dominant firm often assumes the role of a **price leader**, dictating the price in the market, while the smaller firms assume the role of **price followers**. This brings considerable benefits to the firms in the market. If all of them 'know their place' and act in accordance with their allotted role then much of the uncertainty can be removed. Firms in oligopolistic markets live in a very uncertain world since the outcome of any particular action depends on the reaction of rivals. A *modus vivendi* which allows the uncertainty to be reduced brings benefits to all the firms concerned. Such an arrangement is, of course, a form of collusive behaviour.

9.5 Case Study: Price leadership in the car market

In any particular market the largest firm can be described as the **market leader** and will normally take on the role of price leader. The following quotations from the MMC report on the car market illustrate how the supplying firms saw their position within that market when giving evidence to the Commission.

- Most suppliers told the MMC that they regarded either Ford or Ford and Vauxhall as market leaders overall. Renault preferred the term 'main competitive bench-marks' which it saw as applying currently to Ford and Vauxhall.
- Market leadership was more easily identified for a given *segment* of the market.
- We were told by Peugeot that it regarded Ford as the market leader in the small and lower medium segments with the Fiesta and the Escort: Vauxhall in the upper medium segment with the Cavalier; and Ford, Vauxhall and Rover as market leaders in the large segment.
- NMUK (Nissan) said that for its Primera it saw the price leaders as Ford (with the Sierra) and Vauxhall (with the Cavalier).
- VAG (Volkswagen) said that, while Ford might be the market leader overall, Vauxhall's Cavalier held a very important position in the upper medium segment.
- Renault told the MMC that it regarded the Toyota Previa and Range Rover as bench-marks for its Espace.
- Vauxhall said that Ford could be regarded as the market leader as it was the largest supplier of new cars in the United Kingdom. However, Vauxhall said it did not regard the concept of price leadership as useful in analysing competition in the United Kingdom.
- Ford accepted that it was the leader in terms of market share, but that, although it had priced first on a number of occasions, other suppliers had priced first on other occasions. Hence it did not consider itself to be the price leader. It believed, how-ever, that it was normal business practice for suppliers with smaller market shares to wait and see what price adjustments were made by the leader and then to price in a competitive way.

Source: 'New Motor Cars: a report on the supply of new motor cars within the United Kingdom, MMC, February 1992, p. 89.

9.6 Case Study: Predatory pricing – Stagecoach

When you hear the word 'stagecoach' you probably think of cowboys. This may well be what the MMC thinks too, about the bus and train operator that bears that name. Stagecoach is a rags-to-riches company. When it was founded in 1980 it had just two second-hand coaches running a Dundee to London service. Fifteen years later it was Britain's largest bus operator with 6500 vehicles and around 12 per cent of the UK bus market as well as the rail franchise for South West Trains. Its remarkable growth has mostly been through acquisitions. The tactics it has used have been the subject of numerous complaints from rival operators and have led to several investigations by the competition authorities – around twenty referrals to the Office of Fair Trading and four by the Monopolies Commission. A report in 1995 by the MMC described the actions of Busways (a subsidiary of Stagecoach) as 'predatory'.

Predatory action or **predation** is deliberately intended to eliminate a competitor from the market so as to create a monopolistic or quasi monopolistic situation from which the predator can then benefit – for example, by enabling it subsequently to charge higher prices and reduce output. Predatory pricing consists of *temporarily* charging very low prices – often well below cost – so as to get rid of a competitor. Such behaviour is clearly against the public interest because in the long run the consumer is faced with higher prices and a smaller choice of supplier.

The 1995 MMC report on Stagecoach Busways analyses a series of events which took place in Darlington. These actions resulted in the former council-owned Darlington Transport Company (DTC) being forced out of business. The MMC found that Busways had:

1 deliberately poached most of DTC's workforce from them over a short period of time thus depriving them of the ability to operate normally;
2 discouraged potential purchasers of DTC (which at the time was up for sale) by registering its intention to run services on all of DTC's routes;
3 finally, running free services on DTC's routes.

The MMC report judged that these actions were 'predatory, deplorable and against the public interest.' For its part Stagecoach clearly saw them as legitimate business practice. It was well used to such tactics and to such criticism – an earlier MMC report in 1994 had forced the company to give undertakings to limit fare increases and maintain the frequency of its services after its action in Bognor Regis, Sussex, in charging 'uneconomic' fares had forced a smaller operator to leave town.

9.7 Case Study: Cartels – concrete evidence

In 1995 the OFT imposed fines of £8.4m on nine concrete suppliers including RMC, Tarmac, Redland, ARC and Pioneer, all of whom had been engaged in local price fixing agreements and 'serious anti-competitive activity.' The companies had in fact been running a **cartel**.

The cartel had been operating for many years and it was the nature of the business which had encouraged the collusion. Because ready-mix concrete cannot be transported over great distances, deliveries are usually within 15 miles of the manufacturing site, making local knowledge and contacts vital. Salesmen, supposedly in competition with each other, would meet to pool information and carve up the market between them in a pre-arranged tendering system. Such arrangements were described by the judge Mr Justice Brockley as 'endemic'.

The OFT had investigated the market in the 1970s and the companies had given undertakings to the court in 1978-79 that they would not take part in such anti-competitive agreements in future. However, evidence was given to the court that the agreements had restarted almost as soon as the undertakings were given. It was stated that there was knowledge of this at a 'high level' and the directors of the various companies were told by the judge that they would be jailed if found guilty of contempt of court in future.

The case illustrates the difficulty of policing and enforcing judgments laid down by the Restrictive Practices Court.

9.8 Case Study: Petrol retailing

This case study looks at the changes in the market for petrol that have occurred in the post-war period. It illustrates how structural changes – particularly those relating to concentration – bring with them changes in the behaviour of firms within the market.

At the wholesale level the market for petrol in the UK is an oligopoly. However, the market has witnessed a reduction in seller concentration over the last 30 years, such that no firm is now the undisputed price leader. Table 9.1 shows changes in the degree of seller concentration in the period 1953-91. 1953 is a convenient starting point since this date marks the abolition of wartime price controls and the reintroduction of branding.

Market share in Table 9.1 is measured by the percentage of the total retail outlets supplied by each firm. As can be seen in 1953 five firms supplied virtually the whole market. One firm, Shell-Mex and BP Ltd, who at that time shared a joint retailing

Table 9.1 Reduction in concentration (shares of the UK retail market for petrol (%))

	1953	1960	1975	1976	1980	1991
Shell	51.4	49.4	40.8	22.9	16.9	13.6
BP				17.4	11.6	10.2
Esso	28.4	29.8	21.8	22.0	20.0	12.9
Texaco	14.0	12.5	8.0	7.7	8.0	6.5
Mobil	1.1	4.2	4.3	4.4	4.8	4.6
Petrofina	2.2	2.5	3.8	3.7	3.8	4.3
Others	2.9	1.6	21.3	21.9	34.9	47.9

The figures are for the percentage share of total retail outlets, an approximate indication of sales.
Notes: Shell and BP shared a joint retailing organization, Shell Mex and BP Ltd, until 1976, after which their respective market shares are shown separately.

In 1991 the 'others' comprised Burmah (7.0%), Conoco (5.7%), Kuwait (4.5%), UK, Elf, Total, Anglo, Gulf, Murco and others not listed separately.
Source: early years' figures quoted in R. W. Shaw and C. J. Sutton, *Industry and Competition*, Macmillan, 1976 and from R. M. Grant, 'Pricing behaviour in the UK wholesale market for petrol 1970-80: a structure-conduct analysis, *Journal of Industrial Economics*, Vol. XXX, March 1982. Later years' figures from *Retail Marketing Survey*, 1991, *Petroleum Review* and Institute of Petroleum.

Table 9.2 Wholesalers' shares of the retail market for petrol (by gallonage)

Company	Market share (%)					
	1964	*1970*	*1975*	*1976*	*1980*	*1988*
Shell-Mex and BP Ltd	45.0	39.6	35.0	—	—	—
Munster Sims						
Shell UK	—	—	—	19.3	22.6	16.5
Esso	27.4	23.4	19.2	18.7	19.6	19.3
BP Oil	—	—	—	14.7	15.1	12.7
Texaco/*Regent*	11.1	8.0	9.4	9.1	8.2	9.6
Mobil	6.0	7.1	6.6	7.0	7.1	7.7
Conoco/*Jet*	3.5	3.8	4.1	4.2	5.4	6.1
Total Oil	1.5	3.1	4.8	4.5	2.8	3.9
Elf/*VIP/Isherwoods*	0.8	2.1	2.3	2.8	2.8	3.0
Petrofina UK Ltd	2.5	2.4	2.8	2.9	2.2	3.9
Burmah/*Lobitos/Major*	—	2.6	2.9	3.1	1.6	4.6
ICI	—	0.9	2.6	2.7	2.7	0.0
Gulf Oil	0.2	1.0	1.9	2.5	2.3	3.0
Amoco	—	1.2	1.8	1.8	2.5	1.8
Kuwait	—	—	—	—	2.5	2.3
Others	0.8	4.8	6.7	5.9	5.1	5.5

Companies whose names are shown in *italic* type were taken over during the period.
Source: as for Table 9.1 and for later years from MMC Survey Report.

organization, had over 50 per cent of the market. The top three firms – Shell-BP, Esso and Texaco – had a combined market share of almost 94 per cent.

Since 1953, however, concentration in the market has declined continuously, a milestone in this process being the splitting up of Shell-Mex and BP into separate companies in 1976. By 1991 the top four firms had less than 45 per cent of the market and there were numerous smaller players.

The figures in Table 9.1 measure market share rather imperfectly, since they may tend to overestimate the share of firms with a large number of small sites and underestimate the share of firms who concentrate sales into a smaller number of high-volume sites in prime locations. Data on gallonage are a more satisfactory measure of market share and are shown for selected years in Table 9.2. As we would expect, the picture which emerges is one of declining concentration.

Structure – conduct – performance

The reduction in concentration was a key aspect of the change in the **structure** of the industry, which in turn brought with it a change in the **conduct** of the firms operating there. Note the wording of the previous sentence. It says that the change in structure *brought with it* a change in conduct. We could have said that the change in structure *led to* a change in conduct which implies a definite causal link, but this would have been too strong since the causal link, though hypothesized, is by no means firmly established. We could, alternatively, have said that the change in structure *was accompanied by* a change in conduct but this would have missed the whole point, which is that the conduct (and **performance**) of an industry is influenced, if not determined, by its structure, the most important, but not the only, aspect of which is the degree of concentration.

As we saw earlier, the behaviour of firms in oligopolistic markets is uncertain because they are torn between the desire to compete and the opposing desire to collude. At any one time a firm's decision as to which of these two strategies to pursue will be influenced by the following considerations.

1   Seller concentration
Other things being equal, the smaller the number of firms in an industry the easier it will be for them to collude if they wish to do so. The recognition of mutual interdependence will be that much greater and communication, both direct and implied, between the firms will be easier. The extent to which firms recognize their mutual interdependence will depend on the degree of cross-price elasticity of demand for their products. In other words, if the output of one firm is a very close substitute for the output of another, the cross-price elasticity, and therefore the recognition of interdependence, will be high. This condition is clearly satisfied in the market for petrol, since petrol is viewed by the consumer as a more or less homogeneous commodity. The introduction in 1969 of the star-rating of petrol by octane level reinforced this.

2   Demand conditions
At the firm level the price elasticity of demand is likely to be high because of the perceived homogeneity of the suppliers' petrol. At the industry level, however, the price elasticity of demand will be an important influence on the extent to which monopoly profits can be earned. If demand is inelastic, price increases will not reduce demand significantly, so that revenue and profits will increase. The demand for petrol appears to be highly price inelastic in the short run – the price of petrol rose by 75 per cent between the beginning of 1974 and the end of 1975 yet consumption fell by only 0.6 per cent. Thus, to the extent that the demand for petrol is inelastic, the incentive for firms to collude in raising prices and reaping monopoly profits is that much higher.

3   Entry barriers
Entry barriers are a way of protecting in the long term the monopoly profits discussed above. In the market for petrol, barriers to the entry of new firms existed by virtue of the fact that at the beginning of the period under consideration existing firms – the 'majors' – were vertically integrated backwards towards the source of their raw materials. The majors were of course active in oil exploration and production and they also had, and still have, a virtual monopoly on UK refinery capacity. This was not an insurmountable barrier to potential entrants, however, since there was an alternative source of supply, the Rotterdam spot market (and, in fact, many of the smaller independent firms secured supplies through contracts with the majors, though at prices which allowed little scope for price cutting). During the period under review the existing firms also sought to strengthen their position by forward integration. This was achieved by buying up existing retail outlets, particularly those in prime positions, and by exclusive supply contracts with retailers (so-called 'solus site' arrangements).

Thus, the existence of these entry barriers discouraged new firms from entering the market but did not, as it turned out, prevent it. The inability of the existing firms to prevent this entry led to the reduction in concentration we have already noted. This reduced both the incentive for firms to collude and the ease with which they could do so, and was a significant factor in changing the observed price behaviour in the industry.

4   Cost conditions
If one company had enjoyed a clear cost advantage it might have been tempted to compete actively with the others in an attempt to oust them from the market. This was not the case, however, since they all used similar technologies for producing oil and refining it into petrol, so that their costs were similar. This therefore tended to reduce the likelihood of competition and increased the likelihood of collusion.

5   Supply conditions
Over the period studied supply conditions fluctuated between periods of shortage and periods of abundance. During periods when supplies were short the Rotterdam spot market dried up as a source of supply for the independent wholesalers, severely curtailing their ability to penetrate the retail market. However, in the period of abundant supplies between late 1974 and 1977 there was a substantial increase in market penetration by independents.

All the foregoing considerations are relevant to the change in the structure of the industry which took place. The most dramatic evidence of this changed structure is the observed reduction in concentration, but as we have seen there are other aspects which were important. The change in structure brought about a breakdown of the pricing discipline which had been a feature of the industry in the 1960s. During that period the major suppliers (principally Shell-Mex and BP but occasionally Esso) had acted as the price leader with the other firms dutifully following any change in prices. As can be seen from Table 9.3, this behaviour continued until the end of 1973.

Table 9.3   Inner zone scheduled wholesale prices for 4-star motor spirit

Date	Shell	Esso	Texaco	Mobil
16.1.70	6/0	6/0	6/0	6/0
31.7.70	6/0$^{1}/_{2}$	6/0$^{1}/_{2}$	6/0$^{1}/_{2}$	6/0$^{1}/_{2}$
6.11.70	6/1$^{1}/_{2}$	6/1$^{1}/_{2}$	6/1$^{1}/_{2}$	6/1$^{1}/_{2}$
21.2.71	31.75	—	—	—
22.2.71	—	31.75	31.75	31.75
28.4.72	—	—	—	31.15
29.4.72	32.15	—	—	—
1.5.72	—	32.15	32.15	—
9.9.72	32.65	—	—	—
11.9.72	—	32.65	32.65	32.65
29.4.73	33.65	33.65	—	33.65
15.5.73	—	—	33.65	—
4.10.73	34.65	34.65	34.65	34.65
15.12.73	37.35	37.35	37.35	37.35

Table 9.3 contd.

Date	Shell	Esso	Texaco	Mobil
12.2.74	45.25	45.30	45.25	45.27
18.12.74	52.20	52.15	52.20	52.20
2.12.75	55.00	—	—	—
3.12.75	—	55.00	—	55.02
8.12.75	—	—	55.00	—
9.4.76*	13.74	13.745	13.74	13.75
29.10.76	14.51	—	—	—
30.10.76	—	—	14.63	—
3.11.76	—	—	—	14.52
6.11.76	—	14.51	—	—
21.12.76	—	—	—	14.74
1.1.77	—	0	14.76	—
10.1.77	—	14.73	—	—
29.3.77*	15.61	14.83	15.86	15.84
26.4.77	16.08	—	—	—
27.4.77	—	—	16.08	—
29.4.77	—	16.08	—	16.08
8.7.77	15.49	—	—	—
8.8.77*	14.39	14.95	14.98	14.98
27.10.77	—	—	—	14.65
1.12.77	—	14.14	—	—
8.2.79	14.97	—	—	—
12.2.79	—	—	—	15.21
16.2.79	15.08	15.17	15.08	—
6.4.79	—	15.82	16.08	15.82
9.4.79	15.73	—	—	—
26.5.79	—	—	18.58	18.42
12.6.79	18.45	—	—	—
18.6.79	—	18.43	—	—
2.7.79	—	19.60	—	—
3.7.79	19.81	—	—	—
4.7.79	—	—	20.08	—
5.7.79	—	—	—	20.41
29.11.79	20.20	—	—	—
28.12.79	—	20.30	—	—
29.12.79	—	—	20.50	—
1.1.80	—	—	—	20.41
17.1.80	21.08	—	21.20	21.20
18.1.80	—	21.07	—	—
19.2.80	21.08	21.64	—	—
20.2.80	—	—	21.84	21.85
26.3.80*	23.75	23.54	23.74	23.75
17.5.80	—	—	—	24.35
21.5.80	—	—	24.29	—
23.5.80	24.13	—	—	—
24.5.80	—	23.92	—	—

Table 9.3 contd.

Date	Shell	Esso	Texaco	Mobil
3.6.80	24.66	—	—	—
7.6.80	—	24.61	24.63	24.66
5.7.80	24.28	24.23	—	—
9.7.80	—	—	24.28	—
13.8.80	—	—	—	23.90

Notes: 1970 prices in shillings and old pence per gallon: 1971–5 prices per gallon: 1976–80 prices in pence per litre.
Asterisks show changes in excise tax.
Prices include duty, exclude VAT.
Source: R. M. Grant, 'Pricing behaviour in the UK wholesale market for petrol 1970-80: a "structure-conduct" analysis', *Journal of Industrial Economics*, Vol. XXX, March 1982.

Between 1970 and 1973, as Table 9.3 shows, firms charged identical prices and changed prices by the same amount. The response to a price change in most cases occurred either the same day or the following day. This 'well-orchestrated parallelism' was a clear example of collusion. Any price competition that did occur during this period took place by way of the discounts which wholesalers granted to retailers rather than through the posted wholesale prices shown in Table 9.3. Since the magnitude of these discounts was confidential, any competition between the wholesalers was thus furtive rather than open.

The Arab-Israeli war of late 1973 brought a brief period of shortage of supplies of petrol and a rapid increase in prices which was followed by a period of plentiful supplies. With supplies obtained from the Rotterdam spot market, where prices had dropped dramatically because of the glut, the independents were able to undercut the existing firms and increase their market share. This increased the pressure on the major suppliers to defend their position by price competition and, as can be seen from Table 9.3, the collusive pricing behaviour degenerated into more open competition.

The 1980s and 1990s saw a complete breakdown of pricing discipline and a continued erosion of the share of the majors by the independents, most noticeably by the large supermarket chains who began selling petrol at significantly lower prices. The profits made on these sales were very small but the supermarkets reckoned that the availability of 'one-stop shopping' would encourage additional customers into their stores. By the mid-1990s the supermarkets had built up a market share of around 20 per cent. In 1996 Esso embarked on an aggressive 'Pricewatch' campaign promising to match the lowest prices within a three-mile radius of each of its outlets. This sparked off a period of intense competition as the other suppliers matched these low prices in an attempt to hold on to market share.

9.9 Oligopolistic behaviour: game theory

'All the world's a game and all the men and women merely players.'

Shakespeare could have said this – but didn't. He was unfamiliar with the work of Von Neumann and Morgenstern who developed the so-called **Theory of Games**, an analytical apparatus with widespread applications, not the least of which is in analysing oligopolistic market situations.

First we outline the main features of a game. This is best illustrated by the classic game known as the **Prisoner's Dilemma**. Two prisoners, Smith and Brown, are held in custody, accused of committing a serious robbery together. The evidence against them is not particularly strong and the prisoners know that without some sort of confession by one of them the case against them is unlikely to succeed. They are also aware, however, that if they are found guilty their sentence will be considerably less if they pleaded guilty in the first place. They are held *incommunicado* – that is, they cannot talk to each other.

Figure 9.3 illustrates the dilemma facing Smith. He has two strategies – to plead guilty or to plead innocent. The outcomes will depend not just on the strategy he adopts but also on what Brown does. The elements of the matrix in Fig. 9.3 show the **payoffs** to Smith – the number of years of imprisonment. Obviously the best outcome is for both men to plead innocent. Then the prosecution case fails and Smith goes free (as does Brown). But this is a high risk strategy because, if Smith pleads innocent and Brown pleads guilty, then Brown's evidence will be enough to convict Smith who will therefore receive the maximum 15-year sentence. It may be better for Smith to plead guilty. Then he will certainly be convicted but the maximum sentence he will receive is only ten years and he may get as little as seven years if his evidence helps to convict Brown. What should Smith do? Remember, the two men cannot communicate (feminists, please note: they are almost certain to be men, since over 96 per cent of the prison population in Britain is male. See *Social Trends*).

In this situation there is no 'best' strategy because the payoffs to Smith depend on Brown's action. Pleading guilty is the strategy involving least risk. We call this the **minimax strategy**. It minimizes the maximum sentence Smith could receive. Pleading innocent could be called the **minimin strategy** (minimizing the minimum sentence).

The strategy chosen will depend, among other things, on a player's attitude towards risk. Risk lovers will take a chance and opt for the minimin strategy (Smith pleads innocent). But Game Theory suggests that risk averse behaviour may be more common and more sensible. A risk averse player, known technically as a **conservative gamesman**, will choose the minimax strategy (in this case, to plead guilty).

		Brown's actions	
		Plead guilty	Plead innocent
Smith's strategies	Plead guilty	10	7
	Plead innocent	15	0

The elements of the matrix show the payoffs to Smith (in terms of years of imprisonment)

Figure 9.3 The Prisoner's Dilemma

This example demonstrates why it may be difficult to achieve the best outcome, which is for both men to plead innocent and therefore go free. If only they could have agreed between themselves before they were caught that they would both plead innocent this could be achieved. But even if they had come to such an agreement there is no guarantee that each of them would stick to it. As is well known, there is no honour among thieves.

Note, finally, that this particular game is symmetric. That is, although the matrix in Fig. 9.3 shows the payoffs to Smith we could draw a similar matrix from Brown's point of view, showing his payoffs. This will not always be the case. Some games are non-symmetric.

The Prisoner's Dilemma is the classic game. It is easy to imagine how the principles illustrated here could be extended to many other situations, including pricing behaviour in oligopolistic markets.

Figure 9.4 illustrates a situation in which firm A has three possible strategies – to lower prices, leave prices unchanged, or to raise prices. Firm A is a duopolist – there is only one other major player in the market, firm B. The payoffs to firm A depend not just on the strategy A adopts but also on the response of firm B. The payoffs shown in the matrix are the changes in A's sales revenue resulting from the adoption of a particular strategy.

Consider strategy S_1 (raising prices). Provided B responds by also raising prices this produces the best possible outcome, which is an increase in revenue of 30. But it carries great risk because, if B responds by cutting prices, then many of A's former customers will switch to firm B and as a result A's revenue will fall by 15. S_1 is therefore a high risk strategy. It is the **maximax strategy** and it is unlikely to be adopted by a conservative player.

Now consider strategies S_2 and S_3. Careful study of the payoffs in the matrix shows that S_3 is always inferior to S_2. That is, no matter what B does, the payoffs from S_2 are always better than those from S_3. We say that S_2 **dominates** S_3. Therefore, strategy S_3 will not be pursued by any rational player, whatever his attitude towards risk.

	Firm B's response		
	Raise prices	Leave unchanged	Lower prices
S_1 (raise prices)	+30	+5	-15
Firm A's strategies S_2 (leave unchanged)	+8	0	-4
S_3 (lower prices)	+7	-1	-30

The elements of the matrix show the payoffs to firm A (in terms of the change in sales revenue)

Figure 9.4 Pricing strategies: a game

In the Prisoner's Dilemma we identified a minimax strategy. To find the minimax strategy it is necessary to look at each *row* in Fig. 9.4 and identify the *worst outcome*. Then choose the row with the *smallest* worst outcome. Here the minimax strategy is S_2. It minimizes the maximum loss of sales revenue that could be suffered by A. This is the strategy that will be pursued by a risk averse oligopolist.

The payoffs shown in Fig. 9.4 are merely illustrative, but they do make sense. The game theory approach to the analysis of oligopolistic behaviour illustrates two key features of oligopolistic markets. First, such markets are likely to be characterized by price stability. Aggressive price cuts or price increases are risky strategies likely to be shunned by risk averse players. Such strategies are not unknown, however. The reader may wish to construct a matrix in which the rewards from price cutting make it a tempting, if risky, strategy.

Secondly, the payoffs shown in Fig. 9.4 illustrate that the potential benefits of collusion between players are very great. If they could agree among themselves the players could jointly raise prices, and both firms' profits would increase substantially. However, there is no honour among oligopolists either, so this behaviour will be uncommon, though not unknown. It would, of course, be construed as an anti-competitive tactic, and hence deemed illegal by the Monopolies and Mergers Commission.

9.10 The kinked demand curve in oligopoly

In the previous section we saw that in oligopolistic markets the outcome of a particular pricing strategy would depend upon the reactions of rivals. The analysis developed by Sweezy, known as the **kinked demand curve**, focuses upon the response of rivals to price changes. He assumes that rivals will match any price cuts but will not respond at all if rival firms raise prices. The demand curve facing such a firm will therefore be kinked, as in Fig. 9.5.

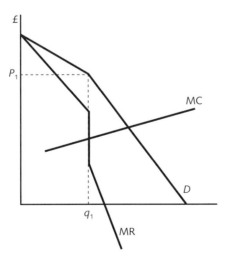

Figure 9.5 The kinked demand curve

The existing price is P_1. Below this price the demand curve is rather inelastic (illustrated by the steepness of the curve) since any price cut will be matched by rival firms. Price cuts therefore do not lead to any change in market shares. But if the firm raises its price above P_1 then rival firms will *not* match this price rise. This leaves the firm exposed. Customers switch to rival suppliers, and the firm loses market share. The demand curve is therefore rather elastic above price P_1 (illustrated by the less steep slope).

As we saw earlier (in section 6.1) there is a technical relationship between the demand curve and its associated marginal revenue curve. Marginal revenue is related to the slope of the demand curve. At P_1 the slope suddenly changes. The associated MR curve therefore has a discontinuity at this point. The profit maximizing firm will of course equate marginal cost with marginal revenue and produce an output level Q_1. This output level corresponds to the existing price P_1.

As can be seen from Fig. 9.5 small changes in costs will have no effect on the profit maximizing price and output levels. Thus the theory is quite consistent with the price stability which is characteristic of oligopolistic markets.

9.11 A game with probabilities

As is so often the case in economics, the analytical techniques have an applicability which extends beyond strictly economic situations. Game theory is one such technique. Decisions are almost always associated with risk and uncertainty. Identifying and adopting the minimax strategy is a decision rule which can be applied to such situations. But it is by no means the only rule.

Some writers distinguish between the terms **risk** and **uncertainty**, defining the former as a situation in which **probabilities** can be assigned and the latter as a situation in which it is not possible to assign probabilities. What is the nature of these probabilities? Suppose, for example, that we are in the Prisoner's Dilemma illustrated earlier, where the payoff to Smith depended on whether Brown pleaded guilty or not. Suppose we said that the probability of Brown pleading guilty was 0.3 and the probability of his pleading innocent was 0.7 (the probabilities must sum to 1.0). These probabilities indicate that Brown is more likely to plead innocent but on what are they based? They may be based partly on past behaviour (perhaps Brown has been in similar situations before) or on some assessment of Brown's character. In other words they are partly objective and partly subjective.

Suppose, for example, that Brown comes from a long line of felons. His father was a felon, as was *his* father before him, and none of them ever pleaded guilty to anything, even when caught red-handed. With this additional information we may wish to amend the probabilities to:

probability that Brown will plead guilty   = 0.05
probability that Brown will plead innocent = 0.95

It seems therefore that the chances of Brown's pleading guilty are pretty remote – only one chance in twenty. If Smith knows this, should he take it into account in deciding upon his plea?

States of the world

	Warnings false prob. = 0.95	Warnings true prob. = 0.05
Take action	$50 bn per annum	$50 bn per annum
Ignore warnings	Zero	Incalculably high

The elements of the matrix show the payoffs – the future costs to the world community

Figure 9.6 Global warming: a game

Recall the possible payoffs to Smith from a strategy of pleading innocent. If Brown also pleads innocent then both men go free. There is only a 5 per cent chance that Brown will not plead innocent, in which case an innocent plea by Smith would lead to the full 15-year sentence. A guilty plea by Smith will result in a 7–10 year sentence. In this situation it seems silly to ignore the extra information provided by these probabilities. The chances of the worst possible outcome occurring (a 15-year sentence) are only one in twenty and many people in Smith's predicament would surely take a chance and plead innocent.

Whether this is wise depends on whether the estimated probabilities do in some sense reflect the likelihood of the different states of the world occurring (that is, of Brown pleading guilty or innocent). The game theory approach implicitly assumes that we have no information on the likelihood of different states of the world occurring or rather it treats them as equally likely.

Paradoxically it is the severity of a particular outcome, rather than its probability, which is likely to influence our choice of strategy. Consider the following game where the world community has two choices – to ignore the warnings of scientists about the threat of global warming or to take action now to limit its effects. Figure 9.6 presents the game in a schematic form. In our example note that the warnings of scientists are in all probability false. But there is a small probability – five per cent – that they are true. If they are true the costs to humankind are incalculably high. What is the correct strategy?

9.12 Security and growth: diversification and integration

Firms are in business to do business, and it makes but little difference what business they do. There is no reason therefore why they should limit the range of their activities to those currently undertaken. Firms, particularly large firms, can move into new markets or withdraw from existing ones; they can move into or out of areas connected in some way with their main trading activities; they can even develop interests in areas which are totally alien to their existing activities. Normally, however, firms expand by developing in areas in which they already have some expertise. For example, DIY ('do it yourself') was a rapidly expanding sector of the retail market which was entered by two firms – Sainsbury and W.H. Smith – who previously had no knowledge of DIY but did have plenty of expertise in retailing other products – food in the case of Sainsbury and books in the case of W.H. Smith. Both firms tackled the market in a similar way, by building very large supermarkets (hypermarkets) devoted to DIY products. When firms grow by expanding into new areas in this way it is known as **diversification**. The reason for choosing this development strategy is twofold. First, it increases security since the overall risk is lessened by being spread: the old adage about not putting all your eggs in one basket (clearly relevant in the case of Sainsbury). Secondly, it allows the firm to grow as fast as its internal finances and its borrowing ability allow, rather than being constrained to grow at the same speed as the market in which it is currently operating (which may, of course, be stagnant or even declining).

Growth and security can also be achieved by a different form of expansion: **integration** (often known as **vertical integration**). Integration is achieved where the firm expands either backwards towards its source of raw materials or forwards towards its retail outlets. For example, if Sainsbury acquires a pork-pie factory (and sells the pork pies in its supermarkets) this is an example of backwards integration. Similar examples of backwards integration are the chocolate manufacturers, many of whom own cocoa plantations, and the major rubber manufacturers who own rubber plantations. Forwards integration occurs when the brewers acquire public houses – the 'tied houses' – in which to sell their beer. British Airtours, a wholly owned subsidiary of British Airways, provides a further example of forwards integration. British Airways' main business is running a scheduled airline service but the establishment of British Airtours, a company which sells package holidays by air, provides a useful (captive) retail outlet for its services.

Note that integration, both forward and backward, can often serve to provide the firm with barriers to the entry of new firms into its existing markets. As such, these developments could be viewed as forming part of an anti-competitive strategy.

Both diversification and integration are examples of expansion into areas related in some way to the firm's existing activities. However, some firms – known as **conglomerates** – have interests in a number of unrelated areas. Lonrho, for example, is a major international company with interests in mining, newspapers (*The Observer*) and retailing. Perhaps better known is the Virgin group, owned by the colourful entrepreneur Richard Branson, who made his fortune through Virgin Records before expanding into unrelated areas including air transport (Virgin Atlantic), radio, and soft drink (Virgin Cola). In the 1980s with the Aids scare at its height the group acquired – and subsequently disposed of – a manufacturer of condoms (which for some reason were sold under the *Mates* brand-name rather than the Virgin brand-name), and in 1996 Virgin acquired one of the rail franchises.

Another conglomerate, less well known to the general public, is Pearson who own the *Financial Times*, Penguin Books, Madame Tussauds and Thames TV – and Addison Wesley Longman who publish the book you are reading now. The archetypal conglomerate, however, was a fictitious company invented by the economist J.K. Galbraith. His company – Universal Global Enterprises or UGE for short (to emphasize its size) – was an amalgam of several real American corporations. UGE had subsidiary companies operating in every conceivable sphere of human activity, from 'cola' to computers and from detergents to defence. The activities of conglomerates like UGE will be discussed in greater detail in Chapter 11 when we consider multinational corporations.

It should be clear that the three avenues of expansion we have identified – diversification, integration and conglomeration – are different ways in which the firm tries to achieve both a more secure future for itself and faster growth of sales and profits. What is also clear is that the three types of expansion normally result from merger activity between two companies or takeover activity. Since mergers and acquisitions are such an important aspect of the growth of firms, they are considered in greater detail in the following section.

9.13 Mergers

An important element in the growth of firms is **merger** activity. Mergers may be motivated by the desire to diversify the firm's activities – so-called conglomerate mergers. They may involve the firms in vertical links (forward or backward vertical integration). Finally, they may take the form of the acquisition of former competitors.

Merger activity involving the acquisition of competitors will clearly result in increased concentration in the industry in question, together with a concomitant rise in the market power of the newly merged companies. Vertical integration will often also result in an increase in market power even though it does not increase concentration *per se*. Of course, mergers may also result in improved efficiency through rationalisation and through an improved ability to benefit from economies of scale. Indeed, this is the major justification which is cited to explain merger activity.

Part of the remit of the Monopolies and Mergers Commission is to decide whether a proposed merger is '**in the public interest**.' Its remit allows it to investigate any proposed merger where:

1 The merger would lead to an increase in market concentration.
2 The merger would increase the ability of firms to engage in anti-competitive tactics (as a result of increased concentration or through vertical links).
3 The value of assets taken over exceeds a certain sum, set at £30 m in 1984. This condition allows the MMC to investigate conglomerate mergers.

In recent years public policy towards mergers as carried out by the MMC has tended to evolve, albeit slowly, in two ways. First, the 1980 Competition Act (which concerned itself with competition rather than with mergers) encouraged the MMC to pay more attention to **anti-competitive behaviour**, both actual and potential, rather than with market concentration *per se*.

The second shift in emphasis in public policy towards mergers has been away from a presumption that mergers are in the public interest (unless the MMC can prove otherwise) and towards a more neutral attitude towards mergers. This results partly from accumulated evidence which shows that the claim that mergers increase efficiency is non-proven. Some of the evidence is contained in the 1978 Green Paper, *A Review of Monopolies and Mergers Policy*. Table 9.4, reproduced from the Green Paper, summarizes the results of a study by Meeks of the post-merger profitability of 213 larger quoted companies which merged in the period 1964–72. The method employed by Meeks was

Table 9.4 Post-merger profitability and the proportion of firms showing a decline in profits

Year after merger	Number of firms	Change in profitability	% of firms with lower profits
0	213	+0.15	34
1	192	−0.02	54
2	174	−0.01	52
3	146	−0.06	53
4	103	−0.10	66
5	67	−0.11	64
6	44	−0.07	52
7	21	−0.07	62

Column three shows the change – relative to the average of the three pre-merger years – in the ratio of the profitability of the merged companies to the profitability of the industries to which they belonged.
Source: G. Meeks, *Disappointing Marriage: a study of the gains from merger*, CUP, 1977 (quoted in 1978 Green Paper).

to compare the profits of the combined company in the six years following the merger with the profits of the acquiring and acquired firms in the three years prior to the merger. As Table 9.4 shows, average profits declined after the merger. Only in the year of acquisition did recorded profits rise, and too much weight should not be attached to that finding since measurement problems are particularly acute in that year. These findings, which are now somewhat dated, may seem surprising but they are in fact in accord with the weight of evidence (in the Green Paper and subsequently), both for the UK and internationally.

Notwithstanding these findings, merger activity continues unabated. Acquiring companies often claim that the proposed merger will lead to **synergy** – the profits of the merged company will be more than the sum of its parts. This may occur (although the evidence does not support this) but, even if it does, one may question whether the increased profitability results from higher prices made possible by market power rather than from lower costs stemming from increased efficiency. It is on this basis that the MMC has to decide whether a proposed merger is 'in the public interest.'

9.14 Case Study: Mergers – Cross-Channel ferries (and the Tunnel)

The market for cross-Channel ferry services was the subject of a considerable amount of merger activity during the 1980s and 1990s and there were several references to the MMC, the latest being in 1997.

In 1981 a company then known as European Ferries was operating nine routes (trading under the name of Townsend Thoresen) and was the owner of a number of ports. The other major operator was Sealink (then a subsidiary of British Rail) who also owned ports. There were a few other operators, the largest of which was P&O Ferries.

There existed a considerable amount of excess capacity on most routes and this had led to cut-throat price competition in order to attract passengers. In 1981 European Ferries had applied to the MMC for permission to acquire Sealink in order to rationalize services and eliminate excess capacity. Failure to do so, they argued, might result in the withdrawal of services as a result of losses or continued low returns on investment. However, the MMC refused permission for the merger on the grounds that it would have produced a monopoly (using the MMC's criteria). The merged company would have had over 50 per cent of the whole cross-Channel market and an even larger market share on other routes. In addition, their ownership of many of the Channel and North Sea ports might have been used to discriminate against existing competitors and new entrants into the market.

The proposed merger was deemed to be against the public interest. In coming to this decision the MMC clearly took the view that any benefit resulting from rationalization and increased efficiency would be outweighed by the costs to consumers of increased market power.

Mergers and acquisitions 1984–90

In 1984 Sealink UK was officially put up for sale as part of the Government's privatization programme. European Ferries asked to be allowed to bid, promising to cut cross-Channel ferry prices by 15–20 per cent if it were allowed to buy Sealink. However, both European Ferries and P&O were barred from bidding for Sealink, which was eventually acquired by the Swedish-owned Stena Line.

In 1987 further rationalization took place when P&O acquired the whole of European Ferries, the new company being known as P&O/European Ferries.

By the late 1980s the market was more or less evenly divided between these two principal operators (P&O/European Ferries and Stena) with around 80–90 per cent of the market. In anticipation of the opening of the Channel Tunnel they applied to the MMC to be allowed to combine their operation. The MMC turned down the application in 1989, clearly believing that in the four-year run-up to the opening of the Channel Tunnel some competition was desirable. However, commentators believed that before 1994 the MMC would reconsider its ruling so as to allow P&O/EF and Stena to rationalize and combine their activities to compete more effectively against Eurotunnel, whose marginal costs were at that time estimated to be only 20 per cent of the ferries' costs. All the ferries invested heavily in the late 1980s/early 1990s in larger, more luxurious ferries designed to promote the pleasurable aspect of crossing by sea.

Enter the Tunnel

The opening of the Channel Tunnel in 1994 created a huge amount of excess capacity in the market for cross-Channel services and changed the competitive environment. However, it had become clear soon after Eurotunnel commenced trading that the cost of building the Tunnel could never be recouped through ticket sales. The debt burden was approximately £9 billion. One could easily calculate (assuming a 10 per cent rate of interest) that the interest payments on this debt would be of the order of £0.9

Table 9.5 Eurotunnel's financial position (as reported in 1995)

- Revenue from Le Shuttle drive-on trains for cars and freight in 1995 estimated at £300m
- Annual revenue from Eurostar London-Paris, London-Brussels trains £60m
- Annual operating costs of the Tunnel £260m which gives a net income (after operating costs) of about £100m
- Owes £8 to £9 billion to syndicate of 225 banks around the world. Annual interest on that rumoured to be around £730 million
- Owes additional £0.3 billion borrowed to cover operating costs and other expenditures since opening. Annual interest bill a further £27 million

Source: derived from *The Observer*, 17 September 1995.

billion per annum. In 1995, the first full year of operation, it became clear that income (less operating costs) was only about one-tenth of that figure, as Table 9.5 shows.

It is clear from this table that the Tunnel is hopelessly uneconomic, technically bankrupt and – from a purely financial point of view – should never have been built in the first place. However, even if Eurotunnel as a company were to go into liquidation, the asset (the Tunnel) would still remain in existence. This is an asset which has no alternative use. A new company would acquire the asset and would recommence trading, but without Eurotunnel's huge debt burden. This is the scenario which the ferries fear most because they would find it difficult to match the low marginal costs of such a competitor, who might then engage in predatory pricing to squeeze their profits and drive them out of the market.

In 1996 P&O and Stena again applied to the MMC to be allowed to merge their activities and in 1997 the MMC gave the proposed merger the green light, acknowledging that any obstacles preventing the ferries from competing effectively against the Tunnel would have to be removed. At the time P&O Chairman Lord Sterling likened the merged ferry company to a David competing against the Eurotunnel Goliath. He is quoted as saying: 'Once the £12 billion Eurotunnel was dumped into the ferry market it was clear there would have to be rationalizations. This became particularly true when Eurotunnel decided not to pay interest and to buy its way into the market by slashing fares.'[2]

Summary

The MMC has the responsibility for investigating monopolistic situations and proposed mergers and of judging whether these are 'against the public interest'. The classic case against monopoly is that prices will be higher and output lower than would be the case in a competitive market. However, large firms in concentrated markets often benefit from substantial scale economies which result in increased efficiency and lower prices than competitive firms would charge. The MMC looks not only at the actual degree of concentration but also at the potential for new firms to enter or leave the market.

In some cases, there is clear evidence of anti-competitive behaviour such as predatory pricing or price fixing cartels. In other cases, the evidence is less clear cut –

sometimes there may be evidence of price leadership by the dominant firm with other firms following suit so that the industry as a whole acts as if it were controlled by a single firm. At other times the firms within an industry compete more openly against each other. The Theory of Games illustrates the dilemma faced by the oligopolistic firm torn between the desire to compete and the opposite desire to collude. The theory suggests that risk averse firms will tend to avoid outright competition, which tends to imply that oligopolistic markets will be characterized by price stability, a conclusion which is also in accord with another theoretical model, that of the kinked demand curve.

Notes

1   See Davies, G. and Davies, J. (1984) 'The Revolution in Monopoly Theory', in *Lloyd's Bank Review*, July 1984.
2   Quoted in *The Guardian*, 4 October 1996.

Key terms

Review questions

9.1   If a competitive industry is replaced by a monopolistic one, which of the following statements are true? Correct the false ones.
(a) Prices in the industry will inevitably rise.
(b) The monopolist may choose not to maximize profits, so prices may not rise.
(c) The monopolist will have lower costs by virtue of his size so prices will fall.
(d) The monopolist may have lower costs by virtue of his size, but prices will rise if the monopolist exploits his market power.

(e) The MES in the industry may be quite small so that further concentration does not lead to significant cost reductions.

(f) Increased concentration at firm level will result in increased concentration at plant level. Unit costs will therefore fall.

9.2 Which of the following definitions of a 'monopoly situation' is used by the Monopolies Commission?

(a) One firm supplies the whole market.

(b) One firm supplies over 50 per cent of the market for a particular good.

(c) A single firm, or a group of firms acting together so as to restrict competition, controls over 25 per cent of the market.

(d) The 3-firm concentration ratio exceeds 90 per cent.

9.3 In addition to the current level of seller concentration, what other factors does the MMC consider relevant in assessing whether a monopoly situation exists?

9.4 If Boots the chemist took over a manufacturer of shampoo this would be an example of:

(a) vertical integration

(b) forward integration

(c) backward integration

(d) both (a) and (b)

(e) both (a) and (c).

9.5 If Boots the chemist started to sell package holidays in their retail outlets this would be:

(a) forward integration

(b) diversification

(c) 'a logical extension of their existing activity in retailing'.

9.6 Suppose two former competitors merge and the subsequent profitability of the merged companies exceeds the profits that could have been expected if the two companies had remained separate. Consider whether the following statements are true.

(a) Since profits have increased, the merger must have increased efficiency. Therefore the merger was in the public interest.

(b) If profits have increased, it is evidence that market power has increased. Therefore the merger was against the public interest.

9.7 Of what relevance is the concept of MEPS in assessing the desirability of a proposed merger?

9.8 What motivated the oil companies to re-introduce the branding of petrol in 1953? What was the reason for the introduction in 1969 of the star-rating of petrol by octane level?

9.9 Firms in oligopolistic markets are torn between the desire to compete and the opposing desire to collude. Consider each of the following factors and state whether it will increase or decrease the likelihood of collusion:

(a) The degree of seller concentration is high.

(b) Demand for the industry product is inelastic.

(c) There are no effective barriers to the entry of new firms.

(d) One firm enjoys a significant cost advantage.

9.10 List the scale economies which you think large supermarket chains enjoy. Which of these are real and which are purely financial economies of scale? Is the increasing concentration in food retailing therefore in the public interest?

9.11 Which of the following are examples of vertical integration? State whether they are forwards, backwards or neither.

(a) The acquisition by British Airways of the package tour operator, Airtours.

(b) The ownership of pubs ('tied houses') by the major brewers.

(c) The expansion by Sainsbury into the DIY market (Homebase).

(d) The ownership by the major ferry operators (P&O and Stena) of harbour facilities at Dover.
(e) Expansion by Richard Branson's Virgin Group into the financial services industry.

9.12 The following matrix relates to a duopolistic market and the elements of the matrix show the payoffs to firm A – that is, the change in revenue that results from the adoption of certain pricing strategies.

Firm B's response

		Raise prices	Leave unchanged	Lower prices
Firm A's strategies	S1 Raise prices	+24	+13	–5
	S2 Leave unchanged	+10	0	–4
	S3 Lower prices	+8	–3	–6

(a) What is A's minimax strategy? Explain why this is the case.
(b) Will strategy S3 ever be pursued and if not why not?
(c) What inference can one draw from this about the elasticity of demand for the industry as a whole?

10 Trade

Preview

In theory if countries specialize in producing those things in which they have a comparative advantage, and trade their surpluses with others, then all countries can enjoy a greater volume of goods and services than would be the case if each were to be self-sufficient. This goes some way towards explaining why countries trade and what goods they choose to specialize in producing. It is also the basis of the argument used by those who favour free trade as opposed to protectionism. In practice trade flows cannot be fully explained by the simple theory of comparative advantage. Moreover, there are cogent arguments which can be adduced in support of some form of protectionism.

10.1 Specialization

In 1776 Adam Smith, a Scottish professor of moral philosophy, published the book now regarded as the most important foundation of neo-classical economic analysis. This book was *An Inquiry into the Nature and Causes of the Wealth of Nations*. In 1776 long titles were very much in vogue. Nowadays we refer to it simply as *The Wealth of Nations*.

Smith was writing in Britain at a time when industrial processes had begun to make available a vastly increased amount and variety of goods. Articles which before the Industrial Revolution had been made by hand, and were hence expensive and in short supply, were now made by machines and were available cheaply to everyone. Smith's great achievement was to stand back and see in perspective the changes that were taking place in his society. In particular he was able to focus on the essential characteristics that made possible this flow of industrial goods.

Smith realised that the key to wealth creation lay in the **division of labour**. In other words products were no longer produced in their entirety by single craftsmen as they were in pre-industrial times. Rather, separate *stages* of the production process were performed by individuals each one of whom specialized, and therefore became adept and efficient at producing only a small fraction of the item being manufactured.

Smith used the example of a pin factory to illustrate this. It seems that even in Glasgow in 1776 the manufacture of pins was a highly specialized business. It consisted of no less than eighteen separate operations each one of which would have been performed by separate individuals, using specialized machines. It was this specialization which enabled mass production to take place, enabling nations to increase the amount of goods ('wealth') they created and enabling ordinary men and women to consume quantities and varieties of products which previously had only been available, if at all, to the very rich.

All of this may seem fairly obvious to twentieth-century man. Mass-produced goods, which involve specialization and the division of labour, are now the norm, hand-crafted articles the highly priced exception. Smith's great genius was in recognizing that it was specialization that made possible the wealth of nations. More than two centuries later in 1990 the Toshiba electronics company produced a television commercial which, inadvertently, makes the same point. A kimono-clad Japanese girl explains that she 'makes the chickambop for NICAM TV' for it is well known, at least in the advertising industry, that Japanese people cannot pronounce the word 'thingumybob'. The (English) voice then explains:

She's the girl that makes the thing
That holds the oil
That oils the ring
That takes the shank
That moves the crank;
That works the thingumybob.

It's a ticklish sort of job
Making a thing for a thingumybob
Especially when you find out what it's for ...

But she's the girl that makes the thing
That fills the hole
That holds the spring
That works the thingumybob that makes the engines roar ...

And it's the girl that makes the thing
That holds the oil
That oils the ring
That makes the thingumybob that's going to make some more.

The nature of specialization is illustrated very effectively by this television commercial. Interestingly, the song is not original. Rather, it was a popular song in the Second World War, when of course lots of British women were engaged in making thingumybobs to use against the chickambops made by the Japanese.

The wartime version was of course slightly different. The last line for example 'that's going to make some more' originally read 'that's going to win the war.'

More importantly for our present purposes, the wartime version hinted that many female operatives working in factories may not have known the nature of the end product which they were helping to make. Sociologists have talked about the alienation in the workplace that results from this. The wartime song-writer expressed it rather differently for the second verse originally read:

It's a ticklish sort of job
Making a thingumybob
Especially when you <u>don't know what it's for</u> ...

Notice that in the Toshiba advertisement '*don't know*' is changed to '*find out*', a subtle but essential change. Advertising is all about image. If one spends £2.5m on promoting a company's image as Toshiba did in this campaign you would not want to suggest that the division of labour necessary to produce high-quality products cheaply may unfortunately involve workers in tedious repetitive tasks. Production line workers in electronics factories may be unaware – or may not care – whether they are producing television components, burglar alarms or weapons guidance systems. One printed-circuit board – PCB in the trade – looks much like another.

10.2 Specialization and trade

The previous section explained how specialization can enable a vastly increased flow of goods to be produced. The corollary of **specialization** is **trade**. This is because the makers of thingumybobs will not of course want to consume all of their output themselves. Rather they will want to trade their thingumybobs with the thingumybobs made by someone else.

The word 'trade' as used here can mean either international trade or simply trade between people and firms in the same country. The only difference between the two types of 'trade' is that in the former (international trade) different currencies are involved, which at some stage have to be exchanged, one for another, on the foreign exchange market at some rate of exchange.

10.3 Comparative advantage

In the nineteenth century, the neo-classical economist David Ricardo considered the question of why countries choose to trade. His analysis extended Smith's ideas on the division of labour. He explained that in a bilateral trading situation *both* countries would gain from trade since the total amount of goods available would be greater than if each country chose to be self-sufficient. He enunciated what is known as the **theory of comparative advantage**. This theory has become a very important part of the economist's analytical apparatus. Ricardo first developed this theory in the context of specialization and trade between countries with different currencies – that is, what we call 'international trade'. But it applies with equal force to specialization and trade within a country, or between countries with the same currency (as may eventually be the case in the European Union). In fact, it applies to all questions of resource allocation, even those facing the individual, for example, as we shall shortly show.

First, however, we shall develop the theory of comparative advantage in the context of a hypothetical example in which two countries, say France and Spain, each produce only two commodities, say wine and cars. For simplicity we assume for the moment that both countries share a common currency and we also assume that both wine and cars are homogeneous commodities.

We also need to make a number of other simplifying assumptions. First, assume that the only factor of production which is important is labour, so that labour costs are the only relevant costs in the production of wine and cars. Secondly, assume that in the production of both wine and cars there are constant returns to scale, which implies that production levels of wine and cars can be varied without altering unit costs. These unit costs – which of course consist only of labour costs – will by definition be both average and marginal costs. It may also help if we assume perfect competition in the product markets where these goods are sold so that price is equal to these marginal costs. Finally, we shall also assume for simplicity that the wage rate is the same in France and Spain, though neither of these last two assumptions is strictly necessary.

Table 10.1 shows the labour requirements in both France and Spain to produce one unit of each of the commodities – that is, it takes 20 man-hours in France to produce one unit of wine, 80 man-hours to produce one car and so on. Since we have assumed that the wage rate is the same in both countries, and that labour is the only relevant cost, the figures show that France is more efficient than Spain both in wine production and in car production, since it takes 30 man-hours to produce wine in Spain (and only 20 in France) and 90 man-hours to produce a car in Spain (and only 80 in France). Thus we say that France has an **absolute advantage** in the production of both wine and cars.

Table 10.1 Labour requirements in the production of wine and cars (hours per unit produced)

	France	*Spain*
Wine	20	30
Cars	80	90

Despite this absolute advantage, however, it would benefit France to specialize in producing that commodity in which she has a comparative advantage. To get some feel for this, consider the concept of **opportunity cost** (introduced in section 6.5). We define the opportunity cost of a good to be the number of units of other goods which must be given up to make one unit of the good in question. Thus in France the opportunity cost of one car is four units of wine whereas in Spain the opportunity cost of one car is only three units of wine. To repeat:

opportunity cost of one car in France = 4 units of wine
opportunity cost of one car in Spain   = 3 units of wine

In other words, in France cars are expensive to produce because you have to give up more to produce them than you do in Spain.

Similarly, wine is expensive to produce in Spain because there the opportunity cost of one unit of wine is a third of a car whereas in France it is only a quarter of a car. Thus France has a comparative advantage in the production of wine and Spain a comparative advantage in the production of cars.

10.4 The gains from trade

Since France and Spain each have a comparative advantage in different products we can show, following Ricardo, that total output will be increased if each country specializes in doing what it does best. That is, France should specialize in the production of wine, in which she has a comparative advantage, and Spain should specialize in cars. To demonstrate this, consider the following, where we are continuing to assume that the unit labour requirements (ULRs) are those shown in Table 10.1. France could reduce her car production by one unit, freeing 80 man-hours. These resources could be transferred into wine production which would therefore increase by 4 units (since ULRs in French wine production are 20 hours per unit produced). Spain for her part could give up 3 units of wine production, freeing a total of 90 man-hours (3×30) enabling her to produce an additional car (ULR = 90 man-hours for Spanish cars). The effect of all this is to lead to a net increase in total wine production of one unit without any loss of car output. The situation is summarized in Table 10.2.

Table 10.2 The gains from specialization

France gives up one unit of car output and uses the resources thus freed to produce 4 extra units of wine	− 1 car + 4 wine
Spain gives up 3 units of wine output and uses the resources thus freed to produce an extra car	− 3 wine + 1 car
net increase in world output = 1 unit of wine	

The net increase in world output of one unit of wine represents the **gains from specialization and trade**. Car output can be increased in a similar way – though the numbers in our example would not work out so neatly. Clearly, if we continue to assume constant returns to scale in the production of wine and cars our analysis suggests that world output could be increased further if further specialization were to take place. If France switched 800 (rather than 80) man-hours from cars to wine the net increase in world output would be 10 units of wine (rather than one). Switching 8000 would result in 100 extra units of wine and so on.

What this analysis demonstrates is that it is possible to have more of *both* wine and cars if countries specialize in producing those goods in which they have a comparative advantage. Note that France has lower ULRs in both wine and cars – she has an absolute advantage in both. This is not important, however. It is the *relative* efficiency with which she produces one good in comparison with the other which is important.

To demonstrate this simple truth we had to assume away a number of complexities which would enter into our consideration were this a real-world rather than a hypothetical example. A number of questions present themselves:

1 What determines whether the extra units of output accrue to France or to Spain? Or if they both benefit, do they benefit equally, or does one benefit more than the other?
2 What difference would it make if we assumed they used different currencies and what would determine the exchange rate between these two currencies?
3 How realistic is the assumption of constant returns to scale? If it is realistic, is it desirable that specialization should continue until the whole of France is covered in vineyards and the whole of Spain in car factories?
4 What difference would it make if we dropped the assumption that labour was the only relevant factor and explicitly recognized that capital and land may be important too?
5 More fundamentally, what determines the ULRs shown in Table 10.1? That is, *why* is France relatively more efficient at producing wine than producing cars? Do French people have large feet specially suited to treading grapes and is the Spanish national character ideally suited to work in car factories? Or are other factor endowments important?

If we did relax some of our simplifying assumptions we would find that our analysis became considerably more complex, but the basic result would be the same. France should give up car production (or at least reduce car production) because she is comparatively disadvantaged there. She should concentrate on wine. Spain should concentrate on cars. If this happens, total output will be greater than would otherwise have been the case – there will be gains from specialization and trade.

This was Ricardo's message, developed as we have seen in the context of international specialization and trade. But the theory of comparative advantage is a general principle which has much wider, indeed almost universal application in all questions of resource allocation.

Consider two individuals, Sam and Janet. Janet is better at everything than Sam who is rather slow and clumsy. Janet is good at house-painting and she is also good at typing.

When it comes to house-painting Sam is not as good as Janet but at typing Sam is very poor indeed.

Janet, of course, could try to do everything herself, spending some time typing and some time painting her house. But she is *comparatively disadvantaged* at house-painting. Since she enjoys a comparative advantage in typing she should specialize in this. In so doing she will make enough money to pay someone else to paint her house (maybe even Sam) and still have enough money left over for something else.

The principle, of course, is that of comparative advantage. Suppose now that Sam and Janet get married to each other (though goodness knows what she could possibly see in him) and that they have children. Who should stay at home to look after the children? Janet is better at looking after the children (because she's better at everything) but she can also earn more money in her job than Sam can in his. Will Sam become a house-husband?

10.5 Trade flows: avocados, tomatoes and dry-cell batteries

The theory of comparative advantage explained in the previous section can by no means provide a complete explanation of all trade flows. In this section we consider the reasons behind trade flows in three products selected at random: a horticultural product (avocados); a horticultural product produced using intensive techniques (tomatoes); and a manufactured product (dry-cell batteries).

Avocados are pear-shaped fruit grown in tropical and sub-tropical climates. It is not surprising therefore that all avocados sold in the UK are imported (mostly from South America, California and South Africa). The UK has a comparative disadvantage in the production of avocados since she is not naturally endowed with a suitable climate, and it would be very expensive to produce artificially the conditions necessary to grow them.

The same holds true, ostensibly, for tomatoes but a moment's reflection reveals that the tomatoes that we purchase in our supermarkets are cultivated in glasshouses. Until recently major suppliers of tomatoes to the UK were the Channel Islands of Guernsey and Jersey. Situated off the French coast and enjoying an enviable amount of sunshine, these small islands had a comparative advantage in tomato production by virtue of their natural endowments. In recent years, however, the Channel Islands' horticultural industry has undergone a dramatic decline. At the same time the Dutch horticultural industry has grown in size. Much of the horticultural produce that the UK used to import from the Channel Islands is now imported from Holland.

If the theory of comparative advantage has any validity we would therefore have to investigate why the Channel Islands have lost their comparative advantage in tomato production while Holland has gained a comparative advantage. Clearly, the answer does not lie in climatological change. We need to look at the abundance or scarcity of the other factors of production involved.

Horticultural products, even those grown intensively, require large amounts of land. Therein lies the problem for Jersey and Guernsey. These are small islands. They enjoy a good climate and being outside both French and British jurisdiction are a tax haven.

Many people, particularly retired people, would like to go and live there. This therefore means that the demand for houses – and hence for land – is very high, driving up its price. Because the price of land has become so high in the Channel Islands the costs which growers face have risen. Therefore they can no longer compete with other producers – particularly the Dutch. At the same time the Dutch have been gaining comparative advantage as a result of low energy costs used to heat the greenhouses (the Dutch have large supplies of natural gas). Do not shed any tears for the inhabitants of the Channel Islands, however. Their comparative advantage now lies in offshore banking as a result of their tax-free status.

In analysing some trade flows, therefore, the theory of comparative advantage does have some explanatory power. In the market for many manufactured products, however, the UK both imports and exports a substantial fraction of the goods consumed and produced. A typical example is provided by the market for dry-cell batteries.

As can be seen from Table 10.3, in 1994 approximately three-quarters of the batteries consumed in the UK were imported (mostly from within the EU). However UK producers also sold exports to the value of about a quarter of all UK sales – £91m compared with about £419m. There was thus a substantial two-way flow in batteries. Two-way flows such as this are quite typical in the market for manufactured goods and the theory of comparative advantage is of little help in explaining them. Here more detailed knowledge of the battery market is required.

Table 10.4 gives some information on market shares in 1995.

As can be seen, 50 to 60 per cent of the market (depending upon whether it is measured in volume or in value terms) was supplied by just two firms, Duracell and EverReady.

Dry-cell batteries can in fact be made of any two dissimilar metals. Traditionally zinc and carbon have been used and this market was dominated by EverReady until the early 1980s when Duracell entered the market with a higher performance alkaline manganese battery. Duracell quickly became established as the major manufacturer of this superior product, without any serious competition until the launch of EverReady's Gold Seal alkaline battery in 1983. The market for zinc carbon batteries has declined continuously as consumers switch to the higher performance (and higher priced) substitute. This reflects in part higher incomes (alkaline batteries are a superior product) and also to some extent changes in the use of batteries (a quarter of all batteries are now used in cassette players and recorders which require higher performance alkaline batteries). In 1993 EverReady re-launched in the alkaline sector with its Energizer brand. This replaced the Gold Seal brand, which had not always been recognized by

Table 10.3 Imports, exports and UK sales of all dry-cell batteries (£m 1994)

Imports	293.7
Exports	91.6
Total UK sales	419 (estimate*)

Source: Mintel.

*Manufacturers use a variety of different sources to evaluate the market so the estimate of the overall size of the market may not be very reliable.

Table 10.4 Brand shares for all dry-cell batteries, by volume and by value (1995)

	Volume Million units	%	Value £m	%
Duracell	120.9	26	142	34
EverReady	116.3	25	117	28
Rayovac*	41.9	9	29	7
Kodak	18.6	4	21	5
Panasonic	14.0	3	8	2
Varta	9.3	2	4	1
Other brands	23.3	5	21	5
Own label	120.9	26	75	18
Total	465.0	100	417	100

*Rayovac own label included in own label total.

consumers as the superior alkaline type because of its link with the Blue Seal and Silver Seal brand names used for zinc carbon batteries.

The own label sector, which EverReady initially refused to supply, is becoming increasingly important. Rayovac are the major supplier, manufacturing about 40 per cent of all own label batteries including those for Asda, Woolworths and Boots. A number of smaller manufacturers entered the UK battery market in the 1980s and 1990s including Panasonic, Kodak, Phillips and Ring. The combined effect of these changes has meant that the market for batteries has become increasingly competitive, with a larger number of suppliers in the market, often sourcing their products from outside the UK.

10.6 Trade flows: aggregates

In the previous section we looked at trade flows in three specific products. In the last of these, dry-cell batteries, we discovered that a *two-way* flow took place. The theory of comparative advantage was insufficient on its own to explain the relative magnitudes of the inward and outward flows. Additional factors were important in explaining these flows.

In this section we broaden the focus of our analysis. Previously we considered specific products in the context of the UK economy. We now consider broad groups of products (classified by industrial sectors) in the context of a wider economic grouping – that of the European Union as a whole.

Table 10.6 identifies a number of industrial sectors. The contribution of a particular sector to total manufacturing exports is shown in column 1. Alongside this, column 2 shows that sector's share in total imports. By comparing the percentage figure shown in each column it is possible to get some idea of those industrial sectors in which the EU specializes, as a result of comparative advantage or for some other reason. Thus for example we see that in pharmaceuticals the export share is larger than the import share suggesting that this is a sector in which the EU specializes. In contrast, in office and EDP machinery the import share exceeds the export share, indicating that other countries (probably Japan) are strong in this area and therefore specialize in it.

Table 10.6 EU exports and imports, and export specialization, by sector (1993)

	Share in total exports	Share in total imports	Export specialization
Mineral oil refining	1.9	2.2	1.40
Ferrous metals	3.1	1.5	1.12
Non-ferrous metals	1.6	5.3	0.57
Non-metallic mineral products	2.0	1.1	1.46
Basic chemicals	5.5	4.9	1.03
Pharmaceuticals	2.8	1.6	1.70
Specialty chemicals	4.7	2.8	1.22
Manufacture of metal articles	3.3	2.5	1.36
Mechanical engineering	16.0	7.5	1.14
Office and EDP machinery	2.8	6.7	0.60
Electrical equipment for industry	4.8	4.4	0.89
Telecom equipment/prof. electronics	3.2	3.0	0.85
Consumer electronics	2.6	6.1	0.52
Household appliances	0.9	0.7	1.51
Motor vehicles & parts	8.7	6.0	0.70
Aerospace equipment	4.3	4.1	1.19
Other means of transport	1.4	1.1	0.76
Instrument engineering	2.3	3.2	0.73
Food, drink, tobacco	6.5	5.3	1.13
Textile	3.9	5.4	1.46
Leather & leather goods	0.9	1.0	1.97
Footwear & clothing	2.7	6.0	1.89
Timber & wooden furniture	1.4	3.7	0.73
Pulp, paper & paperboard	1.5	4.1	0.47
Printing & publishing	0.9	0.5	1.42
Processing of rubber/plastics	2.7	2.3	1.11
Manufacture of jewelry	3.2	4.2	1.58
Other manufacturing	4.4	2.8	1.26
Total manufacturing	100.0	100.0	1.00

Note: column 3 (export specialization) shows the share of each sector in total EU manufacturing exports divided by the same share calculated for the OECD.
Source: Panorama of EU industry 1995/6.

The third column of Table 10.6 provides what is perhaps a more satisfactory way of assessing the nature of the EU's specialization by comparing it with the average OECD export pattern. Remember that the OECD is comprised of all of the world's industrialized countries. Thus in column 3 a value of 1.0 indicates that the weight of that sector in total exports is the same as the OECD average, indicating that the EU shows no specialization in that sector compared with the OECD average. A value greater than one indicates that the EU specializes in that sector, and a value less than 1.0 indicates that other industrialized countries – probably the United States and/or Japan – specializes there. Thus we see a value of 1.70 for pharmaceuticals and 0.60 for office and EDP machinery.

One can infer from columns 1 and 2 of Table 10.6 that in some product areas the EU is a net exporter (such as mechanical engineering) and in others a net importer – areas such as timber and wooden furniture, and paper, pulp and paperboard. The latter is easily explained in terms of factor endowments and the theory of comparative advantage. Most of the EU imports of timber products come from Norway and Sweden, which were both non-EU countries in 1994, the year to which the table relates (though Sweden subsequently joined in 1995). These Nordic countries are sparsely populated with people but densely covered with trees. The climate in these regions makes them ideally suited to forestry but unsuited to other forms of agriculture.

10.7 Hecksher-Ohlin and the Leontief paradox

In other industrial sectors, however, it is not so easy to explain why the EU is a net importer or a net exporter. One might expect to find that the EU would be a net exporter of **capital-intensive**, high-technology products and a net importer of **labour-intensive**, low-technology products. A development of the theory of comparative advantage by Hecksher and Ohlin suggests precisely this. The Hecksher-Ohlin theorem seeks to explain why some countries have a comparative advantage in the production of some products while other countries have a comparative advantage in other products. The explanation they put forward focuses on **initial factor endowments**, and in particular endowments of labour and capital. They argue that developed economies such as those of the United States, the EU and Japan will tend to specialize in producing capital-intensive products and will therefore be net exporters of such products because they are comparatively well endowed with capital. In contrast, poorer countries such as those of the Third World will tend to export labour-intensive products since they are comparatively well-endowed with labour.

Empirically, however, this theorem is not always supported by the evidence, at least not at first sight. The economist Wassily Leontief observed what he described as a paradox, namely, that the United States was an exporter of wheat and rice, products characterized ostensibly by labour-intensive production techniques. In fact, the **Leontief Paradox** is easily resolved. Goods can be produced by a variety of techniques, some of which are more capital-intensive than others. In less-developed countries labour-intensive techniques are used to produce agricultural products such as rice. But in the United States and most of Western Europe agricultural products are produced using large amounts of capital and very little labour. Thus it is probably too simplistic to characterize some products as intrinsically labour-intensive and others as intrinsically capital-intensive.

However, some of the net trade flows which can be inferred from Table 10.6 do accord with the naive version of the H-O Theorem. For example, the EU seems to be a net importer of footwear and clothing, as we would expect, since these are normally produced using labour-intensive production methods. Similarly it is a net importer of consumer electronics which involve similar labour-intensive production techniques, even though they are ostensibly 'high-tech' products.

10.8 Trade shares

There is of course an additional dimension to all this. Most trade takes place not between developed countries and developing countries but between one developed country and another. The developed countries dominate world trade, particularly in manufactured goods. Table 10.7 shows that the developed market economies of the world account for around 70 per cent of world trade.

It is worth pausing for a moment to note our definition of 'developed market economies'. Here this is taken to be synonymous with the economies of the OECD (the Organisation for Economic Co-operation and Development). This now comprises the following countries:

The original member countries namely Austria, Belgium, Canada, Denmark, France, Germany, Greece, Iceland, Ireland, Italy, Luxembourg, the Netherlands, Norway, Portugal, Spain, Sweden, Switzerland, Turkey, the United Kingdom and the United States. In addition, the following countries have become members (accession dates in brackets): Japan (1964); Finland (1969); Australia (1971); New Zealand (1973); Mexico (1994); the Czech Republic (1995); Hungary (1996); Poland (1996); the Republic of Korea (1996).

It is also worth noting two more definitions. The term 'G7' countries refers to the group of seven countries whose economies are the largest in the world, that is the United States, Canada, Japan, Germany, France, the UK and Italy. In 1996 the G7 countries had about 72 per cent of OECD exports. The term 'Triad' is used unofficially by some authors to refer to the three main economic blocs – the United States, Japan and the 15 countries of the EU. In 1996 the Triad countries accounted for about 88 per cent of OECD exports.

Inter-regional and international trade

It is important to note that the data shown in Table 10.7 may give a misleading impression of the relative size of the three members of the Triad. This is because statisticians only record as 'foreign trade' those flows which involve goods or services which pass from one nation state to another – for example, from France to Germany.

Table 10.7 Shares of world trade (% of total exports, 1996)

	$bn	*% of total*
United States	624	11.4
Japan	411	8.0
EU15	2112	40.2
OECD total	3575	69.3*
'Developing countries'	1692*	30.7*

*Estimates. The data shown with asterisks are intended only to show broad orders of magnitude and should not be relied upon for accuracy. Hence some of the calculated percentages may also be inaccurate.
Source: derived from OECD *Main Economic Indicators*, May 1997, *International Financial Statistics*, December 1996 and *IFS Yearbook*, 1996.

Table 10.8 Comparative size of the most important economies and economic groupings (GDP 1996)

	GDP $bn	Percentage of OECD total GDP
United States	7263.2	32.4
EU15	8586.7	38.3
Japan	4597.2	20.5
equals 'Triad'	20447.1	91.1
Major seven (G7)	18685.2	83.2
OECD total	22442.6	100.0

Source: derived from OECD *Main Economic Indicators*, May 1997. The data shown are at current prices and exchange rates.

They do not record trade flows when goods pass from one part of a nation state to another part of the same nation state – for example, from England to Wales, or from Texas to California. This means, therefore, that the statistics shown in Table 10.7 have to be interpreted with caution. Table 10.7 shows that the United States accounts for around 11 per cent of world trade and the EU around 40 per cent. This does not mean that the EU economy is nearly four times as large as that of the United States – in fact as Table 10.8 shows the combined output of the EU is not much larger than that of the United States. The reason why the USA appears to have much less trade than the EU is because most of the 'trade' in the United States is from one state to another and hence is not recorded as international trade. Similarly if a 'United States of Europe' were ever to be achieved what was formerly international trade would be reclassified as inter-regional trade. The specialization and exchange which formed the basis of that trade would not have been diminished, however. Indeed, the removal of barriers to trade would almost certainly lead to greater specialization within the EU – and this is part of the rationale for the European Union.

Table 10.8 gives some indication of the comparative size of the most important economies and economic groupings.

10.9 Free trade versus protectionism

We began this chapter by examining the benefits that could flow from specialization and trade. The analysis relied heavily on the Theory of Comparative Advantage. The implications of the analysis for economic policy are quite clear, namely that free trade is to be encouraged and any restraints on trade between nations should be eliminated.

It should be borne in mind, however, that the Theory of Comparative Advantage was developed by a British economist at a time when Britain was the most powerful industrial nation, having been the first to industrialize. As such Britain was the country most likely to benefit from the free trade doctrines which she preached. Other countries, struggling to industrialize, did not share Britain's enthusiasm for free trade particularly where their **infant industries** were concerned. Rather, they strove to protect these industries with tariff barriers until the day when they became sufficiently mature to compete on equal terms with the foreign competition.

The argument between the advocates of free trade and the advocates of protectionism lives on to this day. Those who call for protection are invariably those whose livelihoods are being threatened by exposure to low-cost foreign producers: thus French farmers demonstrate against agricultural policies by slaughtering British lambs on the dockside at Calais; American car workers demonstrate against the flood of Japanese imports; and Japanese farmers campaign to retain restrictions on the import of low-cost American rice. In contrast the advocates of free trade are those most likely to benefit from that freedom: they are the traders themselves, often transnational companies seeking to exploit the global market.

Although the Theory of Comparative Advantage provides a clear endorsement of free trade the analysis is static, ignoring dynamic considerations. That is, it takes the comparative advantage of one country over another in particular products as a given datum without considering how this arose or how it might change in the future as a result of policies undertaken now. Moreover, it ignores the trauma associated with the decline of an industry exposed to lower-cost foreign competition. In the long term, as the Theory of Comparative Advantage suggests, there may indeed be a net increase in output as resources transfer from a declining sector to an expanding one. Many of these resources are people, however, and the short-term trauma of redundancy and unemployment is not inconsiderable, particularly when work is for many people the most important facet of lifestyle, as it is for farmers for example.

10.10 Policies designed to restrict trade

The advocates of free trade have often been faced by an equally vociferous group arguing in favour of policies deliberately designed to restrict trade. Sometimes this has been based on the infant industry argument but more recently, particularly in Europe and North America, advocates of trade restrictions have justified their position by appealing to an interesting variant – the **senile industry** argument. This states that certain mature industries (such as steelmaking and car manufacture) have been allowed to decline as a result of chronic underinvestment so that they are now uncompetitive in comparison with those industries in some other countries (particularly the Asian Pacific countries). It is therefore necessary to protect such industries behind tariff walls temporarily until they can be restored to a position where they can compete effectively.

This argument has been applied to car manufacture in Europe and the United States. By the 1980s the Japanese car industry had become highly efficient in comparison with North American and particularly European producers. This was mostly as a result of a high level of automation and greater scale economies. As a result the European car makers sought to protect their industry by asking the Japanese manufacturers to limit the number of vehicles exported from Japan to Europe. These **Voluntary Export Restraints (VERs)** were in effect self-imposed quotas.

One of the consequences of this policy, however, was that Japanese cars sold on the European market and particularly in the UK were more expensive than the same vehicles sold in Japan. In effect, if Japanese cars had been sold in Europe at the same price as in Japan the demand would have outstripped the supply available under the VER. Japanese manufacturers were able to choke off the excess demand by charging higher prices (and by not supplying the cheapest models in the range). The prices set by Japanese manufacturers were in line with those charged by European manufacturers who were less efficient and had higher costs.

European consumers would probably have benefited – in the short run at least – from the removal of VERs. Although it is by no means certain what the result of this would have been it is probable that it would have led to a reduction in the price of Japanese cars in Europe and that to maintain market share the European producers would have responded by cutting prices to the further benefit of consumers. Thereafter the dynamic of the situation becomes less clear and it is this lack of clarity which gives such scope for the arguments between the advocates of free trade and those of protectionism. One scenario is that competitive pressures will force European producers to become more efficient. Another is that competitive pressures will force them to close down, leaving Europe increasingly dependent on imported vehicles. This of course would worsen the Trade Deficit and lead to unemployment among car workers. In the longer term, however, these resources would flow to other sectors where Europe enjoys a comparative advantage, at least in theory, though some resources might not find an alternative use.

An additional consideration of course is that Japanese firms have increasingly sought to overcome tariff barriers by establishing production facilities in Europe. This was already well under way by 1991 when Nissan UK became officially classified as a UK producer, the **domestic content** of its vehicles produced in Sunderland having risen above the minimum percentage required for such classification. Nissan, like Ford and General Motors before it, had become a multinational, which is the subject of the next chapter.

Summary

Adam Smith was the first economist to talk about the benefits to be derived from the division of labour and from specialization. His successor, David Ricardo, explained how counties too could benefit by specializing in the production of those goods and services in which they had a comparative advantage. If they did so, and traded their surpluses, they would be able to consume a greater volume of goods than would have been the case had they been self-sufficient. Ricardo's theory of comparative advantage therefore explains why countries trade, and goes some way to explaining which goods and services they will specialize in. The Hecksher-Ohlin theorem sees the source of comparative advantage in terms of initial factor endowments. Leontief noted a paradox, however, namely that some seemingly capital-rich countries export what are apparently labour-intensive products.

The theory of comparative advantage is also used by the advocates of free trade to support their position but there may be valid arguments for protectionism, especially to protect infant industries.

Key terms

Review questions

10.1 Whatever happened to Renaissance Man?

10.2 Many manufactured products which are sold under the label of Western companies are in fact manufactured elsewhere. Bicycles, for example, and particularly mountain bikes, are often designed in America or the UK but made in the Far East as the following table illustrates:

Manufacturers used by Western cycle companies

Cycle company	Manufacturer
Specialised (USA)	Giant (Taiwan)
Ridgeback (UK)	Taioku (Taiwan)
Kona (Canada)	Fairly (Taiwan)
Marin (USA)	Marvel (Taiwan)
Saracen (UK)	Tai Huei (Taiwan)
Trek[1] (USA)	Ideal/Merida (both Taiwan)
Fusion (UK)	Ideal (Taiwan)
Gary Fisher (USA)	Anlen (Japan)
Scott (USA)	CBC (China Bicycle Company)
Schwinn (USA)	CBC
Emmelle (UK)	CBC
Diamond Back[2] (USA)	CBC
Muddy Fox[3]	various (Taiwan and Korea)

1 Entry model levels only.
2 Now owned by CBC.
3 Acquired in 1992 by a consortium comprising Sitac (UK) and TI Cycles of India.
Source: Based on *International Business: text and cases*, J. Preston (ed.). The data relate to 1992.

What factors account for the decision of Western cycle companies to use manufacturers in the Far East?

10.3 The following table shows the number of units of labour input required to produce one unit of output in the clothing and domestic appliance industries in two hypothetical countries Alphaland and Betaland.

	Alphaland	Betaland
Clothing	5	7
Domestic appliances	50	63

(a) Does either country have an absolute advantage in both clothing and domestic appliances?

(b) In Alphaland what is the opportunity cost of one domestic appliance? What is it in Betaland?

(c) Which country has a comparative advantage in appliance production?

(d) Which country has a comparative advantage in the production of clothing?

(e) What should Alphaland specialize in?

(f) Suppose a multinational conglomerate owns clothing factories and appliance factories in both countries. Assume that redundant appliance workers are always redeployed in the conglomerate's clothing factories, and *vice versa*. How much extra output could the conglomerate produce if it closed down its 1000 unit appliance factory in Alphaland and transferred appliance production to Betaland?

(g) The ULRs shown in the table above are in physical units (man-hours or whatever). We could also show them in *value* terms (i.e., money terms) but we could only compare them if both countries used the same currency, or if we converted them into a common currency. Suppose we do the latter and choose the ECU to be that common currency.

If one man-hour costs one ECU the figures would remain unchanged.

Suppose now, however, that wage rates in Alphaland increase by 50 per cent. The input requirements *measured in money terms* (in this case ECUs) would become:

	Alphaland	Betaland
Clothing	7.5	7.0
Appliances	75.0	63.0

Which country now has a comparative advantage in the production of appliances?

(h) What would a profit seeking multinational company do as a result of the wage rise described above?

(i) Suppose now the value of the alpha falls by 20 per cent on foreign exchange markets (the value of the beta remaining unchanged). What then would the multinational company do? (Construct a table similar to those above.)

11 Multinationals

Preview

Economic activity is now dominated by multinational companies. This chapter examines the growth of multinational activity in the twentieth century. It investigates the reasons why firms began to establish production facilities overseas, and what specific advantages multinational companies now enjoy in comparison with firms operating within domestic boundaries. Some of the problems that MNCs pose for national governments are discussed.

In Chapter 9 we looked at the behaviour of firms operating in oligopolistic markets. A typical feature of such firms is their large size, but size in itself is not the only characteristic. A related feature of such firms is that they tend to be multinational. The word **multinational** means something specific and is not merely a synonym for 'international'. A multinational company – otherwise known as an MNC or MNE (multi-national enterprise) or TNC (transnational company or corporation) – is one that has production facilities in more than one country. Thus Ford, which has car plants all over the world, is by definition multinational. In contrast, a company like Rover which produces in only one country and then exports part of its output is by definition not multinational. The difference, though seemingly trivial, is very important, as we shall see.

11.1 A brief history of the multinational company: the product life cycle

Multinational companies began to develop in a significant way in the inter-war period when companies based in America expanded their operations by establishing production facilities outside the United States. Initially most of this expansion was in Europe. There are several reasons why such companies adopted this strategy rather than choosing to export to Europe goods produced in America. Many of these reasons are illustrated by Vernon's **product life cycle** theory[1] (though there is no suggestion that a single rather simplistic theory can adequately explain the historical reasons for the growth and diversity of multinational activity). Vernon's theory suggests that all products go through a number of evolutionary phases during their life cycle. The cycle is initiated by the discovery or invention of a new product – for example, the sewing machine, the telephone, the motor car, the microcomputer, and so on. The discovery is then refined to the stage where a product can be sold to the mass market. When Vernon first put forward this theory, the United States economy had a position of pre-eminence such that most research and development leading to the discovery of new products took place there. The American mass market was also by far the most important market because of its size and the level of income per capita. Hence new products were developed in America and the American market was the first to be exploited. The products which Vernon had in mind were consumer durable products. As the name implies, such products tended not to wear out very quickly so that the growth of sales of, say, vacuum cleaners had a time profile rather like that in Fig. 11.1.

Sales increased more or less exponentially up to point A and then started to tail off as the market became satiated. At point B every household that wanted a vacuum cleaner would already own one, so that the potential for further sales was limited to replacing those that were worn out. Although with experience some manufacturers became more adept at making their products wear out more quickly, the scope for this was restricted since products which wore out too quickly would be perceived by consumers as being of low quality and sales of that brand would suffer as a result. 'Built-in obsolescence' could also be achieved by major technical advances which brought a significant improvement in the performance of new versions of the product, but there was little scope for this in vacuum cleaners or in many other consumer durables. 'Design improvements' were thus limited to cosmetic changes which failed to persuade even the most gullible of consumers that they should replace their old model with a new one.

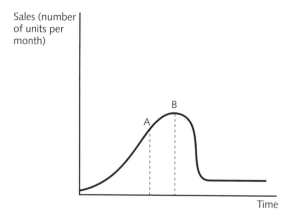

Figure 11.1 The product life cycle

With the domestic American market saturated, manufacturers sought new markets overseas – particularly in Britain and continental Europe. They could, of course, have exported to Europe products made in America. They preferred, however, to establish production facilities in those countries whose markets they wished to exploit. The advantages of so doing were many. First, it overcame the problem of import restrictions which some governments had imposed. Secondly, it reduced transport costs. Thirdly, labour costs in Europe were generally lower than those in America so that products could be produced more cheaply. By establishing production facilities in Europe, American firms were able to compete not on equal terms with European rivals but on superior terms, since the research and development expenditure associated with the new product had already been amortized (written off) in the American market. Because American firms in Europe had this significant advantage over their European competitors, they prospered. The age of the multinational had begun.

On the European market of course the growth of sales of a particular product had a time profile similar to that illustrated in Fig. 11.1. When the European market had been satiated, therefore, the American multinationals had again to look around for new markets to exploit, and these they found in the Far East, in Africa, in South America and Australia – in short, in all corners of the globe.

Although Vernon's theory is introduced here as a (partial) explanation of the emergence of the multinational company, it has a much wider and more general application since many products do seem to experience a life cycle which can be broken down into three phases: rapid growth of sales, satiation and then stagnation. Some products have an extremely short life cycle – the hula hoop and the Rubic Cube for example. Other products have a life cycle extending over several decades – the motor car for example. It is suggested that the current worldwide overcapacity in the car industry is partly the result of the approaching satiation in the demand for cars. In products like cars, however, the replacement demand is still substantial since obsolescence is built into the car, both because it is designed to wear out and because technical improvements, though modest, are sufficient to convince consumers that the new model is an improvement on the old. Note that cars and many other durable goods could be designed to wear out more slowly but that this would generally lead to lower performance and higher cost. Finally, it should be noted that, although certain products do appear to have a life cycle like that illustrated in Fig. 11.1, some writers argue that there is no empirical support for the theory. Clearly for non-durable products, and even for durable products where significant scope for design improvement exists, there is no reason why saturation should ever by reached. In other words, one is always operating on the upward-sloping portion of the life-cycle curve.

11.2 The size of multinationals

The product life cycle helps to explain the reasons for the initial emergence of the multinational company. It is, of course, an over simplification and many of the most important multinationals do not fit into this model. Some are European-based multinationals like Unilever and Philips. Others are Japanese, like Mitsubishi, and many are oil companies whose activities naturally lend themselves to a multinational format.

Multinationals have distinct advantages over purely national companies. These advantages (which are discussed in section 11.3) have resulted in the growth rate of such companies far exceeding that of companies which stick to national boundaries. A corollary of this is that companies who wish to grow rapidly are forced, sooner or later, to extend their activities beyond their own frontiers. Initially they do this by exporting, but to secure the advantages of the truly multinational company they must eventually establish or take over subsidiary companies in other countries. Hence, when we look at the statistics we find that the growth rate of MNCs exceeds that of other companies both because existing MNCs have advantages over other companies, and because other companies are themselves forced to become multinational to secure these advantages.

There is therefore a resulting tendency for MNCs to become the dominant organizational form both in world trade and world economic activity generally. The world's largest multinationals are now very large indeed. Table 11.1 lists the top fifty industrial companies in 1995/6 which, with few exceptions, are multinational. It is not easy to appreciate just how large these companies are. One way of doing so, however, is to compare the annual income of a typical large multinational with the annual income of a medium-sized nation state. This is done in Table 11.2 where we compare the GDP of a number of countries with the annual sales revenue of General Motors. Although not the largest of the MNCs as measured by capital employed, GM is the archetypal large multinational. Its turnover in 1995-96 was about $180bn (£107bn) which is roughly the same as the GDP of a country such as Denmark.

Table 11.1 The world's top 50 industrial companies

Rank	Company	Headquarters	Sector	Capital employed £bn
1	General Electric	USA	electricals	84.1
2	Tokyo Electric Power	Japan	electricity	79.7
3	Nippon Telegraph & Telephone	Japan	communications	76.4
4	General Motors	USA	transport – manufacture & distribution	73.2
5	Royal Dutch Shell	UK/Netherlands	oil, gas & nuclear fuels	54.7
6	Electricité de France	France	electricity	47.6
7	Toyota Motor	Japan	transport – manufacture & distribution	47.5
8	East Japan Railway	Japan	transport services	43.3
9	IRI-Istituto per la Ricostruzione Industriale	Italy	other financial	41.3
10	Exxon	USA	oil, gas and nuclear fuels	41.1
11	Matsushita Electric	Japan	electronics	39.8
12	Hitachi	Japan	electronics	38.7
13	Kansai Electric Power	Japan	electricity	37.4
14	Chubu Electric Power	Japan	electricity	33.3
15	Mitsubishi	Japan	soga sosha[1]	31.6
16	AT&T	USA	communications	27.4

Table 11.1 Contd

Rank	Company	Headquarters	Sector	Capital employed £bn
17	Nissan Motor	Japan	transport – manufacture & distribution	28.2
18	Siemens	Germany	electricals	27.7
19	France Telecom	France	communications	27.4
20	RWE	Germany	electricity	26.6
21	Daimler-Benz	Germany	transport – manufacture & distribution	25.9
22	Veba	Germany	oil, gas & nuclear fuels	24.8
23	Volkswagen	Germany	transport – manufacture & distribution	24.7
24	Mitsui	Japan	soga sosha[1]	23.7
25	Kyushu Electric Power	Japan	electricity	23.1
26	Fiat	Italy	transport – manufacture & distribution	22.7
27	SNCF	France	transport services	22.4
28	IBM	USA	communications	22.1
29	Hydro-Quebec	Canada	electricity	22.0
30	Elf Aquitaine	France	oil, gas & nuclear fuels	22.0
31	Istituto Finanziaro Industriale	Italy	miscellaneous	21.7
32	Philip Morris	USA	food manufacturing	21.3
33	British Petroleum	UK	oil, gas & nuclear fuels	21.2
34	Ford Motor	USA	transport – manufacture & distribution	20.6
35	Petroleos de Venezuela	Venezuela	oil, gas & nuclear fuels	20.1
36	Telefonica de Espana	Spain	communications	20.1
37	Tohoku Electric Power	Japan	electricity	19.9
38	Toshiba	Japan	electronics	18.6
39	Itochu	Japan	soga sosha[1]	18.3
40	Marubeni	Japan	soga sosha[1]	18.2
41	Hoechst	Germany	chemicals	18.1
42	Mobil	USA	oil, gas & nuclear fuels	17.9
43	Nippon Steel	Japan	metal & metal forming	17.8
44	ENI – Ente Nazionale Idrocarburi	Italy	oil, gas & nuclear fuels	17.5
45	Wal-Mart Stores	USA	stores	17.2
46	British Telecom	UK	communications	16.4
47	Southern	USA	electricity	16.1
48	Alcatel-Alsthom Generale d'Electricité	France	communications	16.1
49	Sony	Japan	electronics	16.0
50	Fujitsu	Japan	electronics	15.8

1   Soga sosha = conglomerate, generally with interests in industry and finance.
Source: The Times 1000, 1997.

Table 11.2 Sales revenue of General Motors compared with the GDP of some countries (1995-96 $bn)

General Motors (sales revenue)	180
GDP	
Denmark	175
Norway	156
Portugal	105
Ireland	69
Greece	122
New Zealand	64
for comparison	
United Kingdom	1135

Source: derived from OECD *Main Economic Indicators*, May 1997 and *The Times 1000*, 1997. The latter source reports corporate income in sterling and the data have been converted back to dollars at an exchange rate of £1 = $1.682.

The large multinational companies therefore represent a concentration of economic power which, for many writers, is cause for concern and alarm. The importance of the multinational enterprise in world trade is particularly striking. One author[2] has estimated that in 1981 just 72 firms accounted for half of Britain's exports, and only 18 per cent of Britain's exports were not accounted for by multinationals. In the following two sections we examine why MNCs have prospered. Section 11.3 considers some of the specific advantages they possess in comparison with national companies, and section 11.4 considers particular aspects of multinational activity.

11.3 The advantages of being a multinational

Some of the advantages enjoyed by MNCs exist simply by virtue of the size of such companies rather than as a result of any particular organizational form. Size in itself facilitates further growth for a number of reasons. For example, the cost of acquiring funds for investment may well be lower for the large firm than it is for the small firm. This is so because large firms have access to privileged sources of funds only available to large, financially secure firms. One such source of funds is the Eurodollar market where large sums are borrowed and lent by multinationals at interest rates which are generally lower than elsewhere. Furthermore, there is no exchange rate risk since the funds are borrowed and lent in dollars and are never converted into any other currency. Large firms are also able to finance much of their investment through internally generated funds, that is, through retained earnings. Such advantages are, of course, just one of the economies of scale enjoyed by the large firm. It is important to distinguish however between **real economies of scale** and **pecuniary economies of scale**. Real economies benefit both the firm and society at large because there is a saving in the resources required to do a particular job. Pecuniary economies, on the other hand, benefit the firm itself but society does not benefit because such 'savings' do not result from increased efficiency. Financial economies are the most obvious example of a pecuniary scale economy which results from the market power and bargaining strength of the large firm. This market power may enable it to negotiate more favourable credit terms on loans, or to purchase materials and other goods more cheaply than the small firm is able to do. These financial economies, then, are mostly pecuniary in nature rather than real. However, a not insignificant part of the financial economies results from the lower transaction costs per unit associated with the bulk purchase of materials or the negotiation of larger loans rather than small. These are real economies.

The decision as to whether a particular financial saving should be classified as 'real' or 'pecuniary' becomes more difficult when one recognizes that lending to large firms is less risky than lending to small ones. Large firms are less likely to default. The lower risk explains in part the cheaper interest rates available to the large firm. However, on reflection it can be seen that the reason that lending to large firms is less risky than lending to small ones is because large firms are able to internalize the risk within the firm and thus bear the risk themselves rather than impose it on the lender. Thus in the two cases the risk is borne by different parties – by the bank when loans are made to small firms and by the firm itself when loans are made to large firms. The risk inherent in the investment to which the loan relates is the same, however, regardless of who is undertaking it. This inherent risk depends on the nature of the investment project itself.

Risk spreading

The ability to spread the risk inherent in business activity, and hence to reduce its overall impact on the company is, of course, one of the major advantages conferred by size. The multinational company, however, can add an extra dimension to this risk-spreading activity by diversifying its activities over several countries and continents as well as over several product ranges and types of business activity. Thus the Ford Motor Company, an American multinational, has subsidiary companies (Ford would probably call them 'affiliates') in many parts of the world. The 1980s saw a period when Ford of America was making losses but was being supported by the profits being repatriated to it from Ford of Europe who at that time were highly profitable. By spreading risk in this way the multinational is thus less susceptible to the effects of cyclical fluctuations in economic activity. These fluctuations – recessions and booms – tend of course to be a worldwide phenomenon affecting all those countries linked by trade. However, the timing of these fluctuations and their magnitude differ from country to country. Moreover, the impact which these fluctuations will have on the multinational and its affiliates will depend on a complex set of factors, one of the most important of which is the behaviour of exchange rates.

11.4 Aspects of multinational activity

The important point to note is that a multinational format allows a company to take advantage of movements in economic activity. Being 'footloose and fancy free', without any ties or allegiances, the multinational is able to turn to its own advantage those movements in economic activity which, for purely national companies, would present severe problems. These movements in economic activity may be cyclical, such as the short-term recessions mentioned above, or they may be secular – that is, part of a long-term trend.

Investment flows

The multinational will, for example, respond to secular movements in economic activity by adjusting its investment flows accordingly. That is, investment will flow to those areas where the rate of return is highest. If, for example, the American or the South African economy is growing faster and offering greater investment potential than the UK economy, then UK-owned multinationals will tend quite naturally to direct their investment flows out of the UK and towards the USA and South Africa. This investment in itself facilitates economic expansion, of course, and raises the growth rate of these other economies, thus confirming the multinational in its belief that the rate of return on investment overseas was greater than that in the UK.

Sourcing

Multinational companies involved in manufacturing activity, such as the motor companies, frequently assemble their products utilizing components manufactured by their subsidiaries in other countries. Table 11.3 shows the source of the components used in assembling the Vauxhall Astra in the 1980s. This was a nominally British car built by Vauxhall Motors, the UK subsidiary of the American multinational General Motors. It could validly be described as a British car in the sense that it was assembled in the UK, and if one includes the cost of the manpower involved in its assembly then the local (i.e., British) content is estimated to have been 62 per cent.[3] The remainder was sourced from a variety of GM subsidiaries in Europe and elsewhere.

Table 11.3 Sources of components for Vauxhall Astra, mid 1980s

Front doors	UK	Transmission	
Floor pan	UK	1.3 litre cars	Austria
Rear doors	W. Germany	1.6 litre cars	Japan
Tailgate	W. Germany	Automatics	France
Roof	W. Germany	Electrical wiring	Ireland/W. Germany
Bonnet	UK	Wheels	UK
Glass	UK	Bumpers	W. Germany
Radiator	France	Suspension	W. Germany
Engine		Seat frames	W. Germany
1.2 litre cars	W. Germany	Upholstery	UK
1.3 litre cars	Austria/W. Germany	Interior trim	UK
1.6 litre cars	Australia	Instruments	UK
1.8 litre cars	W. Germany	Headlamps	W. Germany
diesel	W. Germany		

Source: *The Observer*, 21 October 1984.

The procurement of components and materials from subsidiaries in other countries is a common feature of multinational activity. It is sometimes referred to simply as **sourcing**. One implication of sourcing is that products which appear (for example) to be British made may contain a high proportion of foreign-made components. This has implications for the balance of trade since if, for example, Vauxhall Astras are sold on export markets, the net benefit to the balance of trade is much less than the gross benefit since each car contains a high import content. However, it is equally the case that Volvo motor cars contain many British built components so that when such a vehicle is purchased in Britain part of the income from the sale accrues to British companies and workers.

Transfer pricing

Sourcing is, of course, a legitimate business practice. It has been alleged, however, that some multinationals source their products so as to maximize the profits of the group by engaging in **transfer pricing**. That is, the prices which are charged by one subsidiary to another for the transfer of components are such as to benefit the group, that is the multinational parent, possibly at the expense of one of the subsidiaries. To see how this could work out in practice, consider the following hypothetical example.

Suppose that, for example, two countries which we will label Hightax and Lowtax have different rates of corporation tax. Both countries are host to the subsidiaries of an American multinational car company. Both countries also assemble cars which are sourced both locally and abroad. The price at which components are transferred from one subsidiary to another will clearly affect the cost and therefore the profitability of the subsidiaries. Specifically, if components are transferred from the Lowtax subsidiary to the Hightax subsidiary at an inflated price, then this will increase the costs and reduce the profitability of the Hightax subsidiary. Similarly, the profits of the Lowtax subsidiary will be increased by an equivalent amount. Since the rate of corporation tax is lower in Lowtax than it is in Hightax, the overall tax liability of the group is therefore reduced.

It should be stressed that this is a hypothetical example and, for obvious reasons, few data exist to support the allegation that internal prices are deliberately distorted in this way by multinational companies. Given the informational requirement that needs to be satisfied for the practice to benefit the company, it seems unlikely that the practice is either widespread or carried out in a systematic way. Moreover, the discussion of costs in Chapter 5 illustrates the difficulty of defining how the cost of a particular component should be defined and therefore what constitutes a fair price to be used in internal transactions within the company. Having said this, however, it is clear that companies (and individuals) do take advantage of such things as differences in tax rates, investment incentives and the like, and that such behaviour will influence, to a lesser or greater extent, key macroeconomic variables like investment flows, growth rates and the balance of trade. However, it has been estimated[2] that 30 per cent of Britain's exports are to related concerns – that is, to subsidiaries of UK parents or to other subsidiaries of foreign-based MNCs. The scope for engaging in transfer pricing is therefore considerable.

Summary

A multinational company is defined as one which has production facilities in more than one country. The first phase of multinational expansion began in the early years of this century when American firms established production facilities in Europe. These firms prospered because they enjoyed the advantages of scale economies but there were also specific advantages that resulted from their multinational format.

Today almost all large firms are multinationals and they dominate world trade. There is a large concentration of economic power in the hands of a few hundred major corporations operating on a global scale.

Notes

1 A survey of product-cycle theories is provided in Vernon, R. (ed.) (1970) *Technological and International Trade*, National Bureau Committee for Economic Research.
2 Locksley, G. and Minns, R. (1985) 'Multi-nationals and the failure of economic management', *The Guardian*, 3 April 1985.
3 *The Observer*, 21 October 1984.

Key terms

multinational	145	pecuniary economies of scale	150
product life cycle	146	sourcing	153
real economies of scale	150	transfer pricing	153

Review questions

11.1 'All multinationals operate on an international scale but not all international companies are multinationals.' Explain.
11.2 Assess the extent to which the product life cycle hypothesis can be applied to:
(a) video recorders
(b) home computers
(c) colour televisions
(d) washing machines
(e) coffee-making machines.
To what extent have design improvements been able to stave off the day when the market for these products becomes satiated?
11.3 In 1986 the Nissan car company established a major production facility in the UK. Why did it do this rather than continue to export vehicles assembled in Japan?
11.4 As a small company producing only within the UK the Rover car company suffered specific disadvantages in comparison with firms operating on a world scale such as Ford and General Motors (Vauxhall). What specific disadvantages did Rover suffer in comparison with these multinational rivals?

11.5 A multinational sells cars in two national markets, Alphaland and Betaland. All cars are assembled by the Alphaland subsidiary using gearboxes produced by the Betaland subsidiary. Corporation tax is 40 per cent in Alphaland but only 30 per cent in Betaland. The following are the national prices which could be charged for internal transactions within the company:

price at which gearboxes are transferred from Beta to Alpha	300	250
price at which cars are transferred from Alpha to Beta	4000	5000

If the company wishes to maximize the post-tax profits of the group, which prices will it charge?

12 The consumer

Preview

This chapter presents a theoretical model of a utility-maximizing consumer. A condition for utility maximization is derived. The chapter also explores the concepts of income and substitution effects, which are important in analysing the effect of a price change on the demand for a good.

12.1 Diminishing marginal utility

In the last few chapters we have been concentrating on the supply side of the market. In this chapter we shall focus our attention on the demand side by considering in greater depth some of the points introduced in Chapter 2. Specifically, we shall be investigating the factors which influence consumption behaviour.

The concept of **utility** is central to the economic analysis of consumer behaviour. Utility, in an economic sense, means the satisfaction or pleasure which results from some act of consumption. Goods and services are therefore said to possess utility. Consumers, if they are rational, will spend their income in such a way as to maximize the utility they get from the goods and services they purchase. This statement is a very general proposition, so general in fact that it is axiomatic. Nevertheless, it deserves some comment. Different people derive utility from different things and the statement is by no means inconsistent with the observation that, while some crave a lifestyle of glamour, excitement and extravagance, others derive utility from solitude and contemplation – one man's meat is another man's poison. Nor is the assumption of rationality in any way inconsistent with the observation that some individuals engage in activities which to others appear to be acts of sheer lunacy. Rationality in this context simply means that, when faced with a choice, the consumer will follow that course of action which will give him more utility rather then less.

Utility of course is not capable of being measured on a scale like temperature or barometric pressure. The Utilitarian school under John Stuart Mill, who introduced this concept, argued however that it was not in principle impossible to do so. A device for measuring utility – a 'hedonometer' or 'pleasure-meter' – has even been talked about. If it were possible to measure it on a scale, that is to measure it cardinally, the units of measurement would, of course, be **utils**. More realistically, utility could be measured **ordinally**; that is, one could rank consumption bundles in order of preference – first, second, third, and so on. Note that the distinction between cardinal and ordinal utility is the same as that between the cardinal numbers (one, two, three, etc.) and the ordinal numbers (first, second, third, etc.).

Goods generally are said to possess **diminishing marginal utility**, which means that the increments to utility provided by additional units of consumption become less and less as consumption increases. Consider Fig. 12.1, noting carefully the axes. The horizontal axis shows the total number of chocolate bars ('Zip bars') eaten per day, and the vertical axis the satisfaction or utility derived from them, measured of course in utils. Note that the curve shows the total utility derived, whereas the slope of the curve shows how much extra utility is derived from eating an additional chocolate bar. That is, the slope of the curve shows the **marginal utility**. (The relationship between total and marginal utility is of course the same as that between total cost and marginal cost, and total revenue and marginal revenue. It may be helpful to re-read section 5.3 if you are unsure about this.) It is easy to see from Fig. 12.1 that the extra satisfaction – the marginal utility – derived from the first bar is greater than that derived from the second. Similarly, the third and fourth bars yield less extra utility than those which came before. The marginal utility of the fifth bar is very small and beyond this point satiation is reached and additional units of consumption reduce rather than increase total utility – that is, marginal utility has become negative (the slope of the curve is negative): too much chocolate makes you sick.

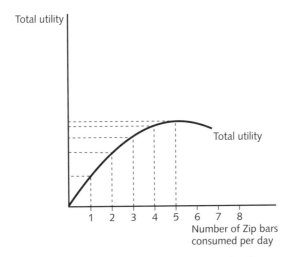

Figure 12.1 Diminishing marginal utility

It seems not unreasonable to accept that all goods and services possess this property of diminishing marginal utility. It is perhaps a little more difficult to accept that income has diminishing marginal utility since additional large increments to income may make possible consumption experiences which were impossible previously and from which the individual may derive considerable satisfaction. This is not a proposition which can be refuted, of course, since utility in practice cannot be measured; at least, it cannot be measured cardinally. In passing, it is worth noting what Shakespeare had to say on the subject of diminishing marginal utility. He of course pre-dated the Utilitarians by some two centuries so would not have been able to use the same terminology but, in *Antony and Cleopatra* he explains Antony's infatuation with the Goddess of the Nile with these words:

> Other women cloy the appetites they feed,
> But she makes hungry
> Where most she satisfies. (II.ii.241)

For Antony, then, Cleopatra had increasing rather than diminishing marginal utility.

12.2 Utility maximization

As we saw in section 12.1, the consumer is assumed to be a **utility maximizer** and, as we argued there, the assumption that the consumer attempts to maximize his utility is axiomatic. It is another way of saying that people act rationally, not necessarily in a coldly calculating way, weighing up the amount of satisfaction derived from each pound's worth of expenditure, but rather they are rational in the sense that they do what they like doing. They buy those things, and engage in those pursuits, which give them satisfaction. In this section we shall derive the formal condition which needs to be satisfied in order that utility is maximized.

Consider an individual who spends all his income on just two commodities, cakes and ale, which are the only two things which give him satisfaction. Suppose the price of cakes, P_C, is 10p per cake and the price of ale, P_A, is 20p per pint. Both these goods of course possess diminishing marginal utility. At current consumption levels, however, suppose that the last cake yields an increase in total satisfaction of 5 utils and the last pint of ale yields an increase in total satisfaction of 8 utils. That is, at current consumption levels the marginal utility of cakes is 5 utils and the marginal utility of ale is 8 utils. In summary: $P_C = 10$; $P_A = 20$; $MU_C = 5$; $MU_A = 8$.

Has the consumer arranged his consumption spending in such a way that he is maximizing his utility? Clearly not, for if he reduces his ale consumption by one pint he can afford two more cakes. As a result of the drop in ale consumption his total utility will fall by 8 utils but the additional cakes he buys will increase his satisfaction by $2 \times 5 = 10$ utils, thus giving him a net increase in total utility of 2 utils. By transferring expenditure from ale to cakes he will therefore increase his total utility.

However, since both cakes and ale have diminishing marginal utility, the increase in cake consumption will reduce the marginal utility of the last cake consumed (to somewhat less than 5 utils) and the reduction in ale consumption will increase the marginal utility of the last pint of ale consumed (to somewhat more than 8 utils). The increase in the marginal utility of ale and the reduction in the marginal utility of cakes thus sets a limit to the extent to which total satisfaction can be increased by substituting cakes for ale in consumption. If this were not the case of course, that is, if the goods in question did not possess diminishing marginal utility, then the rational consumer should give up ale altogether and spend all his income on cakes.

A few moments' reflection will show that the consumer maximizes his total utility when he arranges his consumption set in such a way that the ratio of marginal utility to price is the same for all goods. That is, the following condition must be satisfied:

$$\frac{MU_A}{P_A} = \frac{MU_C}{P_C} \qquad\qquad [12.1]$$

In other words, total utility is maximized when the last penny spent on cakes yields the same increase in total satisfaction as does the last penny spent on ale. If this condition is not satisfied, the consumer can increase his total satisfaction by substituting cakes for ale in the way described above, and this process of substitution should be continued until equation 12.1 is satisfied. Clearly equation [12.1] can be extended to any number of goods, not just cakes and ale. In a more general form it can be rewritten as:

$$\frac{MU_A}{P_A} = \frac{M\acute{U}_B}{P_B} = \ldots = \frac{MU_n}{P_n} \qquad\qquad [12.2]$$

where A,B,...,n are all the goods and services in the economy.

12.3 Income and substitution effects: the choice of family size

The previous section showed how the rational consumer could maximize his utility when faced with a choice between cakes and ale. In the real world, of course, consumers have to make choices between an enormously wide range of goods and services, all of which make some claim on their income and have the potential for yielding utility. The consumer, in short, is faced with what in the jargon is called a **choice problem**; and economics is about making choices.

An area of application of economic analysis recently explored is that of fertility rates. Underlying this analysis is the notion that family size is the result of a choice process or, in other words, couples (or individuals) choose whether or not to have children, when to have them and how many to have.

The question of family size may seem an improbable area of application of economic analysis. Can the cold logic of the economic calculus really be applied to this most fundamental of human desires? What about unplanned pregnancies? Should one really analyse reproductive behaviour as if people acted in a rational and considered manner? If one considers the question more deeply, however, it is clear that these objections are not valid. In a biological sense, birth follows conception, which follows intercourse in a natural sequence. In a social or a statistical sense, however, they are not linked in this strict sequence. Most acts of intercourse are not followed by conception – the birth rate would be very much higher if they were. This is not to deny of course that there are some unplanned pregnancies. However, the dividing line between planned and unplanned pregnancies is not easy to draw. Some pregnancies are planned but do not occur due to infertility. Some pregnancies are planned by one partner but not by the other. But all pregnancies occur because effective contraceptive measures are not taken, and herein lies the choice. If you choose not to take a raincoat when going out you run the risk of getting wet, not normally a serious risk. If you choose not to take waterproof clothing with you when going hill-walking you run the risk of getting wet and chilled, a more serious risk which may even prove fatal. Since most people would be more likely to take seriously the consequences of getting wet when hill-walking than when walking down a city street, they are more likely to guard against that eventuality. The perceived seriousness of the consequences will determine how carefully you plan against those consequences occurring. Similarly, women for whom conception is seen as extremely undesirable will take effective contraceptive measures, even to the extent of sterilization in certain circumstances.

Of course, in individual cases the best-laid plans often go awry. Some pregnancies do occur which were not 'planned' and other pregnancies which were 'planned' do not occur. That is why the economic analysis of choice behaviour cannot predict or explain the size of any one particular family. It can, however, attempt to explain the size of families on average or, if you like, it can be applied to the study of fertility rates.

Children as a consumption good

Children, at least in developed Western societies, can to some extent be regarded as a consumption good. That is, parents derive utility or satisfaction from the rearing of children in much the same way as they derive utility from their material possessions such as their house, car, TV and from the services which they consume such as holidays or going to the zoo. The amount of satisfaction derived from child rearing depends of course on personal tastes and circumstances. Some people like children, others do not. Other things being equal, therefore, those individuals that like children will tend to have larger families. Other individuals will prefer to spend their time and income in different ways. In formal terms of course this implies that the utility-maximizing consumer will arrange his consumption set such that:

$$\frac{MU_A}{P_A} = \frac{MU_B}{P_B} = \ldots = \frac{MU_K}{P_K} = \ldots = \frac{MU_n}{P_n} \qquad [12.3]$$

where A and B are any two other goods from the n goods available and good K is the consumption good, children. In words, the last pound devoted to children will yield exactly the same increase in total satisfaction as does the last pound devoted to consumer good A, good B, and so on for all *n* goods. In reality, of course, the utility-maximizing consumer will have a much more difficult task than if he were simply choosing between cakes and ale. Children are more akin to a consumer-durable good like a house which yields a stream of services through time, as opposed to goods which yield immediate satisfaction, like cakes and ale, and are then used up. Moreover, the consumer will have to base his decision on very imperfect information – he will probably already have tasted cakes and ale and be contemplating repeat purchases. He (or she) may never have experienced parenthood and the complete experience takes a lifetime to acquire. Nevertheless, even though our rational individual will not achieve the condition set out in equation [12.3] we could argue that if she is rational she will strive towards it.

The price of children

Children of course do not have a purchase price but child rearing does involve a cost. Certain complementary goods have to be acquired – a cot, a pram, nappies, toys – but the cost of these items is normally fairly insignificant in comparison with the main item in the cost of having a child, which is the *income forgone* by the parent who stays at home to look after the child rather than engage in paid employment. Thus the main cost of having a child is the *opportunity cost* of not working during the child's pre-school years (and possibly the difficulty of re-entering the labour market thereafter). This realization immediately leads to two interesting and possibly testable predictions. First, following the birth of one child the cost of producing a second child is low. The necessary capital equipment has already been acquired (pram, cot, etc.) and this can be used for more than one 'unit', thus lowering the unit cost. Moreover, if the parent is already staying at home to look after one child the further loss of earnings involved in rearing a second child is comparatively small – perhaps six years' lost earnings instead of four. There are, in short, economies of scale in child rearing. Thus we might expect to find that very large families were commonplace were it not for the fact that, along with other consumption goods, children possess diminishing marginal utility – the more you have of them the less you want more of them. Secondly, we might expect to find that family size is related to socio-economic variables but in a rather complicated way. For example, as income increases would we expect couples to have more children or less? The answer, it turns out, depends on the strengths of the **income and substitution effects**. Assuming that children are not an inferior good (that is, assuming that their income elasticity is positive – a reasonable assumption) then as income rises we would expect couples to have more children, other things being equal. Other things are not equal, however, because the cost of children also tends to rise as income rises, since the major element in the cost of having children is the income forgone by the parent. Thus children become more expensive relative to other consumer goods as one rises up the socio-economic scale and hence we would expect the rational consumer to 'consume' fewer children and to consume more of the substitutes whose price is falling relative to the price of children.

This may produce the result that both low-income and high-income families tend to be somewhat larger than those families in the middle of the income range. This is

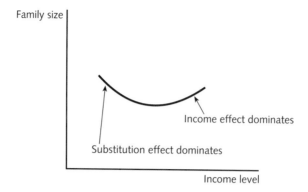

Figure 12.2 Income and substitution effects and the choice of family size

illustrated in Fig. 12.2. The distribution shown in Fig. 12.2 results from the fact that initially as income rises the substitution effect dominates – children become more expensive relative to other goods and therefore the utility-maximizing individual chooses to consume fewer children and more of the cheaper substitutes. As income continues to rise beyond a certain level, however, the income effect begins to dominate and families, by virtue of their high income, can afford more of everything, including children. Very high-income families may even be able to afford to employ a nanny to look after them.

The reason for illustrating the income and substitution effect in the context of the analysis of fertility rates is to show that the analysis of choice behaviour can be applied to many situations which initially appear to be beyond the scope of economics. Note the important (but rather disappointing) result we derived, which was that the substitution effect and income effect potentially working in opposite directions produced a result that was indeterminate.

Summary

People derive utility (or satisfaction) from the goods and services they consume. However, every type of good or service is assumed to possess diminishing marginal utility which means that the extra satisfaction derived from additional units of consumption becomes smaller and smaller as consumption increases. Economic theory assumes that individuals attempt to maximize their utility. If they can get a net increase in satisfaction by transferring income from one good to another they will do so. They will continue to rearrange their consumption bundle until they can no longer achieve any net increase in satisfaction by so doing. They will then be maximising the utility they can get from their given income.

The impact which price changes will have on demand is not always possible to predict. A fall in the price of a particular good will normally lead to an increase in the demand for that good. But the impact on demand will depend on both the substitution and income effects, and if the income effect is negative (as it will be for inferior goods), the net effect of a fall in price may be to reduce the amount demanded.

Key terms

Review questions

12.1 If you look up the word 'utility' in a dictionary you will find:

utility *noun* Usefulness: the power to satisfy the wants of people in general (philos): profit (obs.): a useful thing: a public utility, public service (esp. US): provided in order that the public may be supplied in spite of rise in prices: (of breed of dog) originally bred to be useful, to serve a practical purpose. **utility room** a room esp. in a private house, where things required for the work of running a house are kept.

Which of these definitions corresponds most closely to the meaning of the word in economics?

12.2 'One man's meat is another man's poison'
Which of the following statements illustrates the meaning of this proverb:
(a) You have to be very careful what you eat these days.
(b) Different people derive utility from different things.
(c) Some people prefer to be vegetarian. This doesn't make them weirdos.
(d) Some people prefer fish to meat – especially the French.
(e) Chacun à son goût.

12.3 Which of the following statements illustrates the concept of diminishing marginal utility?
(a) 'When I've eaten one Choc-o-Crunch bar I don't like the second one as much as I did the first. But I still like it.'
(b) 'Once you get the taste for Choc-o-Crunch bars it's difficult to stop eating them.'
(c) 'When I've had one Choc-o-Crunch bar I go right off them.'

12.4 A consumer buys only two commodities, Seven-up and crisps, both of which have diminishing marginal utility. At current consumption levels the marginal utility of crisps is 12 and the marginal utility of Seven-up is 14. The price of crisps is 20p and the price of Seven-up is 28p. Which of the following are true?
(a) The consumer is maximizing his utility.
(b) The consumer would probably increase his utility by buying more Seven-up and fewer crisps.
(c) The consumer should buy more crisps and less Seven-up to increase his total utility.
(d) If the consumer eats more crisps he will get even more thirsty so the utility of Seven-up will rise.

12.5 An electrical retailer records the prices and sales volumes of both colour and black-and-white television sets for 1985 and 1990.

	Price		Sales	
	Black & White	Colour	Black & White	Colour
1985	£70	£250	100	400
1990	£60	£250	80	500

Consider whether the drop in sales of black-and-white sets (despite a drop in price) could be explained in terms of income and substitution effects. (Incomes rose between 1985 and 1990.)

12.6 Delete or fill in the blanks as appropriate:

As a result of the substitution effect an increase in the price of a good will *sometimes/always* lead to a … in the amount consumed. As a result of the income effect a fall in income will normally lead to a … in the amount consumed. Inferior goods are an exception to this. Inferior goods are defined as those for which the income elasticity of demand is *positive/ negative/zero*. Therefore with inferior goods the effect of a fall in income will be to cause the amount consumed to …

Factor markets

13.1 How to build a swimming pool
13.2 What if factor prices change?
13.3 The production function
13.4 What is capital, exactly?
13.5 …and what is labour?
13.6 Marginal productivity theory
13.7 Investment in human capital
13.8 Do labour markets work?
13.9 Discrimination in the labour market

Preview

Economic theory assumes that firms are cost-minimizers and this chapter derives the technical conditions that must be satisfied to achieve this. The way in which firms will combine the various factors of production to produce a given output will depend upon relative factor prices. The chapter then takes a more general look at factor markets, particularly the market for labour.

13.1 How to build a swimming pool

The study of economics gives the student a transferable skill. It provides her or him with an analytical apparatus which can be applied not just to the specific area of economics from which it springs but more generally to a whole panoply of issues. Here we introduce some powerful tools from the economist's tool kit.

Imagine that you have decided to build a swimming pool in your back garden. The basic technology to be employed is straightforward: you dig a big hole and line it with concrete. There are a variety of ways in which this can be accomplished, however. You could go out and buy a shovel and start digging or hire labourers with shovels. Digging is a very labour-intensive activity and you may therefore decide that it would be better to employ a more capital-intensive method of digging the hole, perhaps by hiring a small mechanical digger from your local hire shop. You may even decide, if you are planning a large pool, to contract out the earth-moving operation by hiring a large mechanical digger such as a JCB together with its driver.

The choice of production technique can be characterized as either **labour intensive** or **capital intensive**. Your choice of technique will depend *inter alia* on the cost of hiring labour and the cost of hiring capital.

Having dug your hole you then have to line it with concrete. Again you have a choice of techniques available, some more capital intensive than others. The most labour-intensive technique would be to drive to your local DIY store, buy bags of cement and sand, load them in the boot of your car, drive home, unload them and then proceed to mix the cement using the shovel purchased previously. Alternatively, you may decide to use a bit more capital and a bit less labour, by hiring or buying a cement mixer. You may even decide to use a lot more capital and a lot less labour by arranging to have a load of ready-mixed concrete delivered to your house.

The choice of production techniques available is illustrated in Fig. 13.1 where labour inputs are measured on the vertical axis and capital inputs on the horizontal. Each point represents a feasible way of building a pool of a given size.

The general point is that there is a choice of production techniques available some of which use lots of labour and not much capital, and some which use lots of capital but not much labour. Where a choice of techniques exists it is possible to substitute capital for labour (that is, use more capital and less labour) and *vice versa*.

Imagine a situation in which labour and capital were **continuously substitutable**, that is, at the margin you could use a little bit more of one factor and a little bit less of the other. Clearly this is not the case when building our swimming pool because in that example there are **indivisibilities** – if you decide to order a lorry load of ready mix you have to take the whole load. Nevertheless, conceptually it is feasible to think in terms of continuous substitutability, and it is convenient for the moment to do so. Thus we have joined together the points in Fig. 13.1 with a dotted line. This line

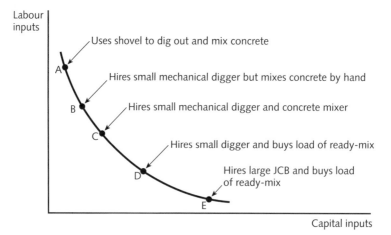

Figure 13.1 Different factor combinations can be used to build a swimming pool

is called an **isoquant** (literally, 'equal quantity') because combinations and capital and labour along this line are capable of producing the same output (in this case, a swimming pool of a given size). In Fig. 13.2 we generalize this idea by drawing a series of isoquants. Isoquants I_2 and I_3 correspond perhaps to larger pools, or to more pools of the same size. As we move in a north-easterly direction the isoquants we encounter correspond to larger and larger outputs.

Note that the isoquants are bent towards the origin rather than being straight lines (some textbooks describe this as being convex towards the origin). Thus in Fig. 13.1 the isoquant is steeper as we move from A to B than it is from D to E. This illustrates what is called a **diminishing marginal rate of technical substitution**. At point A the addition of a small amount of extra capital allows substantial savings in labour inputs (while maintaining the output level intact). At point D, in contrast, it takes a lot more capital to produce comparatively small savings in labour input. The assumption of diminishing marginal rates of technical substitution is one which is normally made. However, it is not necessarily always a realistic description of the technical possibilities, nor indeed may it be valid in the example we are using here. It is a convenient assumption to make, however, since as we shall see it allows us to identify a unique optimal combination of factor inputs.

It is important to emphasize that we are assuming a single objective, namely to minimize the cost of building a swimming pool of a given size. With this in mind what then is the optimal combination of factor inputs? Clearly, the answer to this question will depend upon the price of one factor relative to another.

Suppose you had £1000 to spend on building your swimming pool. If the price of one unit of labour is P_L the number of units you could afford to purchase is $1000/P_L$. Similarly, if the price of one unit of capital is P_K the number of units of capital you could afford to purchase is $1000/P_K$ (note that, following convention, we are using the symbol K to denote capital). This is illustrated in Fig. 13.3 by the dotted line, which some authors refer to as an **iso-cost line** since it shows different combinations of labour and capital

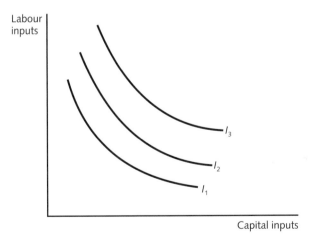

Figure 13.2 Each isoquant corresponds to a given level of output

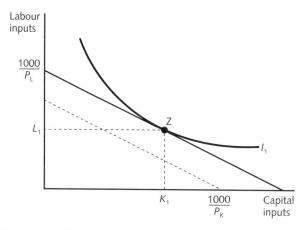

Figure 13.3 The optimal factor combination depends on prices

which cost the same in total. It is worth emphasizing that $1000/P_L$ and $1000/P_K$ are the maximum *amounts* of labour and capital that can be purchased for a budget of £1000.

However, the *slope* of this line also reflects relative prices. The slope is P_L. This is because we measure the slope by the vertical distance divided by the horizontal, which in this case is:

$$\frac{\dfrac{1000}{P_L}}{\dfrac{1000}{P_K}} = \frac{1000}{P_L} \times \frac{P_K}{1000} = \frac{P_K}{P_L}$$

In our particular example this also tells us that £1000 is insufficient to build a pool because our £1000 budget line (or iso-cost line) does not touch the isoquant at any point. We need to spend more. That is, we need to shift our budget line north-east, indicating increasing expenditure but keeping the new budget line parallel to the original one reflecting the same relative prices. The new budget line – the solid line – represents the minimum expenditure that must be undertaken to build a pool. As can be seen, it is tangent to the isoquant at point Z which represents the least-cost method of building the pool. This corresponds to labour inputs of L_1 and capital inputs of K_1. The slope of the isoquant is of course equal to the slope of the budget line at point Z. Since the slope of the isoquant measures the marginal rate of technical substitution, and the slope of the budget line measures relative prices, we can conclude that to produce a given output at minimum cost the marginal rate of technical substitution between capital and labour must be equal to the relative prices of the two factors.

13.2 What if factor prices change?

Once the basic analysis has been understood – and that may require a re-reading of the previous section – it is comparatively easy to see that a change in the price of one of the factors will result in a change in the slope of the budget line. This in turn leads to a change in the least-cost combination of capital and labour required to produce a given output. Consider the effect of a rise in the price of labour. Since we assume that the price of capital is unchanged this rise in the price of labour represents a change in *relative prices* – capital has become relatively cheaper compared with labour. We would expect to find therefore that there is a switch to more capital-intensive techniques as these are now relatively cheaper and hence more cost-effective.

However, the rise in the price of labour means that any technique involving even a small amount of this factor will cost more than it did previously. Hence, even though we economize on the use of labour which is now relatively expensive, it will still cost more in absolute terms to produce a given output than it did previously. To build a swimming pool of a given size we need to spend more. That is, we need a larger budget.

Figure 13.4 illustrates how the **relative price effect** and the **budget effect** can be combined. The isoquant shows, as before, the minimum amounts of capital and labour necessary to produce a given output – a pool of a given size. At the old set of relative factor prices indicated by the budget line AA^1 the least cost method was one which required K_1 units of capital and L_1 units of labour. When the price of labour rises the maximum amount which can be purchased with our pre-existing budget falls from 0A to 0B. Hence our new budget line is BA^1. This new budget line does not touch the isoquant. Hence we need to spend more to build the pool. This is illustrated by an out-ward shift of the budget line from BA^1 to CC^1, the two lines being parallel reflecting the new set of relative prices. CC^1 is tangent to the isoquant at Y where the least-cost combination of factor inputs is K_2 units of capital and L_2 units of labour. As expected, we are now using more of the factor which has become relatively cheaper (capital) and less of the factor which has become relatively more expensive (labour).

The relative price effect (or **substitution effect**) will always result in the increased use of the factor which has become relatively cheaper. However, it is possible that, as a result of the increase in factor prices, you decide to build a smaller swimming pool than the one you had originally planned. This will give rise to an **output effect** illustrated

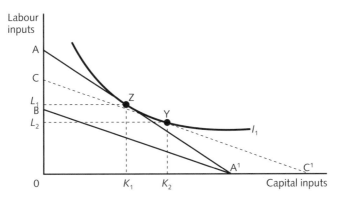

Figure 13.4 The relative-price effect and the budget effect combined

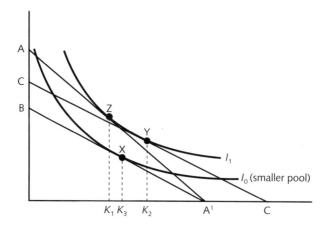

Figure 13.5 The output effect results in less capital being used

in Fig. 13.5 by the isoquant I_0 which represents a smaller pool than I_1. The labelling of the iso-cost lines in Fig. 13.5 corresponds to those in the previous figure. The increase in capital usage from K_1 to K_2 is the substitution effect which we noted earlier. However, the reduction in the size of pool being constructed, indicated by the lower iso-quant I_0, may result in the total amount of capital employed being only K_3. Although more than the K_1 units originally employed, this is less than the K_2 units that would have been employed if the output level had been maintained.

The increase in the price of labour rotates the budget line from AA^1 to BA^1. If you decide to keep expenditures unchanged you will have to build a smaller pool (I_0). If you had built the pool originally planned you would have used K_2 units of capital now that relative prices have changed. However, the reduction in pool size results in only K_3 units being used.

Z is the least-cost combination of factor inputs at the original set of relative prices. Y is the combination you would use following an increase in the price of labour if you were prepared to spend more in total to build the pool originally planned. X is the combination which results when you reduce the size of the pool to fit within your original budget.

It is even possible, as Fig. 13.6 illustrates, for the output effect to outweigh the substitution effect such that the total amount of capital employed falls to K_0 which is *less* than the K_1 units originally employed. For example, because you are now building a smaller pool you may decide not to hire a JCB but to dig it out using shovels.

This is similar to the previous figure except that here the output effect outweighs the substitution effect resulting in a net reduction in capital usage.

The difference between the two figures lies in the technical possibilities for substitution between labour and capital as represented by the shape of the isoquants. The shape of I_0 in Fig. 13.6 is different from that in Fig. 13.5.

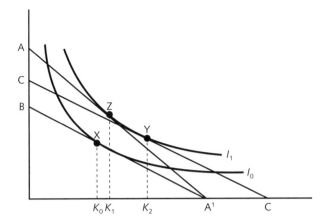

Figure 13.6 The output effect can outweigh the substitution effect

13.3 The production function

The preceding analysis implies the existence of what economists call a **production function**. Used in a mathematical sense the word 'function' means a relationship between two (or more) variables. If those variables are y and x then:

$y = f(x)$

means y is a function of x, or depends on x. If you tell me what x is, then I can tell you what y will be, provided I know what the functional relationship between the variables is.

A production function relates inputs to outputs:

output $= f$ (inputs)

In the previous section we identified two sorts of factor inputs which we called capital and labour. Hence we could write:

$Q = f(K,L)$

where Q stands for output, K for the number of units of capital, and L for the number of units of labour.

The *concept* of a production function is very important in economics though its practical application is beset by difficulties.

A production function implies a **transformation process** whereby inputs are converted into outputs. Firms are a specific example of economic units which transform factor inputs into output. However, the concept of a production function relates more generally to any transformation process, in which inputs – not necessarily capital and labour – are converted into output.

The concept of **efficiency** is an integral part of the concept of the production function. An increase in output not attributable to an increase in factor inputs must by definition be attributable to an increase in the efficiency with which these inputs are transformed.

While the last point may seem painfully obvious, non-economists often fail to distinguish between inputs and output or worse still confuse the two. 'Mr Busy works very hard. He's always in his office by 8 o'clock in the morning and never leaves until 8 o'clock in the evening. All the effort he puts in makes him a real asset to the organization.' No. This is a *non sequitur*. A classic case of equating inputs with output. Mr Busy's output may be very high, but it does not follow from the fact that his input is high. He may, in fact, be the most inefficient worker in the organization so that his output is actually less than that of Mr Clever who comes in at 10 a.m. and leaves at 4 p.m. but uses his time to better effect in the interim.

There are a large number of specific functional forms relating inputs to output. The analysis of the preceding section assumed substitutability between capital and labour – there was more than one way of building a swimming pool, some techniques being more capital intensive than others.

In contrast, we could assume **fixed-factor proportions**. That is, we could assume that there is only one technically efficient way of producing any given output. Suppose, for example, that it takes four units of capital and 30 units of labour to produce one unit of output. The factors must always be combined in this ratio. There is only one combination of factors which is feasible. This would not give rise to the smooth, convex to the origin isoquants we encountered earlier. Rather, the isoquants would be single points or L-shaped as in Fig. 13.7. In the previous section we saw that the optimal factor combination will vary as factor prices vary. This will not happen with the L-shaped isoquants in Fig. 13.7, however. Factors must be combined in fixed proportions. Hence if the firm has only four capital inputs available, having 60 or 90 labour inputs adds nothing extra to production.

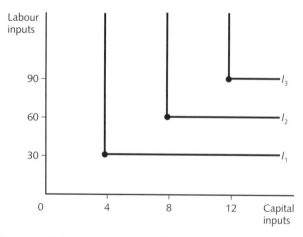

Figure 13.7 L-shaped isoquants illustrate fixed factor proportions

Which type of isoquant is the more realistic description of production relations in the real world – continuous substitutability or fixed-factor proportions? Well, transnational car companies seem to use approximately the same production methods in labour-rich countries (such as Taiwan) as they do in capital-rich countries (such as the USA). So do Macdonalds fast food restaurants. Launching a space satellite is not noticeably more labour intensive in Russia, a country where labour is comparatively abundant, than it is in the USA, where capital is relatively abundant.

On the other hand, there is quite clearly more than one way of building a swimming pool and it would be very surprising to find labour-rich countries using capital-intensive techniques when the same output could be achieved more cheaply using labour-intensive techniques. Normally some substitutability is possible.

13.4 What is capital, exactly?

The production function technique described in the previous section can be interpreted in two ways. First, it can be interpreted as an analytical concept relating output to two types of input, which could be labelled A and B but which here we have labelled 'capital' and 'labour'. Alternatively, it can be taken literally to refer to capital and labour. This then raises the question: what exactly is this stuff which economists call 'capital'? How would one recognize it? In what units is it measured? Is it a homogeneous sort of substance? Similar questions can of course be posed about the other factor, labour.

These fundamental questions about the nature of capital and labour have occupied economists since the beginnings of the discipline. For Marx, capital was 'embodied' labour. It represented the efforts of previous workers, distilled into a tangible form. Thus a machine such as a tractor represented the physical embodiment of many hours of labour time expended in the past by workers in the tractor factory, the oil refinery, the paint factory and so on. Labour, and only labour, was capable of producing value – the so-called Labour Theory of Value. Returns which accrued to capital should rightfully have accrued to the labour which created that capital in the first place.

Capital can be considered as consisting of the durable physical objects created by the production process – for example machines, roads and buildings. Additionally, it can be considered as consisting of **claims**. These claims are pieces of paper, or some other medium, which give the holder the right to own or acquire these durable physical objects. The most liquid form in which these claims exist is money. Less liquid forms include bonds and shares.

Stocks and flows

Capital can be thought of as a stock of assets – some physical and some financial. To this stock there corresponds a flow. This flow is what economists call the **return to capital** – if you like, the earnings of this factor. Financial capital (money, bonds and shares) will earn a financial return (interest, dividends). Physical capital will produce a stream of factor services – a car will provide transportation services, tractors will plough fields, provided of course that they are combined with suitable other factors, such as tractor drivers.

Land is sometimes treated as a type of capital 'provided by nature'. As such it yields a return in the form of rental income (if rented out to another person) or in the form of a stream of services (you can walk on it, grow things on it, build things on it or simply contemplate the beauty of it).

In market economies capital earns a return which in some equilibrium sense approximates to the rate of interest. This is easiest to understand when one considers financial assets. Interest is the reward you receive by lending financial capital (such as money) to others. But this financial capital is merely claims which can be exchanged for real capital, and *vice versa*. You can use your money to buy a tractor; and you can reverse the decision by selling the tractor for money.

In the long run we would expect those people holding assets which produce a lower than average return to dispose of them. Others will buy these assets, but at a lower price than that paid originally. A price in fact which reflects the relatively low returns to be expected from that particular asset so that when we calculate the percentage return it is no lower than that which can be earned elsewhere. This explains why in equilibrium the rate of interest can be described as the **opportunity cost of capital**. It also explains why the rate of return from all assets tends to be equalized. Thus we can talk about *the* rate of return to capital – in practice rates of return will vary but over time competitive forces will tend to make them equal, one to another.

13.5 ...and what is labour?

Defining what is meant by the word 'labour' is perhaps not quite as difficult as defining capital. However, there are operational difficulties, not the least of which is that labour is clearly non-homogeneous – an hour of an accountant's time is not a perfect substitute for an hour of a telephone engineer's time. In this sort of analysis, however, we tend to simplify the real world by assuming that labour is homogeneous, so that we can talk about *the return* to labour. This return is of course the price of labour – or the wage rate.

13.6 Marginal productivity theory

Consider the following example, where a shop manager whose objective is to maximize the profit he gets from his shop can hire as many sales assistants as he wishes at the going rate. Generally speaking, the more staff he has, the greater will be his sales, but the more staff he hires, the smaller will be the extra contribution of each additional assistant. There will come a point when additional staff will actually reduce sales, not because the extra staff are less efficient or more surly, but simply because the size of the shop is fixed and the number of potential customers they could serve is limited. In other words, the staff get in each other's way and put off the customers by their excessive zeal. Clearly, there are too many staff in this situation, but what is the optimal number to hire?

Suppose that the shopkeeper knows the relationship between the number of staff and the net revenue from sales (that is, total sales revenue minus the bought-in prices of the goods he sells) as in Table 13.1 columns 1 and 2. He can, therefore, calculate the extra net revenue attributable to each additional assistant. This is the **value of the marginal product** of each extra assistant (column 3). The number of staff which the manager wishes to hire will depend upon the wage he has to pay. Suppose the going rate is £60 per week. The first assistant will be worth hiring because he adds £100 to net revenue but only £60 to costs, thus increasing profits by £40. Similarly, the second and third assistants add more to net revenue than they do to cost, so that they will be hired. But the fourth assistant adds only £55 to net revenue and a further £60 to costs, so that by employing him the manager will be reducing the shop's profits. Hence, he will not be employed. When the wage is £60, the manager will hire three assistants; that is, the demand for labour is three.

If wages rise to, say, £70 per week but the productivity of the assistants remains unchanged then we can easily check that the third assistant will no longer be employed because the wage that he has to be paid exceeds the value of his marginal product. At the higher wage of £70, the demand for labour drops to two.

In fact, the value of marginal product curve is the manager's **demand curve for labour**, since it shows how many assistants will be hired at each wage level, as in Fig. 13.8. If the four points in Fig. 13.8 were joined up, they would constitute a demand curve for labour. In our particular example, this is a step function rather than a smooth curve, but one can readily appreciate that what Fig. 13.8 illustrates is an inverse relationship between the demand for labour and the wage rate.

This example also illustrates a fundamental conclusion, namely that at the margin the wage rate is equal to the **marginal product of labour**. For example, at a wage of £80 (well, £79.99 I suppose) two assistants will be hired and the wage rate – the price of labour – will be equal to the extra output generated by the second worker. Thus in symbols we could write that in equilibrium:

$$\text{MP}_L = w = P_L$$

that is, the marginal product of labour equals the wage rate (which is the price of labour).

Table 13.1 Shop assistants

Number of assistants	Net revenue from sales (£ per week)	Value of marginal product (£ per week)
1	100	100
2	180	80
3	245	65
4	300	55
5	320	20
6	320	0
7	310	−10

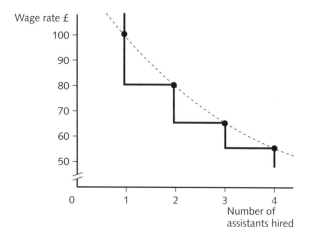

Figure 13.8 How the demand curve for labour is derived

The same will be true of all factors so that we could also write that in equilibrium:

$$\mathrm{MP}_K = r = P_K$$

that is, the **marginal product of capital** equals the interest rate (the rate of return on capital) which is also the price of capital. In general, then, factors earn a return which reflects the value of their output. Factors which are more productive earn a higher return.

13.7 Investment in human capital

We have already noted that labour is a non-homogeneous factor. Marginal productivity theory suggests that factors earn a reward related to their productivity – more productive factors earn higher rewards. Hence we would expect to find that skilled labour earns more than unskilled labour. The question remains, however, as to why some units of labour are more skilled than others. One possible explanation is to do with the influence of education. Educated individuals, so the argument runs, possess **human capital**, so that part of the return which they receive is in fact a return to the capital vested in them rather than a return to labour. Education makes people more productive. Hence they receive higher rewards – that is, earn higher incomes.

Studies that have been undertaken confirm, as we would expect and as Table 13.2 shows, that earnings rise with education. The higher the level of educational attainment, the higher will be the average earnings of the individual in question, other things being equal. Of course earnings are also affected by gender (men earn more than women) and by age (earnings tend to rise with age). To assess the separate influences of education, gender, and age on earnings we can consult the **age-earnings profiles** shown in Fig. 13.9.

Table 13.2 Gross weekly earnings by highest educational qualification attained; and by gender (Index: total = 100; Great Britain 1985)

	Degree or equivalent	Below degree higher education	GCE A-level or equivalent	GCE O-level or equivalent CSE grade 1	CSE other grades/ commercial apprenticeship	No qualifications	Total
Men	145	121	107	101	91	86	100
Women	156	134	106	99	90	81	100

The interpretation of this table is that male graduates tended to earn about 45% more than average males, and so on.
Source: *General Household Survey*, 1985, Table 7.13. Later editions of the GHS do not report data on the link between eduction and earnings.

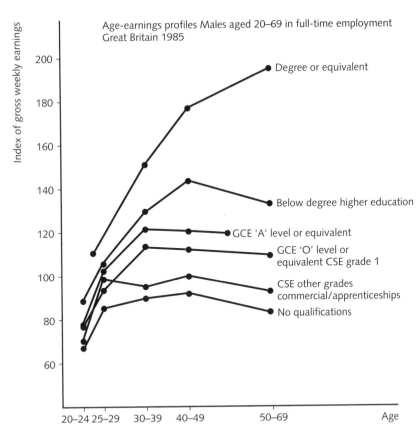

Figure 13.9 Age-earnings profiles (*Source*: derived from *General Household Survey*, 1985)

The figure relates to males only so that we have excluded any gender influences on earnings. Note that earnings tend to rise with age, more steeply in the early years, but to tail off slightly above the age of 50 for all groups except graduates. Similar age earnings profiles have been estimated for women though average earnings are lower. The story told by these age-earnings profiles is very clear: earnings are related (positively) to education.

The question remains, however, as to why educated people earn more than those who are less educated. The analysis of the preceding section suggests that the answer is straightforward. The higher rewards they receive reflect the fact that they are more *productive*. They are more productive because education has made them so. Part of the reward they receive is a reward to the human capital vested in them.

This may be a correct interpretation but a possible alternative explanation suggests that the reason why some individuals earn more than others is because they are innately more able than others – more intelligent and with a greater motivation and capacity for work. Because they have this innate advantage they succeed in the educational process whereas their less able classmates fail. Able pupils overcome the initial hurdle of GCSEs and go on to take 'A' levels. From this group the more able overcome the 'A' level hurdle and go on to higher education where again only the more able succeed in getting good degrees. This view sees the educational process as a **filter**. At each stage the education system filters out the less able, allowing only the more able to pass through. Qualifications serve only to indicate to potential employers which candidates are the ones with more intelligence, ambition, capacity for work – and perhaps willingness to conform. These people secure highly paid jobs because they possess these qualities. So, in this explanation, education identifies them as such but does not confer these qualities upon them.

So, does education make people more productive or is it simply a filter? The answer, probably, is that it does both these things to some extent. But to what extent? The only way of answering this question would be to measure how much earnings rise with educational attainment when we hold all other factors constant – factors such as age, gender, social class – and, most importantly, innate ability. The only way of doing this is to follow a cohort of individuals more or less from birth until the end of their working lives. However, a small number of studies have attempted to do this and the results of one such study conducted in Sweden are shown in Table 13.3. In this study the

Table 13.3 Swedish study (mean incomes before tax of males at age 35 by years of schooling and IQ at age ten; thousands of Kroner (City of Malmo, Sweden 1964))

	Years of schooling			
IQ	*under 8*	*8–10*	*11–14*	*14 or more*
–85	14.6	14.9	17.7	35.5
86–92	17.7	17.5	20.5	—
93–107	15.3	18.2	21.7	31.4
108–114	16.6	19.5	19.4	41.0
115+	17.4	21.9	33.7	43.1

Source: Husen (1968) quoted in Blaug, M., *Economics of Education*.

performance of individuals in intelligence tests taken at an early age was used as a (crude) measure of innate ability. The results of the Swedish study show that even when innate ability is held constant education still increases earnings by a significant amount. This therefore provides strong evidence to suggest that education is indeed an investment in human capital and is not merely a filter.

13.8 Do labour markets work?

Some economists would argue that the foregoing analysis of investment in human capital contains a major flaw. A flaw so profound in fact that it renders the whole analysis invalid. And this it is, namely, that factor markets – and in particular the market for labour – may not in practice ensure that factors are paid a reward which reflects the value of the extra output they produce. In other words marginal productivity theory may simply be an unrealistic account of what happens in the labour market in the real world.

The first reason for suspecting such a flaw is that it is extremely difficult to measure the value of the extra output – the marginal product – attributable to most individuals in the workplace. Difficult for economists trying to analyse the situation, but difficult too for that amorphous mass known as 'the market' which, according to its supporters, is supposed to possess the ability to know what individuals find it impossible to know. The managing directors of large companies receive very large salaries. Who is to say that such salaries do not reflect the contribution of such individuals? It is a mistake, however, to argue that *because* these individuals receive such high salaries this therefore is an indication of the value of the contribution they make to the organization. In other words high salaries do not 'prove' that the individual is worth what he is paid by the organization, particularly if the individual in question has some influence in the process which determines his salary, as is often the case.

A second piece of evidence adds weight to the suspicion that labour markets do not in practice work perfectly, in the sense of ensuring that individuals are paid a wage in accordance with the value of their marginal product. This evidence relates to the existence of **discrimination** in labour markets. This discrimination may be on the basis of race or gender. Here we concentrate on the latter.

13.9 Discrimination in the labour market

On average, men earn more than women. Figure 13.10 shows average gross earnings by gender in 1996. As can be seen, average[1] female earnings are just over £200 per week whereas average male earnings are about £260. [Note: strictly speaking, what we are talking about here is the *modal* income which can be seen as the top of the curve shown in the figure. It would also be true of course that *mean* incomes for men would be higher than mean incomes for women. Note also from the figure that the distribution of incomes for both men and women is highly skewed to the right – indicating that a small number of individuals receive very high incomes.]

United Kingdom
Percentages

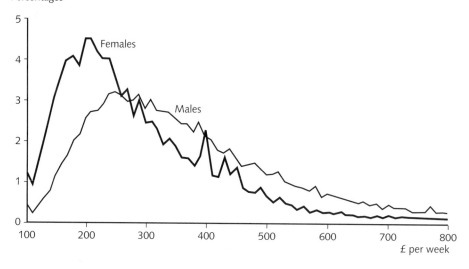

Figure 13.10 Gross earnings by gender, 1996

Earnings differentials are not in themselves proof of discrimination, however, since all of the other factors which affect earnings have not been held constant – factors such as the number of hours worked in a week, age, the number of years of experience and, of course, education. Table 13.5 gives an indication of the influence of each of these factors. The table shows the same educational attainment levels as those in Table 13.2 but now the table has been extended to show the average number of hours worked and the average age. Not surprisingly perhaps, men tend to work somewhat longer hours than women – about 8 per cent higher on average. This in itself could be responsible for an 8 per cent difference in earnings, all other things being equal, but the male/female earnings differential is much larger than this – perhaps nearer 30 per cent rather than 8 per cent.

A more surprising statistical finding, at first sight, is that the average age of men in the workforce is more than three years greater than that of women. This curious statistical fact is presumably because women tend to retire at 60 whereas the retiring age for men in the UK is still 65. This will tend to pull up the average age of men in each group. Since we know that earnings increase with age, especially for graduates, this in itself explains in part the higher earnings of males relative to females. Again, however, it cannot explain all of the differential that exists.

What the table does not record is the average number of years' participation in the labour force. Most women leave the workforce at some time to bear and rear children and this reduces the number of years of accumulated experience which again partly explains their lower earnings. It is interesting to note, however, that in some countries the business of child rearing does not preclude women from participating in the workforce. Figure 13.11 shows the difference in the female participation rates between countries. At the one extreme, in Denmark about 85 per cent of women

Table 13.5 Gross weekly earnings, hours worked, and age by highest educational level attained and gender (persons aged 20–69 in full-time employment; Great Britain, 1985)

	Highest qualification level attained						
	Degree or equivalent	Below degree higher education	GCE A-level or equivalent	GCE O-level/ CSE grade 1	CSE other grades/ commercial apprenticeship	No qualifications	Total
Median weekly earnings £							
men	240	200	176	167	151	141	165
women	174	150	119	110	100	91	112
Earnings of women relative to those of men %	73	75	67	66	67	64	68
Hours							
Mean hours worked per week							
men	42.6	41.4	41.5	42.7	42.4	43.4	42.6
women	39.5	39.0	38.4	38.3	39.0	39.8	39.1
Mean hours of women relative to those of men %	93	94	92	90	92	92	92
Age							
Mean age (years)							
men	38.7	37.0	34.0	35.4	41.7	44.4	39.8
women	32.4	36.4	29.1	30.7	38.0	43.6	36.5

Source: as for Table 13.2.

work and there is no noticeable decline during the child-bearing years (though there was in earlier decades). At the other extreme, in Ireland participation in the workforce slumps with the onset of pregnancy – and most women never return to the workforce.

All of the factors mentioned contributed partly to the differentials we have observed. Estimating the independent effect of each of them is of course a difficult statistical task. It is interesting to note from Table 13.5, however, that differentials seem to narrow as educational attainment increases.

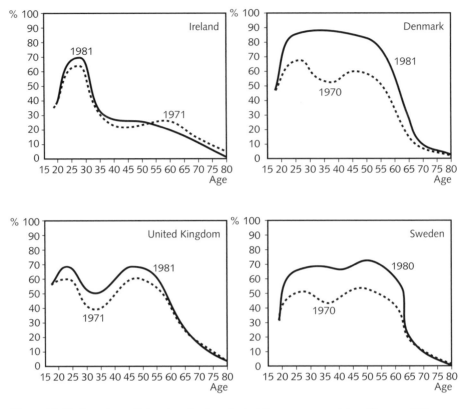

Figure 13.11 Female participants rates in selected European countries. (*Source*: UK *Economic Studies*, Winter 1990)

Summary

In the same way that individuals are assumed to maximize utility, economic theory assumes that firms try to minimize costs. The technical condition that needs to be satisfied if this is to be achieved is that the marginal rate of technical substitution is equal to the factor price ratio (and in diagrammatic terms this is where the slope of the isoquant is equal to the slope of the budget line). If the price of one factor changes relative to the other, this will lead to a change in the optimal factor mix.

Implicit in this analysis is the notion of a production function – a mathematical relationship between inputs and output. This relationship may be characterized by fixed factor proportions or, alternatively, there may be opportunities for substituting one factor with another.

This theoretical model assumes that both labour and capital are homogeneous factors which can be easily measured. In practice, however, there are different types of labour. Capital, moreover, is difficult to measure except in value terms.

Marginal productivity theory demonstrates, under rather restrictive assumptions, that labour will be paid in accordance with the value of its marginal product. Part of the return to skilled labour can however be thought of in terms of a return to the capital vested in the human agent. The presence of gender discrimination in the labour market suggests that marginal productivity theory provides an incomplete explanation of factor rewards.

Key terms

labour intensive	166	efficiency	172
capital intensive	166	fixed-factor proportions	172
continuous substitutability	166	claims (interpretation of capital)	173
indivisibilities	166	return to capital	173
isoquant	167	opportunity cost of capital	174
diminishing marginal rate of technical		value of the marginal product	175
substitution	167	demand curve for labour	175
iso-cost line	167	marginal product of labour	175
relative price effect (substitution effect)	169	marginal product of capital	176
budget effect	169	human capital	176
output effect	169	age-earnings profiles	176
production function	171	filter (education process)	178
transformation process	171	discrimination (in labour market)	179

Review questions

13.1 With a given amount of land a wheat farmer has only two factors of production to consider – fertilizer application and irrigation. Sketch an isoquant map where the isoquants illustrate *continuous factor substitutability*. Explain what this term means and explain why the isoquants will be 'convex to the origin'.

Sketch the budget line which illustrates the relative price of fertilizer and water and demonstrate that the least-cost combination of factor inputs is where the Marginal Rate of Technical Substitution is equal to relative prices. Illustrate on your diagram the likely effect of an increase in water prices assuming the farmer decides to maintain his pre-existing level of output.

13.2 Consider the extent to which the following are characterized by fixed-factor proportions or by opportunities for labour/capital substitution.
(a) car manufacture
(b) teaching
(c) osteopathy
(d) growing daffodils
(e) farming
(f) banking.

13.3 Say whether the following statements are true or false. If false, correct them:
(a) All graduates earn more than non-graduates.
(b) The higher the level of educational attainment, the higher the lifetime earnings, *ceteris paribus*.
(c) Earnings and educational attainment are positively correlated but so are earnings and age.
(d) Earnings and gender are related.
(e) IQ influences educational attainment which in turn influences earnings. Therefore IQ determines earnings.

The price system as an allocative mechanism

Preview

This chapter presents the basic theory of welfare economics first developed by Pareto. It explains that competitive markets will produce an allocation of society's resources which is 'optimal' provided certain conditions are met. Perhaps more importantly it explores in detail why those conditions are unlikely to be satisfied in practice and that therefore in some circumstances state intervention may be desirable.

14.1 Markets and the allocation of resources

It is sometimes said that there are three basic economic questions – **What**? **How**? and **For Whom**? Each of these is considered below.

What?

What sorts of goods and services should be produced? Should society's resources be used to produce guns or butter or motor cars or cakes? And what type of cakes – jam sponges or cream doughnuts – and should they be large ones or small ones?

How?

How should these goods and services be produced? Are capital-intensive methods of production to be used or labour-intensive ones? Should the cakes be made with butter or with margarine and should the motor cars be made with steel, with aluminium or with plastic?

For whom?

How is the output of goods and services to be divided up among the population? Who gets the cream cakes and who gets the motor cars? And how is this decided?

All of these questions relate to the way in which society's resources are allocated. Imagine for a moment a fairytale kingdom which is ruled by an immensely fat and not at all benevolent despot with an insatiable passion for cream cakes. Because of the absolute power that he commands he can prescribe that cream cakes shall be produced. The resources of his kingdom – the labour, land and capital equipment – will therefore be devoted to the production of cakes. And since he decrees that they shall contain the finest cream he also commands that all of his kingdom's agricultural land shall be devoted to dairy farming. The economic questions have been resolved. Cakes will be produced. Society's resources will be devoted to the production of cakes. And he gets them all.

However, when we leave this fairytale kingdom it is not at all clear how the basic economic questions of *What? How?* and *for Whom?* are resolved. One possible solution is to employ some form of state planning such as that practised in the Soviet Union and the Eastern Bloc countries for most of the post-war period. But in capitalist or free-enterprise economies there appears to be no coordinating mechanism. There is no central plan, no despotic ruler, benevolent or otherwise, to dictate how society's resources should be used. The allocation of society's resources seems to be arbitrary, haphazard, almost random rather than planned and coordinated.

And yet – and this the insight which economists from Adam Smith onwards have provided – the working of the market mechanism does result in society's resources being used in a way that is *not* random. The price system does produce an allocation of resources which is not arbitrary and may indeed be superior to that produced by a system of central coordination or state planning. The purpose of this chapter is to examine how the market mechanism does this in theory and to consider whether the theory is a reasonable description of reality. The analytical framework presented here derives from the work of the Italian economist Vilfredo Pareto. It forms the theoretical basis for a branch of study known as **welfare economics** which itself underpins large areas of economic analysis.

14.2 An optimal allocation of resources

Recall our discussion in Chapter 12 of the rational consumer, attempting to maximize the utility to be derived from a given income. This would be achieved by allocating spending between two goods A and B in such a way that the *last penny* spent on good A yielded the same *extra* satisfaction as the last penny spent on good B.

If this were not the case – say, for example, that consumers got more satisfaction out of the marginal penny spent on A than that spent on B – then by transferring a small amount of income from B to A they would experience a net increase in satisfaction, since the gain in utility enjoyed as a result of consuming more of A would more than compensate for the loss of utility suffered as a result of consuming less of B. In formal mathematical terms the condition that had to be satisfied to ensure that the consumer was maximizing his utility was:

$$\frac{\mathrm{MU_A}}{P_A} = \frac{\mathrm{MU_B}}{P_B} = \cdots = \frac{\mathrm{MU_n}}{P_n} \qquad [14.1]$$

In other words, for every good in the consumer's preference set the *ratio* of marginal utility to price should be equal.

Assume now that the goods which our rational consumer buys are sold on markets in which prices reflect production costs. Specifically, assume that, in each market, price is equal to marginal cost. This condition will of course be satisfied in perfectly competitive markets but may not be satisfied in markets where elements of monopoly are present. If price were equal to marginal cost in all markets, however, then we could rewrite equation [14.1] as:

$$\frac{\mathrm{MU_A}}{\mathrm{MC_A}} = \frac{\mathrm{MU_B}}{\mathrm{MC_B}} = \cdots = \frac{\mathrm{MU_n}}{\mathrm{MC_n}} \qquad [14.2]$$

simply by replacing P_A by MC_A, and so on. The interpretation of this equation is similar to that of the earlier equation 14.1. However, whereas previously we were thinking about how the spending of an individual was allocated between two goods A and B we must now think in terms of how *society's* resources are allocated between the *production* of goods A and B. This is because $\mathrm{MC_A}$ represents the cost to society at the margin of producing good A, and $\mathrm{MC_B}$ the cost of producing good B. More explicitly, $\mathrm{MC_A}$ should be thought of as the value of the resources used to produce the extra unit – the marginal unit or the last unit – of good A, and $\mathrm{MC_B}$ the value of the resources used in producing the last unit of good B.

Equation 14.2 will be satisfied for all utility maximizing consumers. We can therefore say that, for each individual, the value of the extra resources devoted to producing good A (that is, $\mathrm{MC_A}$) yields the same increase in satisfaction ($\mathrm{MU_A}$) as does the value of the extra resources devoted to producing good B. Since this equation is satisfied for all consumers it follows that it is not possible to reallocate resources between goods A and B and achieve a net increase in utility for society as a whole. What results is known as a **Pareto optimal allocation** of society's resources.

Of course, a reallocation which shifts resources towards one particular individual at the expense of others will be seen from the point of view of that individual as a preferred or improved allocation. It is always possible to make one person better off by making others worse off. However, a Pareto optimal allocation of resources implies a situation in which *nobody* can be made better off without at the same time making someone else worse off. Of course, it is possible to imagine a Pareto *non-optimal* allocation of resources. In this case a reallocation of resources could make some people better off without changing the utility levels of others. Such a re-allocation of society's resources would be termed a **Pareto improvement** (some people are made better off and no-one is made worse off).

It is not easy for the reader coming to equation [14.2] for the first time to understand exactly what is being said. It is impossible, however, to underestimate its importance since it is a statement to the effect that the price system will produce an allocation of society's resources which is the 'best' that is attainable. 'Best' in this sense means Pareto optimal. What this means is that with any Pareto non-optimal allocation of resources it is possible to imagine a reallocation which could produce a net improvement in society's welfare. The key conclusion is that the market mechanism, that is, the unfettered operation of the laws of demand and supply, ultimately produces an allocation of society's scarce resources which is optimal in the restricted sense of the term employed here. The allocation cannot be bettered. As such, this analysis represents a strong case for private enterprise.

Before we go on to consider the validity of the analysis presented above, it is worth elaborating on its main points.

First, the role which prices play in the resource allocation process is central. Prices act as **signals** to which both producers and consumers respond. We saw in the previous chapter how utility-maximizing consumers would respond to a change in relative prices by modifying their consumption pattern. For example, if the price of cakes rose relative to the price of ale, the rational consumer would then buy fewer cakes and more ale. In a similar way, producers respond to changes in the prices of the factors of production which they use. For example, if the price of steel rises relative to the price of plastic then producers will tend to replace steel components by plastic ones where it is technically feasible to do so. In this way they minimize their production costs in an attempt to maximize profits, in the same way that the consumer attempts to maximize utility.

Prices, then, convey information about relative scarcity. Goods which are in scarce supply and for which there is a high demand will command a high price; goods which are abundant and for which there is little demand, a low price. This is what is meant by 'scarcity' in economics. It is the supply relative to the demand which determines the economic scarcity of a good. For example, the drawings and paintings of Pablo Picasso are quite numerous but there is a high demand for them so they command a high price. In contrast, I myself have produced few drawings and paintings but even for this small number the market demand is zero and hence they command a zero price.

The economic problem exists because scarcity exists. Not everybody can have everything they want, so choices have to be made. The poor man has to choose between bread and potatoes, the rich man between a new yacht and a villa. Choices have to be made not only in consumption, however, but in all other situations characterized by scarcity – the individual has to decide how to allocate his time between work and leisure, the investor how to allocate his funds, the firm how to produce its goods and what and where to sell. All of these decisions have two things in common. First, they are decisions based on the information about relative scarcities which is provided by the set of relative prices. Secondly, each decision is goal-orientated. It has some purpose to it. The consumer seeks to maximize his utility, the firm seeks to maximize its profits. In all cases, however, decisions are motivated by self-interest rather than by philanthropy. In pursuing their selfish ends, individuals inadvertently bring about an allocation of society's resources which is 'optimal'. They do good by doing well, since the price system channels and coordinates their myriad selfish actions in such a way that society as a whole benefits.

14.2 Market failure

If the analysis of the previous section is correct, then it does indeed seem that the market mechanism will produce an allocation of society's resources which is 'optimal' in the restricted sense that we have used this term. Indeed, advocates of the free-market mechanism have used Pareto's analysis to support their contention that the greatest happiness of the greatest number can be secured if the state refrains from intervening in the market and simply allows market forces to rule. On the other hand, those who believe in some state intervention have pointed to the very restrictive – and unrealistic – assumptions under which such a Pareto optimal allocation of resources will be produced. There are four key criticisms which can be levelled at these underlying assumptions.

1 Price not equal to marginal cost

In perfectly competitive markets price will be equal to marginal cost. Such markets are rare, however. In most markets, in practice, price will diverge from marginal production cost (even assuming that marginal cost can be identified) and in many cases price will bear almost no relation to production costs. The extent to which price could diverge from marginal costs obviously depends on the extent to which the firm enjoys monopoly powers. Monopolists – or, to be more correct, oligopolists – are price makers rather than price takers, so their price need not reflect the element of economic scarcity embodied in the marginal cost concept.

2 Income distribution

A Pareto optimal allocation of resources is predicated upon a particular initial distribution of society's resources or, in other words, upon a particular distribution of income. Different income distributions will produce different Pareto optimal allocations of resources. In other words, there is not just one Pareto optimal allocation of resources but many Pareto optima – as many in fact as there are possible distributions of income. When consumers spend their income, each pound spent is like a vote cast for the production of a particular commodity. A pound spent on cakes is a vote for cake production. A pound spent on ale is a vote for ale production.

Suppose, for the purpose of this example, that society is composed of two groups, those who like cakes and a second group who like ale. If the cake lovers are rich and the ale lovers poor then the allocation of society's resources will be heavily biased towards cake production. If, on the other hand, the ale lovers become rich and the cake lovers poor then the resulting increased expenditure on ale would result in a shift of society's resources away from cake production and towards ale production. The allocation of society's resources which results from the operation of the market mechanism is therefore clearly dependent on the initial distribution of income.

3 Untraded goods

Some goods which affect consumers' utility are not traded. That is, not only are they not sold on perfectly competitive markets, they are not sold on markets at all. Thus, for example, a consumer's utility may be affected by the level of noise pollution to which he is exposed, by oil pollution on holiday beaches or by the level of street violence. In other words some producers and consumers impose **external costs** or **externalities** on others. These externalities are not traded on markets. Hence the amount of society's resources devoted to producing them – or in this case controlling them – is not the result of a set of preferences expressed in the market. In other words, the consumer cannot vote for more resources devoted to reducing pollution by spending more money on reducing pollution. In summary, there is an area in which the market does not work.

4 Public goods

A further area in which the market works only imperfectly, if at all, is **public goods**. The term 'public goods' as used by economists refers to certain goods and services often – but not invariably – supplied by the public sector rather than the market. Services such as policing, street lighting, roads and flood protection schemes can be considered as public goods. Because such goods possess the characteristics of **non-excludability** and **non-rivalness** (to be explained in section 17.3) they may not be supplied in the quantities which consumers' preferences would dictate because consumers cannot effectively express their preferences by purchasing or not purchasing the good in question.

Two related conclusions follow from the foregoing analysis. First, the operation of the market mechanism may not produce a Pareto optimal allocation of resources because of the ability of some sellers in oligopolistic markets to set prices which diverge from marginal cost. Secondly, even if the allocation of resources in society were Pareto optimal there might be some citizens, or indeed a majority of citizens, who would prefer those resources to be allocated in a different way – for example, they might prefer the distribution of income to be more equal (or less equal) or they might wish society's resources to be directed to areas which the market mechanism did not adequately serve, such as the control of pollution.

Summary

The theory of welfare economics demonstrates that if all goods are sold on perfectly competitive markets the resulting allocation of society's resources will be Pareto optimal – which means that no-one can be made better off without making someone else worse off. This seems to be a powerful theoretical justification for arguing that market forces should be allowed full sway and that any form of state intervention should be avoided. However, the theory is based on restrictive assumptions which will not be met in practice. In particular, the market fails to produce an optimal allocation of resources when there are externalities and where some goods are non-excludable and non-rival.

Key terms

Review questions

14.1 Say which of the following are correct:
A Pareto optimal allocation of resources:
(a) cannot be achieved under a planned system;
(b) is automatically achieved in a market system;
(c) is never achieved in reality;
(d) could be achieved if prices conveyed information about relative scarcities.

14.2 Suppose the price of aluminium rose relative to the price of nylon. Which of the following statements are correct?
(a) The government would have to instruct firms to use less aluminium.
(b) Manufacturers would try to use nylon rather than aluminium where it was feasible to do so. The demand for aluminium would go down.
(c) Products which used aluminium would become more expensive. People would buy less of them so the demand for aluminium would go down.
(d) Only those consumers who were concerned about environmental issues and who knew that aluminium was becoming scarce would economize on its use. The rest would not.

14.3 In a market system, in pursuing their selfish ends individuals 'do good by doing well'. Why was this not true of Al Capone (the gangster who was so successful in America in the 1930s)?
(a) It was true. Al gave people what they wanted.
(b) Because the statement does not apply to things like alcohol and gambling.
(c) Because people were not free to choose whether they dealt with Al Capone or not.
(d) Because, by acting selfishly, people cannot possibly do good.

14.4 Market failure occurs because:
(a) not everyone has heard of the concept of Pareto optimality;
(b) the distribution of incomes is unequal;
(c) market prices do not always reflect the true resource costs involved.

14.5 A country produces only two types of goods – defence goods (guns) and consumer goods (butter). Both these goods possess diminishing marginal utility (the more that is produced the less *extra* satisfaction does society derive from them). At current production levels the marginal utility of guns (i.e., the extra satisfaction derived from the last unit of defence output) is 20 utils and the marginal utility of butter is 17 utils. The marginal cost to society of producing the last unit of defence output is £40 and the marginal cost of the last unit of butter is £30.
   Which of the following is/are true?
(a) Society would be better off if it transferred some of its resources from gun production to butter production.

(b) Society is already achieving a Pareto optimal allocation of resources (it is maximizing the satisfaction it can get).

(c) Social satisfaction would be increased if resources were switched from butter production to gun production.

14.6 Which of the following are reasons why a Pareto optimal allocation of resources may NOT be achieved by a market system:

(a) Because consumers place their own interests above those of society.

(b) Because there is no such thing as society, only individuals and families.

(c) Because some companies have market power and as a result they can charge prices which are in excess of marginal cost.

(d) Because individuals and companies base their decisions on prices which do not reflect social costs.

(e) Because some individuals derive lots of utility from things which don't cost any money, like a walk in the park.

14.7 A market system gives people what they want. You want a flame-grilled Big Whopper with extra relish and french fries. You got it.

People don't like sitting in traffic jams. So why cannot the market provide a solution and give people what they want?

Comment on the following statements. You can say whether you think they are true, false or irrelevant. If you wish, you can choose the statement(s) which provide(s) the best explanation.

(a) The problem is that the government has failed to provide the roads that the people want.

(b) This is an instance of market failure – people cannot 'vote' for the production of roads by purchasing roads, in the same way that people vote for fast food by buying hamburgers.

(c) Because the market only provides an optimal amount of 'private goods'. It doesn't work so well with 'public goods' like roads.

(d) You could correct for market failure if people were able to purchase road space. After all, they have toll motorways in France and in Italy. Italian motorways were built by private companies and are run by them.

(e) The problem is that the private sector for some reason will not invest enough in public transport.

(f) People will always prefer the independence and mobility that their cars give them.

(g) Most car journeys are made by men. Only a small proportion are made by women.

(h) It is something to do with prices and the fact that prices don't properly reflect social cost. Motorists don't pay the full social cost of their actions. Diners at Burger King don't impose a cost on others by eating hamburgers, but motorists do impose a cost on others by driving their cars.

(i) Building more roads simply encourages people to use their cars more.

15 The economy and the environment

Our species is only a tiny part of the whole natural world...
Nature is not our enemy to be fought against, but it's part of us
And we're part of it.

(Geoff Hamilton, presenter of BBC's *Gardeners' World*)

This chapter explains that the economist regards pollution as an example of market failure. Classical economists like Pigou saw the solution in terms of taxes which would force polluters to pay the full social cost of their actions. But there are practical difficulties with this and direct regulation is often a more effective option.

15.1 Pollution as an example of market failure

In Chapter 14 we presented the theory which lies at the heart of welfare economics – the theory of Pareto optimality. This stated that the market mechanism will produce an allocation of society's resources which is 'optimal' but that this happy outcome can only be assured provided certain key assumptions are satisfied. The most important of these assumptions is that *all* of the things which affect *each* individual's utility are bought and sold on competitive markets. In the real world this assumption may be violated – indeed *will* be violated – and there are three related reasons for this.

Missing markets

Some of the things which affect an individual's utility – such as the quality of the air he or she breathes, the level of street crime and the cleanliness of the bathing waters around the coast – are not bought and sold on markets. The individual cannot buy better quality air, and because it cannot be bought the individual cannot 'vote' for its production, and therefore producers will not respond to the demand for higher quality air by producing more of it. The market fails to respond to the wishes of consumers because there is no market in air quality – but nevertheless air quality affects the individual's utility. This is an example of a **missing market**.

Existence of externalities

A firm which pollutes the environment imposes **external costs** – or **externalities** – on the neighbourhood. For example, by discharging toxic effluent into a watercourse, the polluter kills fish, thereby reducing the income of fishermen further downstream, and increasing costs for the water company who will now have to install a more expensive treatment plant to clean up the water and restore it to drinking quality. These additional costs, then, are borne by society at large but not by the polluter. However, the polluter will base his decisions (about how much to produce, where to produce and so on) on his **private costs** and will not take these external costs into account.

A socially optimal allocation of society's resources cannot result if decisions are made on the basis of private costs which understate the true **social costs** of production. The presence of negative externalities means that social costs will exceed private costs.

Existence of public goods

A **public good** possesses the characteristics of *non-excludability* and *non-rivalness*. The air in a city can be thought of as a public good. No-one has property rights over it – no-one owns it – and therefore no-one can be excluded from using it, to breathe, or as a medium into which to discharge wastes such as smoke or other toxic chemicals. As long as the level of pollution is not too high this public good remains non-rival. But when pollution reaches a certain level the air becomes a rival public good. Now there is a paradox: it is in everyone's interest to restrict their use of this public good but in no one individual's interest to do so. This paradox arises because public goods are non-excludable.

The three points mentioned above – the absence of markets, the existence of externalities, and the presence of public goods – are all related. They are all aspects of **market failure**. Conceptually one can summarize the problem by saying that if the decisions of consumers and producers are based on prices which reflect social costs then all will be well – an optimal allocation of society's resources will result. But because of market failure the prices of some goods will not reflect the true resource cost. Therefore a mis-allocation of resources will result. The level of pollution, for example, will be too high, and the market cannot in itself correct for this failure.

15.2 An 'optimal' level of pollution

Consider a situation in which a firm produces two types of output. One is a good from which consumers derive utility – say, plastic – and the other is a 'bad' which causes disutility – say, smoke. These two outputs are produced in fixed proportions. In this example, therefore, there is no possibility of a 'technological fix' which will enable the firm to double its output of plastic without at the same time doubling its output of smoke. In Fig. 15.1 the output of both plastic and smoke is measured along the horizontal axis.

Consider first the downward sloping curve labelled *marginal benefit to producer*. This shows the marginal benefit (the extra profit) which accrues to the producer as a result of increasing output by a small amount. The profit maximizing level of output, which the firm would choose if it bore none of the costs associated with the smoke, is labelled q_{pm}.

To understand why the producer's marginal benefit curve is drawn in this way, recall that any firm, regardless of market structure, will increase output until the extra revenue that it gains by so doing (its marginal revenue) is equal to the increase in cost which results (its marginal cost). Consider Fig. 15.2 which illustrates the simplest case, that of a perfectly competitive firm facing a horizontal demand curve for its product. Profit is the difference between total revenue and total cost. The change in profit – the extra profit to be gained from producing more – is the difference between marginal revenue and marginal cost (the vertical distance between MR and MC in Fig. 15.2). Notice how this becomes less and less as we approach the profit maximizing level of output q_{pm}. This level of output is the same as that labelled q_{pm} in the earlier Fig. 15.1.

Now consider Fig. 15.3 which also shows the marginal cost to the neighbourhood. This is drawn so as to indicate that the disutility associated with the smoke pollution

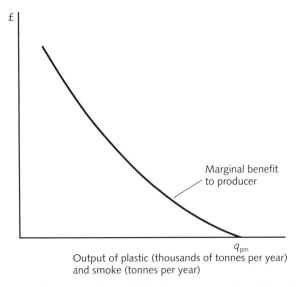

Figure 15.1 The marginal benefit to the producer of plastic and pollution

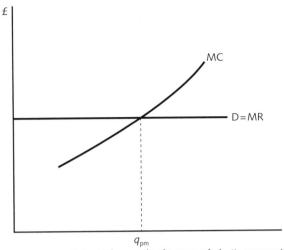

Figure 15.2 The profit-maximizing output of plastic and smoke

rises as the level of that pollution rises (though in fact it is not necessary for our analysis that the curve should have exactly this shape). Note that the curve does not start from the origin – the firm is allowed a small amount of smoke output (labelled 'absorptive capacity') before the costs that this imposes on the neighbourhood are discernable, though again this is not necessary for our analysis.

As we noted earlier there is not, generally, a market in pollution. But imagine for a moment that such a market did exist, and that this enabled the two parties affected by

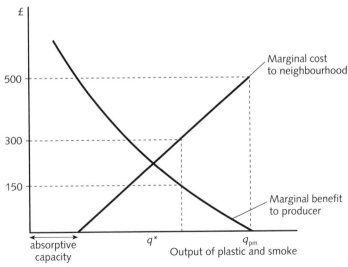

Figure 15.3 Marginal cost to the neighbourhood and marginal benefit to the producer

it to bargain over how much should be produced. For example, suppose that the neighbourhood was in a position to bribe the producer to reduce his output of smoke. At the level of output q_{pm} each additional tonne of smoke output causes £500 worth of damage to the neighbourhood. The neighbourhood would therefore be prepared to offer a bribe up to a maximum value of £500 to persuade the producer to reduce his output by this last tonne of smoke. The producer for his part would be quite happy to accept such a bribe and to reduce his output because at q_{pm} the last tonne of output yields an increase in profit which is only slightly greater than zero. Similarly, if the current level of output is, say, q_1 each additional tonne of smoke causes damage which the neighbourhood values at £300. This therefore is the maximum amount of money that the neighbourhood would be prepared to offer in order to persuade the firm not to produce this extra tonne of smoke. For his part the producer would be happy to accept any bribe greater than £150 since this is the amount of extra profit he gets from this last tonne of output. Finally, consider the level of output labelled q^* where the two curves cross. At this unique point the *maximum* bribe that the neighbourhood would be prepared to offer (to persuade the producer to cut pollution by a small amount) is equal to the *minimum* bribe that the producer would be prepared to accept to do so. This is the level of pollution that would be arrived at if there were a market in pollution. We can therefore refer to it as the **optimal level of pollution**.

Note that the optimal level of pollution is not equal to zero. Notice also that this is the level of pollution which would be arrived at even if the firm had to purchase the right to pollute from the neighbourhood rather than the other way round – the neighbourhood purchasing the right to clean air from the firm, as in the preceding paragraph. This can be confirmed by Fig. 15.4. If the firm were currently producing at q_2, for example, it would be prepared to offer a bribe as big as £350 to persuade the neighbourhood to allow it to pollute a little more, and the neighbourhood would accept any

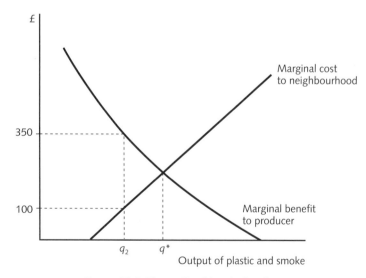

Figure 15.4 The optimal level of pollution

bribe bigger than £100 since this is the amount of damage it suffers. Thus, again, if trade in pollution were possible the optimum amount arrived at by bargaining between the two parties would be $q*$.

15.3 Pigovian taxes

A. C. Pigou was the economist who first emphasized the importance of externalities as a source of market failure. In our example these externalities are the extra costs imposed by the producer on the neighbourhood – labelled 'marginal cost to neighbourhood' in Figs 15.3 and 15.4. The producer ignores these costs, because they are external to him, and as a result decides his level of output purely on the basis of his private costs and revenues (labelled marginal benefit to producer). How can the producer be forced to take these external costs into account in his decisions? The answer, according to Pigou, is for the government to impose a tax on the producer, the magnitude of which is equal to the size of the externality. Such a **Pigovian tax** is illustrated in Fig. 15.5. At the socially optimal level of pollution $q*$ the size of the externality is £250 and this therefore is the size of tax required to correct for this market failure. The imposition of a per unit tax of £250 pounds per tonne of smoke produced will have the effect of shifting the producer's marginal benefit curve vertically downwards by the amount of the tax. This is because the producer will have to remit to the government £250 for each tonne of output, reducing his net-of-tax benefit by this amount.

The imposition of this tax corrects for market failure by adjusting the prices on which the firm bases its decisions – adjusting these prices so that they reflect more accurately the true social cost of the firm's actions. In addition to its private costs the firm must now also pay these external costs. The tax has in a sense 'internalized' the

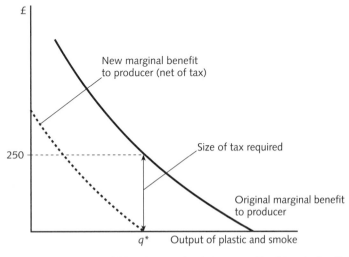

Figure 15.5 Imposition of Pigovian tax leads to an optimal level of pollution

externality. The firm will now find that the new profit-maximizing level of output is at q^* – the socially optimal level of pollution. The Pigovian tax has therefore succeeded in correcting the market failure.

15.4 The practicality of Pigovian taxes

In practice, there are a number of difficulties involved in the application of Pigovian taxes. The first of these is the **problem of valuation**. In the preceding figures we have sketched out curves labelled 'marginal cost to neighbourhood' as if the cost were in fact known with a degree of certainty. In practice, this will not be the case. To place a money value satisfactorily on the disutility associated with a specific pollutant requires a large amount of scientific and economic data. This large informational requirement is unlikely to be satisfied in practice. Specifically, one would need to know:

- The technical relationship between the firm's output of goods and its output of pollution (or to be able to measure the output of pollution directly).
- What the physical effect of this pollution is on the environment in the short term and, if it accumulates in the environment, the effect in the longer term.
- The human 'damage response' to this exposure, in physical and biological terms.
- The 'damage response' of non-human species (though some economists would ignore this, arguing that it should not be taken into account. The well-being of other species does, however, enter into the utility function of some humans (*sic*).
- The monetary evaluation of the pollution exposure identified.

Because pollution problems are seldom purely localized they have a global as well as a local dimension and are therefore characterized by a high degree of uncertainty. Consider, for example, discussions about the desirability of a **carbon tax** – a classic example of a Pigovian tax on carbon-based fuels such as oil and coal. Such discussions are dogged by disagreement about the impact of carbon dioxide emissions on the global eco-system – that is, disagreements about the reality or the seriousness of global warming, and the contribution which carbon dioxide emissions make to this.

15.5 Who pays the tax?

When using Pigovian taxes to correct for market failure the general rule that should be applied is the **Polluter Pays principle** – which simply means that the external cost associated with the output of a particular pollutant should be paid for by those responsible for producing it. Will not a polluting firm simply pass on the pollution tax to its customers, however, in the form of higher prices? The answer to this is that a *part* of the tax will be passed on and a part will be absorbed by the firm in the form of lower profits. Consider Fig. 15.6 where we illustrate the effect of the imposition of a per unit pollution tax in a competitive market. Initially the industry is in equilibrium producing q_0 units of output at a price of p_0. The effect of the imposition of a per unit pollution

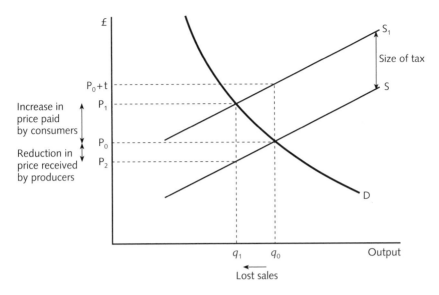

Figure 15.6 The effect of the imposition of a pollution tax

tax is to shift the industry supply curve vertically upwards by an amount equal to the magnitude of the tax (since the amount actually received by producers will be net of tax, the tax being passed directly to the government). Notice that as a result of this the price does not rise by the full amount of the tax to p_0+t. Rather, it rises to only p_1 (and output falls to q_1). In Fig. 15.6 about two-thirds of the tax is paid by the consumer in the form of higher prices and about one-third is paid by the producer in the form of lower net-of-tax prices.

What then determines the proportion paid by the consumer and the proportion paid by the producer? The answer is that this will be determined by the *elasticity of demand* for the product. If the demand for the product is inelastic (as in Fig. 15.7a) most of the tax will be paid by the consumer and there will be only a small drop in demand. In contrast, if the demand for the product is elastic (as in Fig. 15.7b) the pollution tax will cause a large drop in demand and most of the tax will be paid by the producer. The market price will rise by only a small amount.

What determines the elasticity of demand for a product? The answer, as we saw in Chapter 2 when we first introduced this concept, is that it is the *availability of substitutes* that determines the elasticity of demand. Therefore the demand for petrol is shown to be rather inelastic in Fig. 15.7a because there are few substitutes available, at least in the short run. A pollution tax imposed on petrol retailers requiring them to pay, say, an extra £1 for each gallon sold will result in the price to motorists rising by almost the full £1. In contrast, the demand for, say, phosphate washing powders can be thought of as quite elastic since there are close substitutes available (non-phosphate powders) so that the imposition of a pollution tax would result in most of the tax being absorbed by the producer in the form of lower net-of-tax receipts.

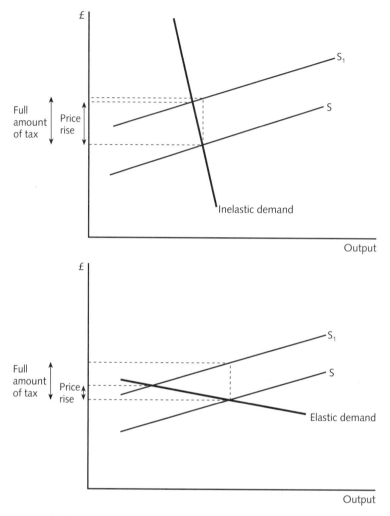

Figure 15.7 Whether the tax is borne by the consumer or the producer depends on the elasticity of demand for the product

15.6 The advantages and disadvantages of Pigovian taxes

The consideration of the elasticity of demand for a product also gives us an important insight into how **effective** a tax will be in reducing pollution. As can be verified by Figs 15.7a and b in the previous section, if the demand for the good in question is inelastic then an increase in price brought about by a pollution tax will have very little impact on the amount purchased – consumers will continue to buy more or less the same amount as before so the tax is ineffective in reducing pollution. A carbon tax may suffer from this problem. Suppose, for example, that the elasticity of demand for petrol is only –0.1 (an estimate which is consistent with most empirical studies of this parameter).

Doubling the price of petrol (a 100 per cent increase and a tax change which would be political suicide for any government which imposed it) would therefore result in a drop in consumption (and therefore of pollutants) of only 10 per cent.

The international (or **transfrontier**) nature of many pollution problems may also call into question the effectiveness of Pigovian taxes. Pollution from motor vehicles creates both local problems (air quality in cities) and global problems (global warming resulting from CO_2 emissions). In considering the effectiveness of carbon taxes we must therefore take into account the impact of such policies in counties other than those which impose the tax. Suppose for example that a number of developed countries sign up to an international convention in which they undertake to reduce carbon dioxide emissions by the imposition of carbon taxes. Further suppose that these taxes are successful in reducing the demand in signatory nations. This will have the effect of lowering the worldwide demand for oil, depressing oil prices and thereby *increasing* the demand for oil in non-signatory nations (and in signatory nations as well to some extent). Thus, paradoxically, the more successful a policy is in reducing oil consumption the more it encourages greater oil consumption.

In comparing Pigovian taxes with alternative approaches to the control of pollution one should also take into account the effect of such policies on the distribution of income. In as much as they are passed on to the consumer in the form of higher prices, pollution taxes are similar in their impact to sales taxes such as VAT and excise duties. These are invariably **regressive** in their impact in the sense that they take a larger proportion of the income of poor households than they do of rich ones. Consider, for example, the proposal to impose VAT on domestic heating fuel. This can be thought of as a 'green tax' since by raising the price of gas and other fuels consumers will be encouraged to use less, thereby reducing the amount of carbon dioxide emitted by burning these fuels. However, low income households (especially pensioners living on their own) spend a much larger proportion of their income on heating than do richer households. The tax therefore bears down particularly hard on this group. However, economic theory would argue that this is not a valid reason for eschewing the use of such taxes, since the adverse distributional impact could in theory be offset by compensating changes elsewhere. For example, the extra revenue raised by the imposition of VAT on fuel could be used to fund additional payments to those on low incomes – such as state pensions and other income maintenance programmes.

15.7 Market-based incentives versus 'command and control'

In addressing the problem of pollution we can distinguish two basic approaches. Pigovian taxes are an example of the first of these which we can refer to as **market-based incentives (MBIs)**. Such policies work by changing the set of relative prices faced by consumers and producers, but these economic agents are still free to act so as to maximize their utility or maximize their profits in whatever way they see fit. In contrast, those anti-pollution measures which go under the general heading of **'command and control' (CAC)** use legislation to prohibit certain pollutants or to stipulate that activities must be carried out in a way prescribed by the law. Examples of such policies include the Clean Air Acts (introduced in Britain, making it illegal to burn coal in urban areas); Health and Safety Regulations which control the use of asbestos; regulations compelling car manufacturers to fit catalytic converters to the exhaust system of petrol engined vehicles; and banning the use of chloro-fluoro-carbons (CFCs) as propellants in aerosol cans and as refrigerants.

In comparing the effectiveness of MBIs and CAC policies in reducing pollution, a number of factors must be taken into account. First, it is helpful to distinguish **flow pollutants** from **stock pollutants**. Those pollutants which are absorbed into the environment where they break down into harmless substances are known as flow pollutants. They are also known as **bio-degradable** – a term which has however been hi-jacked by the advertising industry. Examples of flow pollutants include sewage, oil discharged at sea, and CO_2 emissions. In contrast, stock pollutants include materials such as asbestos, plutonium, mercury and other heavy metals which are not absorbed into the environment but which, when released into the environment, simply stay there and accumulate.

In addressing the problem of flow pollutants the use of MBIs may well be appropriate. A tax on such a pollutant will increase its price and therefore slow down the flow. If the tax were high enough the flow could be reduced sufficiently so as to bring it in line with the ability of the eco-system to absorb it and convert it back to harmless substances. In dealing with stock pollutants, however, MBIs are probably not suitable since the socially optimal level of discharge into the environment of substances such as plutonium and mercury is zero. In this instance, legislation which prohibits the discharge of these substances into the eco-system would be more appropriate.

In assessing the effectiveness of these two approaches one must also consider how easy it is to enforce the policy and to monitor compliance. One must also take into account the so-called **resource cost** of the policy. This can be thought of as the *opportunity cost* of reducing pollution – the goods and services that society has to give up in order to enjoy cleaner air and better water quality. It is on this point that conventional neo-classical economics makes its strongest contribution to the policy debate about how best to tackle the problem of environmental pollution. Economic theory states that – provided certain assumptions are satisfied – economic incentives are preferable to regulation because the cost to society in terms of the other goods and services forgone in reducing pollution will be less with MBIs than it will be with CAC policies. To illustrate this we consider a second type of market based incentive, known as **tradeable permits**.

15.8 Tradeable permits

Suppose a cluster of firms operating in a particular geographical area is currently producing 100 units of pollution. The government wishes to reduce this to 80 which it has decided is the socially optimal level of emissions for the time being. Suppose it issues permits to the firms in the area, giving them the right to pollute, but that only 80 units worth of pollution permits are issued. However, the government also allows firms to trade these permits – those who have insufficient permits are allowed to purchase additional pollution rights from other firms; and those who have permits in excess of their needs can sell these rights to others.

In practice, because the number of permits issued is less than the current level of pollution all firms will find that the quantity of pollution they wish to emit is more than they are allowed to by their current holding of permits. Each firm therefore has two options. Either it can purchase and install a filter (or some other device to reduce the flow of pollution) or it can purchase additional permits and continue with its existing technology. The firm will compare the cost of these two alternatives. If, for the particular firm in question, the filter is comparatively cheap and effective in reducing the amount of pollution it emits, then this will be the cheaper option. It will install the filter and sell any permits it has which are now surplus to its needs. In contrast, a second firm may find that because of the peculiarities of its production process it is technically very difficult and expensive to install an effective filter. The cheaper alternative for such a firm would be to purchase additional pollution rights. Each firm will compare the cost of reducing pollution at the margin (known technically as the **marginal abatement cost**) with the market price of a permit allowing it a marginal increase in emissions. The firm will have an incentive to install a filter and sell permits if the marginal abatement cost is less than the permit price; and it will have an incentive to continue with its existing technology and buy permits if the marginal abatement cost is greater than the permit price.

The net result will be that only those firms who can reduce pollution cheaply (by diverting only a small amount of resources to its control) will do so. The remaining firms, for whom the resource cost of compliance is much greater, will not reduce pollution but will purchase additional rights. If we then consider the amount of resources in total devoted to controlling pollution we can say that the resource cost to society of reducing emissions to the socially optimal level will be minimized. In contrast, a CAC policy will use up more of society's resources because *every* firm will have to comply, both those who can do so at quite a small resource cost and those who can comply only by diverting a large amount of resources to compliance. This therefore is the argument for the claim that a market-based incentive, such as a tradeable permit, will achieve the desired reduction in pollution at less cost to society than could be achieved with a CAC policy.

Tradeable permits are more than a text-book example of an MBI. They are in use in various parts of the world including the USA and Italy (in the latter case in an attempt to clean up the heavily polluted Lagoon in which Venice is situated). They suffer from some important objections, however, at both a theoretical and a practical level. The first is the question of the basis on which pollution permits should be issued in the first place. The practical answer is that when permits are initially issued this is done on the basis of historical levels of pollution (known as **grandfathering**). Thus firms which have traditionally been the worst offenders are given the most rights to pollute, which some critics have argued is inequitable. A second practical problem is that political pressure may be placed on the government to issue a greater number of permits in total than would be consistent with a socially acceptable level of emissions. This is an aspect of what is sometimes called **regulatory capture** – the civil servants and government ministers will be placed under pressure by those firms that they are supposed to be regulating and may well be unduly influenced by them, even though there is no explicit corruption.

Summary

Pollution is an example of market failure. There may be missing markets – for example, there is no market in air quality; there may be externalities which are not taken into account by producers; and certain environmental goods – such as the air in a city – may be non-excludable. Pigou's approach was to imagine that a market in pollution did exist in which the polluter and those who suffered from pollution could bargain with each other. A socially optimal level of pollution could then be defined. Pigovian taxes could be used to achieve this level of pollution by modifying the private costs paid by producers to bring them in line with social costs.

There are practical difficulties associated with this solution. Such taxes are often regressive and it is difficult to place an objective money value on the damage caused by the pollution. Additionally, the producer may simply pass on the tax to the consumer – the extent to which he is able to do so will depend on the elasticity of demand for the product in question.

Pigovian taxes are an example of a market based incentive. An alternative approach, known as 'command and control', consists of setting legal limits and regulations, such as those requiring catalytic converters on cars. Tradeable permits are an example of an MBI, but their effectiveness can be reduced by the problem of regulatory capture.

Key terms

Review questions

15.1 Explain the distinction between operational and accidental pollution using a sentence (or sentences) beginning 'The nuclear power industry…'

15.2 Should the following be classified as stock pollutants or flow pollutants:
   raw sewage discharged into the sea
   discarded dry-cell batteries
   emissions from cars with catalytic converters
   noise from aircraft at Heathrow
   low level radioactive waste, e.g., clothing
   Magnox power stations that have been closed down.

15.3 Explain why the following are examples of transfrontier pollution:
   (a) acid rain (b) the river Rhine.

15.4 The city of York is, allegedly, now more susceptible to flooding from its river than it was a generation ago. The same seems to be true of areas of Holland recently affected by flooding from the Rhine. Explain why this may be the result of 'externality generating upstream activities'.

15.5 Sweden has recently banned the use of two-stroke outboard motors on its inland lakes. What is the rationale for such a policy and why was CAC preferred to an MBI?

15.6 The plan by the former Conservative Government to place VAT on fuel caused a political furore? Why was this? The incoming Labour administration rescinded the policy, but were there any merits in it?

16 The distribution of income

16.1 The distribution of personal income
16.2 The distribution of wealth
16.3 Regional inequalities
16.4 A note on statistical regularity
16.5 Will the market mechanism reduce inequalities?

Preview

The market mechanism rewards success and punishes failure. Small wonder then that the distribution of income which results is unequal. This chapter examines just how unequal that distribution is. It then goes on to examine the extent to which the distribution is changed by the systems of taxation and cash grants. Finally, it presents some data on the distribution of wealth.

16.1 The distribution of personal income

In Table 16.1 we divide the population of households in the UK into **quintile groups**, each group containing 20 per cent of the total distribution. They are then ranked from highest to lowest. If the distribution of income were completely equal, the top quintile group would receive 20 per cent of total income, as would the next quintile group and so on down to the lowest quintile group who would also receive 20 per cent of total income. Clearly, however, the distribution of income is not equal. As can be seen, the top quintile received 50 per cent of total income whereas the bottom 20 per cent of households received only 2.6 per cent of total income.

Note that Table 16.1 refers to what the Office for National Statistics calls 'original household income'. Before proceeding therefore we should define what this means. Note first that the distribution of income which we are considering relates to *households* and not to persons. Statistics on the distribution of personal income would not be very useful because some individuals – children and infants especially – have very little or no

Table 16.1 Distribution of original household income (percentages accruing to each quintile group, UK, 1995–96)

Top fifth	50.0
Next fifth	25.0
Middle fifth	15.0
Next fifth	7.0
Bottom fifth	2.6
	100.0

Source: derived from: 'The effects of taxes and benefits upon household income, 1995–96', *Economic Trends*, No. 520, March 1997.

income. Statisticians are therefore compelled to use households rather than persons as the unit being studied. This is not entirely satisfactory, however, since some households will contain just one person, often a pensioner, whereas others will contain two or more adult income-earners and dependent children. This fact alone would lead us to expect an unequal distribution of household income.

Secondly, we should consider what is meant by the term 'income'. The basic distinction we want to make is between **pre-tax** and **post-tax income** but we also want to take account of receipts of cash grants, such as unemployment benefit, and possibly even the receipt of income in-kind such as free schooling and health care. The ONS defines five categories of income: original income, gross income, disposable income, post-tax income and final income.

'Original income'

Households receive income from various sources, but principally from employment (including self-employment) and from investments (dividends etc.). Income from occupational pension schemes (but not state pensions) is also defined as part of **original income**, as are alimony and gifts.

'Gross income'

For some households, transfer payments, such as state retirement pensions or unemployment benefit, represent by far the most significant part of income received. The addition to original income of these cash payments yields what the ONS calls **gross income**.

'Disposable income'

Most households pay income tax and those in employment will also pay the employees' National Insurance Contribution (NIC). The deduction from gross income of income tax and employees' NIC yields **disposable income**.

'Post-tax income'

In addition to the payment of direct taxes such as income tax, all households pay indirect taxes – such as VAT and customs and excise duties on tobacco and alcohol. By subtracting these indirect tax payments from disposable income we arrive at **post-tax income**.

'Final income'

Most households receive income in kind in the form of free education for their children and free health care under the National Health Service. An estimate of the value of such benefits is added to post-tax income to arrive at an estimate of **final income**.

The various stages of redistribution are summarized in Fig. 16.1.

Armed with these definitions we can now approach Table 16.2 which shows the average income accruing to each quintile group. It uses the five standard definitions of income. Table 16.2 shows how the various forms of government intervention modify household income. As is to be expected, gross income exceeds original income because of the addition of cash benefits; disposable income is less than gross income because of the payment of income tax; the payment of indirect tax means that post-tax income is lower still; and lastly the addition of benefits in kind increases final income.

Unfortunately it is difficult for the reader to gain much more from Table 16.2 because of the way that it is presented. Although we can see (by looking along the rows) that the income of the top quintile was much greater than the income of the bottom quintile it is difficult to judge exactly *how much* greater. A more meaningful way of presenting the data is to express the income of each group as a fraction of the average income of all groups in the economy. This is how Table 16.3 is presented. Here the average income is expressed as 100. It can therefore be seen that the original income of the bottom quintile is only 9 per cent of the average and that of the top quintile is more than 2.5 times the average. In this table it is easier to see the effect that the various forms of state intervention have on the distribution of income. If we look at the bottom row

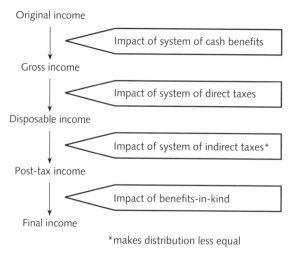

Figure 16.1 The 'stages' of redistribution

Table 16.2 Income accruing to quintile groups, average per household (£ per year) 1995–96

	Bottom	2nd	3rd	4th	Top	All households
Original income plus cash benefits equals...	1590	4870	12 780	22 310	44 470	17 200
Gross income minus income tax equals...	5790	9890	16 190	24 400	45 990	20 450
Disposable income minus indirect tax equals...	4810	8580	13 260	19 280	34 890	16 170
Post-tax income plus benefits in kind equals...	3430	6430	10 080	15 110	29 040	12 820
Final income	5650	9510	13 280	18 490	32 670	15 920

Source: derived from: 'The effects of taxes and benefits upon household income, 1995–96', *Economic Trends*, No. 520, March 1997.

we can see the total effect of intervention, since the final income of the bottom quintile has risen from 9 per cent of the average to about one-third of the average whereas the income of the top quintile has fallen from 2.5 times the average to twice the average.

The table also illustrates that the bottom quintile has very little income from employment (original income). Most of their income comes from cash benefits, and we can see that this form of intervention significantly redistributes income. However, the table also shows that the tax system has very little effect on the distribution of incomes – which the reader may find surprising – since post-tax income is within a couple of per-

Table 16.3 Income accruing to quintile groups of households as percentage of average (= 100) 1995–96 (unadjusted for household size)

	Bottom	2nd	3rd	4th	Top
Original income	9	28	74	130	258
Gross income	28	48	79	119	225
Disposable income	30	53	82	119	216
Post-tax income	27	50	79	118	227
Final income	36	60	83	116	205

Source: derived from: 'The effects of taxes and benefits upon household income, 1995–96', *Economic Trends*, No. 520, March 1997.
Note: The figures shown in Table 16.3 are consistent with those in Table 16.1.
The total income for all households is 17 200 × n (where n is the number of households).
The total income accruing to the top 20 per cent is 44 470 × n/5, so the share accruing to the top quintile is: (44 470 × n/5)/(17 200 × n) = (44 470/5)/17 200 = 52% which is approximately equal to the figure shown in Table 16.1.

Table 16.4 Equivalized income accruing to quintile groups of households as percentage of average (= 100) 1995–96 (adjusted for household size)

	Bottom	*2nd*	*3rd*	*4th*	*Top*
Original income	14	35	80	130	240
Gross income	39	53	84	120	208
Disposable income	38	57	87	120	198
Post-tax income	33	54	84	119	210
Final income	51	64	88	113	183

Source: derived from: 'The effects of taxes and benefits upon household income, 1995–96', *Economic Trends*, No. 520, March 1997.

centage points of gross income for all groups. Note particularly the effect of the system of indirect taxes which *reduces* the incomes of the bottom quintile (as a percentage of the average) and increases the incomes of the top – the opposite to what one might expect.

As might be supposed, differences in household income are partly explained by differences in **household composition**. Households in the bottom quintile are likely to contain fewer persons than those in the middle or top. Statisticians can take account of this by a process called **equivalization**. The equivalized income accruing to each quintile group is shown in Table 16.4 so that the effect of equivalization can be judged by comparing Tables 16.4 and 16.3. As is to be expected – and as can be seen – the major effect of equivalization is to raise the income of the bottom quintile by a significant amount. Note, however, that the result we saw earlier is still apparent – the net effect of the tax system is to reduce the incomes of the bottom quintile (as a percentage of the average) and raise the income of the top quintile.

16.2 The distribution of wealth

The information necessary to compile statistics on the distribution of income is collected from two sources – first, from Inland Revenue data and secondly from the Family Expenditure Survey which covers a sample of about 7000 households each year. Data on the distribution of wealth are, however, not so readily available and therefore any statistics relating to the distribution of wealth should be treated with caution.

A parade of dwarfs

We know, however, that the distribution of wealth is very unequal, much more unequal than the distribution of income discussed in the previous section. It is sometimes difficult, when presented with the raw data, to get a feel for just how unequal the distribution of wealth really is. Because of this the economist Jan Pen suggested an expositional device which consisted of relating each person's wealth to his or her height. Pen suggested that the entire population should file past in the space of one hour, starting with those with the least wealth (who would therefore be the smallest) and ending with those with the most wealth (who would therefore be the tallest). Anyone observing such a procession would see 'a parade of dwarfs... and a few giants'. Because the distribution of wealth is so skewed by those with extremely high incomes the first half an hour or so would consist of people whose stature was that of midgets, tiny people only a few inches high. Only after a full 50 minutes had elapsed would people of normal height begin to emerge, and as the fifty-ninth minute ticked away giants would appear. In the closing seconds people would be seen who were so tall that their heads touched the sky.

You cannot take it with you

The only time in people's lives when they are forced to reveal their wealth is when they die. Bizarre as it may seem, this is the source used to compile data on the distribution of wealth. When a person dies the property left to his or hers heirs is known as an *estate*. Statisticians use data on the estates of dead people to paint a picture of the wealth of the living. Clearly, this **mortality multiplier** method, as it is known, is beset with difficulties and potential anomalies. If a few very wealthy young people die, estimates of the distribution of wealth among the living show a marked increase in inequality. Lysteria in the potted meat sandwiches at a Royal Garden Party would produce a significant increase in measured inequality.

The definition of wealth

In addition to the problem of acquiring data there is the problem of defining what is meant by wealth, and in particular of evaluating the worth of the assets. Some assets, such as stocks and shares, are marketable and are easy to place a value upon. Other marketable assets, such as real property and land, are more difficult to value unless they are sold. Some authors argue that **non-marketable wealth** such as occupational and state pension rights should also be included in a definition of wealth.

Table 16.5 relates to marketable wealth only. If one were to include occupational and state pension rights, the distribution would appear more equal, though the argument for the inclusion of such rights – particularly state pension rights – is unconvincing.

Table 16.5 has two salient features. First, as we have already noted, the distribution of wealth is much more unequal than the distribution of income. Secondly, unlike the distribution of income which is becoming more unequal, there appears to be little change in the degree of inequality associated with the distribution of wealth. In 1993 half the adult population in the UK owned 93 per cent of the wealth. Residential property forms a large part of this personal wealth which means that, if the value of dwellings is excluded from the definition, the distribution of marketable wealth becomes more unequal with over half of total wealth being owned by only 5 per cent of adults.

Table 16.5 The distribution of wealth, UK

	1976	1993
Marketable wealth percentage of wealth owned by:		
most wealthy 1%	21	17
most wealthy 5%	38	36
most wealthy 10%	50	48
most wealthy 25%	71	72
most wealthy 50%	92	93
Marketable wealth less value of dwellings: percentage of wealth owned by:		
most wealthy 1%	29	26
most wealthy 5%	47	51
most wealthy 10%	57	63
most wealthy 25%	73	80
most wealthy 50%	88	93

Note: the statistics relate to persons aged 18 and over.
Source: derived from *Social Trends* 27, based on Inland Revenue data.

16.3 Regional inequalities

We saw in the previous section that a market system produces inequalities in the distribution of income between households. Market systems are often characterized, too, by inequalities in the distribution of income between regions of the same country though such inequalities occur also in planned economies. In the UK there is a 'North-South divide'. The North is poorer than the South. While one could debate where the 'North' starts and the 'South' ends, it is clear from Table 16.6 that certain regions such as the South-East, East Anglia and the South-West are more prosperous than other regions such as the North, Wales and Northern Ireland.

Table 16.6 shows average weekly incomes expressed as an index number for the various regions of the UK. What these statistics show is that incomes in the South-East tend to be about 19 per cent higher than the UK average whereas incomes in Wales are about 23 per cent lower than the UK average. We conclude therefore that people in the South-East have a considerably higher standard of living – at least in material terms – than those in Wales.

We should not be surprised to find that other indices of the *material* standard of living correlate highly with income. One such index of the material standard of living is the ownership of certain consumer durables, which is shown in Table 16.7.

Table 16.7 is presented so that the ranking of the regions is the same as in the previous table – that is, they are ranked according to income. As can be seen, households in richer regions are more likely to have a dishwasher, a telephone, a home computer and a CD player. Of course, the correlation is not perfect but there is a clearly discern-

Table 16.6 Average gross weekly income per person, by region, 1994–95 (index – UK average = 100)

South-East	119	
Greater London	122	
Rest of South-East		118
South-West	101	
Scotland	99	
East Anglia	98	
East Midlands	97	
North-West	93	
Yorkshire and Humberside		91
West Midlands	88	
North	83	
Northern Ireland	78	
Wales	77	

Source: derived from *Regional Trends*, 31, 1996, Table 8.2.

able tendency for the ownership of certain durable goods to rise as income rises, as we would expect. Note, however, that there are some exceptions to the general pattern. In Greater London, for example, only 18 per cent of households have dishwashers though incomes are higher in this region than any other part of the UK. This paradox can probably be explained by differences in household composition – in Greater London a relatively high proportion of households consists of single persons who are less likely to own a dishwasher than households comprising families with children.

It is not surprising to find that the ownership of consumer durables is associated with income. What is perhaps more surprising is that income is also correlated with other indices of the 'quality of life' which relate to less materialistic notions of

Table 16.7 Percentage of households with selected durable goods (regions ranked by average gross weekly income)

	Dishwasher	Telephone	Home computer	CD player
South-East	22	94	27	47
Greater London	18	93	25	45
Rest of South-East	25	94	28	49
South-West	22	92	24	41
Scotland	15	88	21	43
East Anglia	18	92	23	46
East Midlands	16	89	22	39
North-West	14	88	22	39
Yorkshire and Humberside	13	89	23	40
West Midlands	14	89	24	40
North	11	85	25	40
Northern Ireland	15	84	16	26
Wales	16	87	23	40

Source: derived from *Regional Trends*, 31, 1996, Table 8.11.

Table 16.8 Pupils achieving GCSE grades A-C in selected subjects, 1993–94

	English		Any science	
	Males	*Females*	*Males*	*Females*
South-East	46.4	63.0	42.7	43.0
Greater London	42.3	57.7	36.5	37.8
Rest of South-East	48.6	65.9	46.0	45.9
South-West	48.4	65.9	47.8	47.0
Scotland (see text)	55.6	71.6	55.6	59.1
East Anglia	43.5	63.4	45.4	44.6
East Midlands	41.1	58.4	41.7	40.0
North-West	43.7	59.2	40.6	39.9
Yorkshire and Humberside	38.9	56.6	37.8	38.4
West Midlands	39.8	58.5	39.0	40.5
North	39.5	56.5	37.4	36.6
Northern Ireland	—	—	—	—
Wales	34.5	54.4	38.7	38.4

Source: derived from *Regional Trends*, 31, 1996, Table 4.8.

well-being. Table 16.8, for example, shows that there is also an association between income and educational attainment. As with the previous tables, the regions in Table 16.8 have been ranked according to income, and this enables us to see at a glance that there is indeed a correlation between income and educational achievement. Pupils living in regions with higher incomes are more likely to pass GCSE than those living in poorer regions. As with the ownership of consumer durables, the correlation is not perfect but the fact that an association exists is clear.

16.4 A note on statistical regularity

W. Sawyer once described statistics as 'the search for pattern'. Careful scrutiny of the statistics in Table 16.8 reveals an intriguing pattern. Pass-rates correlate with income. It is also clear, however, that in every region girls do better than boys in English, and by a significant margin. In science, however, there is no clear tendency for them to do better or worse than their male classmates.

The pattern we have discovered is a type of 'explanation'. It does not explain the underlying processes which give rise to these differences but the discovery of the **statistical regularity**, in itself, goes some way towards improving our understanding. It teaches us what to look for, and, if we know what to expect, the unexpected stands out.

Two regions of the UK do not fit the typical pattern. The first is Scotland where pass rates in Science and English (of which the Scots speak a variant) are significantly higher than we would expect on the basis of income alone.

This is true for both males and females. This is either because the Scottish educational system is superior to that in England and Wales or simply because the examinations are easier. Inasmuch as Scottish girls score roughly 16 per cent higher in English than Scottish boys, however, the statistical regularity noted previously is still present.

Table 16.9 Infant mortality and perinatal mortality, by region, 1994

	Infant mortality[1]	Perinatal mortality[2]
South-East	5.5	8.4
Greater London	6.3	9.5
Rest of South-East	4.8	7.5
South-West	5.3	7.9
Scotland	6.2	9.0
East Anglia	5.2	7.6
East Midlands	6.9	9.2
North-West	6.2	9.2
Yorkshire and Humberside	7.7	9.4
West Midlands	7.2	10.6
North	6.3	9.0
Northern Ireland	6.1	9.7
Wales	6.2	9.2

Notes:
1   Deaths of infants under 1 year of age per 1000 live births.
2   Still births and deaths of infants under 1 week of age per 1000 live births and still births.
Source: derived from *Regional Trends*, 31, 1996, Table 7.2.

The second region which does not fit the general pattern is Greater London. Incomes in London are higher than elsewhere but educational attainment is much poorer than might be expected on the basis of income alone. The probable reason for this is again to do with household composition and type – a higher proportion of children in London will come from ethnic minorities or households where English is not the first language or will be disadvantaged in some other respect.

The disadvantaged nature of households in Greater London – despite their material affluence – is also evident if we look at other indices of the non-material 'quality of life' – things such as mortality and disability rates. Table 16.9 looks at infant and perinatal mortality. As expected this is correlated with income – poorer regions have a higher rate of infant mortality than richer regions. But Greater London has a much higher rate than might be expected on the basis of income.

An increase in inequalities

Income is a convenient summary statistic. To the experienced economic statistician the predictive power of variations in income to 'explain' variations in other indices of the standard of living is well known, and it comes as no surprise to find the correlations we have observed.

What is perhaps slightly more surprising is that regional inequalities have tended to increase in the UK. As Table 16.10 shows, since the early 1980s the degree of inequality between the regions has increased. The South-East in particular has become relatively richer whereas most of the English regions have become relatively poorer.

Table 16.10 Average gross weekly income per household, by region[1], 1980–81 and 1994–95 (index – UK average = 100)

	1980–81	1994–95	
South-East	115	118	
Greater London		115	118
Rest of South-East		115	118
South-West	94	103	
Scotland	96	98	
East Anglia	95	94	
East Midlands	94	99	
North-West	98	92	
Yorkshire and Humberside		87	93
West Midlands	97	87	
North	90	82	
Northern Ireland	79	88	
Wales	92	77	

Note: Regions ranked by income in 1994–95.
Note the difference between this table and Table 16.6. This table relates to income *per household*, the earlier table to income *per person*.
Source: derived from *Regional Trends*, 31, 1996, Table 8.1.

16.5 Will the market mechanism reduce inequalities?

The period of the Conservative Government from 1979 to 1997 was of course a time when much greater reliance was placed on the market mechanism. Expenditure on policies designed to reduce regional inequalities was cut back. Table 16.11 shows that there was a fall in the assistance given to industries in less favoured regions.

The rationale for this policy of non-intervention has been that the market mechanism, left to its own devices, will tend to reduce and in the long run eliminate regional inequalities in income per capita. The textbook argument which supports this argument focuses on flows of factors between regions in response to regional differences in the prices of these factors. Suppose there are two regions – 'North' and 'South' – as in Fig. 16.2. The North is characterized by relatively low income per capita and relatively high unemployment rates. In the prosperous South in contrast, unemployment rates are much lower and consequently there are labour shortages in some industries

If the market for labour works in the way that competitive markets are supposed to do, then the excess demand for labour in the South will cause the price of labour – that is, wages – to rise. In the North, high rates of unemployment depress wages. It follows therefore that wage costs will be higher in the South than in the North. In pursuit of these lower costs, firms will move North, relocating their factories to areas where wages are lower. In short, there is a movement of physical capital from South to North. This increases job opportunities in the North, raising output and incomes in the region.

For their part workers are attracted by the higher wages in the South. They therefore migrate in pursuit of these higher wages, reducing unemployment rates in the North as they do so.

Table 16.11 Government expenditure on regional preferential assistance to industry
(£ million) (The regions shown in this table are DTI regions which do not correspond with
the standard regions used in earlier tables)

	1987–88	1994–95
South-East	—	1.5
South-West	14.8	9.4
Scotland	153.2	134.4
East	—	0.7
East Midlands	9.4	5.2
North-West	79.0	32.4
Yorkshire and Humberside	38.8	23.0
West Midlands	19.3	14.7
North-East	109.3	38.4
Northern Ireland[1]	126.6	132.9
Wales	132.4	109.2

Note: The system of assistance available in Northern Ireland is not comparable with that
operating in the rest of the UK.
Source: derived from *Regional Trends*, 31, 1996, Table 13.7.

In summary, labour will flow from North to South and capital will flow from South
to North. These flows result from the market incentives provided by regional differences
in wage rates and profit rates. These flows will reduce the inequalities that gave rise to
them, eventually eliminating the inequalities altogether. Clearly, this textbook explana-

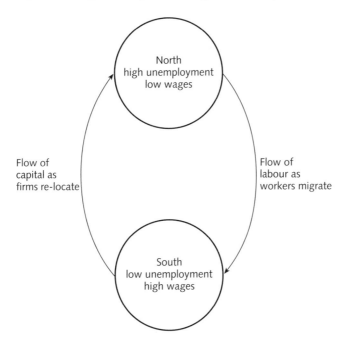

Figure 16.2 The flow of factors between regions in response to regional differences

tion is excessively simplistic. It is, moreover, at variance with the evidence, since, as we have seen, the freer play of market forces in the period 1979–97 has increased rather than reduced regional inequalities. Why, then, do the flows of capital and labour not take place as the theory predicts?

First, labour is a rather immobile factor of production. Migration to a different region in pursuit of work involves the loss of (perhaps) family, friends and familiar surroundings. Nevertheless, labour does move. Paradoxically, however, movements of labour may exacerbate rather than reduce regional inequalities in income. When labour migrates from a low-income region it takes purchasing power with it, further reducing the income of that region. This will affect the residents of the region who are left behind – shopkeepers will suffer since even those formerly unemployed would have spent something in the local shops. Now they are gone. Their spending has gone with them. Since local shopkeepers, estate agents, builders, gardeners and solicitors have suffered a fall in income, they in turn reduce their spending, further reducing the income of the local community. Thus regional income will tend to fall still further as a result of the movement of labour from the low income area, exacerbating regional inequalities. Economists refer to this as a **multiplier effect**.

Moreover, the theory, illustrated in Fig. 16.2, implicitly assumes that labour is a homogeneous factor. In practice, labour is non-homogeneous however. A skilled carpenter is not a perfect substitute for an accountant or a chemist. Unemployed labour in the North may not possess the skills for which there is high demand in the South. Firms, moreover, may rely on specific skills only available in their existing location in the South. A pool of unemployed labour in the North, and lower wages, may not provide sufficient attraction if that labour does not possess the requisite skills.

Capital is a more mobile factor. In fact, it is very mobile and willing to move not just to different regions, but to different countries, sometimes on the other side of the globe. Therein lies the problem with the theory illustrated in Fig. 16.1. Some way off the diagram, off the page in fact, lie other countries with wage costs that are not only lower than those in the South of Britain but are lower than those in the North too – countries such as Taiwan, Korea and Thailand where wages are low and there is a plentiful supply of compliant labour. The market mechanism does work in the sense that capital will flow from the South. But it flows not to the North but to these low waged countries overseas.

Summary

The Office for National Statistics measures the income of *households* rather than *persons*. In doing so it uses a number of different definitions of income – original income, gross income, disposable income, post-tax income and final income. The degree of inequality in the distribution of household income varies somewhat according to which definition is used. The net effect of the tax-benefit system is to make the distribution of income more equal, with the system of cash benefits having the most significant impact. Indirect taxes, in contrast, are regressive. The distribution of wealth is more unequal than the distribution of incomes, but there are similar difficulties in defining what is meant by 'wealth' and in measuring it.

Within the UK there are regional imbalances. In the South-East, and to a lesser extent in East Anglia and the South-West, incomes are higher than in the rest of the UK. Moreover, the statistics seem to show that material prosperity is correlated with other indices of the quality of life such as educational attainment and mortality and morbidity rates.

In theory, imbalances between regions will automatically be corrected by flows of factors of production – capital and labour – from one part of the country to another. But there are reasons why this does not happen or is very slow to occur, which is why governments and supra-national agencies such as the EU give financial assistance to poorer regions.

Key terms

Review questions

16.1 What is the impact on the distribution of income of the following forms of intervention:
    (a) the system of cash benefits
    (b) the direct tax system
    (c) the indirect tax system
    (d) benefits in kind.

16.2 Figure 13.10 (on page 180) shows the distribution of earnings as distinct from the distribution of incomes. This distribution is 'skewed to the right'. Say what you think this means. Would you expect the distribution of incomes to be skewed also? Would the distribution of wealth be more skewed or less skewed than the distribution of incomes?

17 Planning

Preview

This book is about the way the market allocates resources. Paradoxically the study of planning systems – which stand in contast to market allocation – provides additional insights into the way that market systems work. This chapter looks at planning in two very different contexts – the command economies of the former Soviet bloc and planning in wartime Britain.

17.1 Economic planning in peace and war

State planning stands in contrast to the market as a mechanism of resource allocation. In this chapter we look at planning in two distinct, though related, contexts. First, we consider the way resources are allocated in the **centrally planned** or **command economies** of the Soviet type. Secondly, we shall look at the planning methods used in capitalist economies in wartime, the focus of our study being the British economy in the Second World War. These two examples of planning, though distinct, in fact share the common features that they do not use prices and profitability as a means of indicating where resources should flow. In a market system, as we have seen, the myriad decisions of economic agents – firms and consumers – are coordinated by the unseen hand of the price mechanism. Decisions are decentralized but the basic questions which have to be resolved – what is to be produced, by what method and for whom – are resolved because economic agents respond to price signals. Thus, ultimately the allocation of society's resources is the result of decisions which are decentralized and diffused. This is the way of the market.

In a planned system, in contrast, decisions, are taken centrally by some state planning agency. This agency, in effect, dictates the way in which society's resources are allocated in pursuit of some objective which may be either the maximization of economic growth (as was the case in the centrally planned economies) or the winning of a war (as was the case in wartime Britain).

It may seem strange that a book about the operation of market economies should discuss planning, which is in effect the antithesis to market allocation. There are a number of valid reasons for so doing, however. First, a sizeable proportion of the world's population – between a third and a half – have lived, at least until recently, in economic systems which were characterized by central planning: the Soviet bloc, China and many third-world countries. Second, in both the First and Second World Wars the combatants resorted to planning as a means of more effectively promoting the war effort. Third, a study, even a brief one, of the operation of economic planning gives an invaluable perspective to the study of the operation of market economies. The market economy does work. It does allocate resources. But there is an alternative way of doing things – by state planning. Since planning was and remains a preferred development strategy in some countries and is used extensively by market economies in wartime, it is instructive to consider the rationale for economic planning, the mechanisms involved and the experiences of such policies.

Two contemporary developments give increased importance to this chapter. The first occurred in the UK in the 1980s and it related to the way in which the provision of public services such as refuse collection, education and health care was organized. The Conservative Government pursued a belief that the provision of such services by a system of state planning – either centralized or decentralized – was inefficient and that the substitution of market forces or quasi-market forces would increase efficiency, improve resource allocation and the responsiveness to consumer wishes. Typical of this was LMS (local management of schools); the contracting out of local authority services such as refuse collection; and the introduction of trust status for NHS hospitals, freeing them from the control of Area Health Authorities. This is discussed in section 17.4.

The second development, more significant in a global sense, occurred in the economies of Eastern Europe where a *volte-face* took place in the late 1980s. One by one in rapid succession these economies decided to abandon the command systems that they had used for 50 years and espouse the market. This is discussed in section 17.5.

17.2 Soviet planning

Words like 'socialist', 'communist' and 'Marxist' are all adjectives used loosely in the West to describe those economies the essential feature of which is economic planning. Confusingly, however, these terms mean different things to different people. For example, in America the word 'socialist' is applied to many European countries, among them Sweden, France and even Britain, which are essentially capitalist in nature. They are capitalist because, even though there may be some state-owned industries, most resources are privately owned and economic decisions are for the most part taken on the basis of market signals. In command economies, by contrast, the means of production tend to be owned by the state, and decisions about resource allocation are based on administrative fiat. Some centrally planned economies are more 'planned' than others, however. China and the Soviet Union were probably the most centralized of the command economies, with comparatively little private ownership of productive resources and, initially, not much of a role for prices in the allocative process. By contrast, the former Yugoslavia, which stood geographically and ideologically on the edge of the communist bloc, had introduced by the 1960s a sort of 'market socialism' in which factories and other production facilities were owned and run by workers' cooperatives and the decisions of the factory managers about what to produce, in what quantities and by what techniques, were based on market prices.

The history of Soviet planning

It is difficult to appreciate why Soviet central planning developed in the way that it did without knowing something of the historical context within which it occurred. In 1917, the date of the Russian Revolution, Russia was a backward country whose attempts to industrialize had faltered. Between 1914 and 1921 war with Germany and the ensuing civil war had caused a catastrophic worsening of an already bad situation. Industrial output in 1921 fell to a third of what it had been in 1913.[1] Some recovery occurred under the New Economic Policy (NEP) instituted by Lenin in 1921 which reintroduced elements of the free market. However, Lenin's policy of reforms was reversed by Stalin when he came to power in 1928. The Stalin era, 1928–53, marks the period in which the full mechanism of state central planning was constructed. In 1928 Russia felt herself vulnerable, first because she was economically weak in comparison with the capitalist economies and secondly because, being the only communist country, she felt isolated and under threat. Thus it was imperative to build up her economic strength quickly to enable her to withstand the assault which she felt sure would come from the capitalist West. The promotion of rapid economic growth requires that resources that would otherwise have been used to produce consumer goods be diverted into investment – investment in machines, factories, roads, communications, power generation and so on – as well as investment in the human capital required – the trained technicians, doctors, teachers, scientists and all the other specialists that an advanced industrial society needs.

In a market economy, as we have seen, the consumer is sovereign, in theory at least. Consumers ultimately dictate what is produced and they also dictate what proportion of annual output will be devoted to investment. They do this by refraining from consumption, that is, by saving part of their income, thus freeing resources to build up the economy's stock of capital goods. The rationale for central planning, then, was to remove from private individuals the ability selfishly to consume almost all of annual output. Central planning would lower consumption levels in the short term in order to increase the stock of capital assets in society and thereby raise production possibilities in the longer term. Thus during the Stalin era the proportion of Russia's resources devoted to investment (in heavy industry and infrastructure) was comparatively high. Consequently, the rate of economic growth was high in comparison with previously achieved Russian levels and in comparison with most capitalist countries at the same time. This then was the rationale for economic planning in the Soviet Union.

The nature of Soviet planning

A Soviet economic plan started from a set of macro aggregates – the target output of steel, of cement, of men's suits, of trained doctors, and so on. Each of the economic enterprises producing, say, steel was then given an individual production target, the production targets both at the individual (micro) level and at the aggregate (macro) level being related to past years' realized performance. Each of the individual enterprises was then allocated the resources deemed to be both necessary and sufficient to meet its production quota. At this stage inputs and outputs were decided upon in physical terms rather than in terms of the money values of those inputs and outputs. Thus, for example, the target output for steel would be X million tonnes rather than X million pounds' worth of steel; coal input into steel making would be Y million tonnes of coal rather than Y million pounds' worth of coal; and so on for all the other inputs including labour. The physical plan was then translated into monetary terms using prices deemed appropriate by the central planners. Each individual enterprise then purchased the inputs it had been allocated, at the prices decided upon by the planners, and sold the output it produced, again at the prices decided upon by the planners.

Note that in this system the performance (the efficiency) of an enterprise is measured by its success in meeting its production target (which is itself based on levels achieved in the past). Profitability was not a meaningful measure of efficiency, nor indeed was it a relevant concept since it depended on a set of prices which was arbitrarily imposed. Moreover, there was no incentive for the firm to economize on the use of the resources it had been allocated since if it were to do so the resulting surpluses (of income over expenditure) would be appropriated by the state and the firm's allocation of inputs for subsequent years reduced. The incentive to exceed current production targets was slight since this would result in increased targets in subsequent years.

An evaluation of Soviet planning

The foregoing account of Soviet planning is based on methods used in the Stalin era, but the methods used up until 1991 were essentially the same. However, early attempts at planning were characterized by an emphasis on physical planning – the use of prices as part of the planning process was eschewed altogether. The measurement of output in physical terms (often in weight) frequently led to absurdities. Some of the stories which emanated from the Soviet Union about central planning in the Stalin era may have been apocryphal, but the deficiencies of the system were well known and acknowledged by the Soviets themselves. A famous cartoon of the time, much emulated even in the official Soviet press, shows a crane lifting an enormous button. The caption, which loses nothing in translation from the original Russian, reads: '…and with this single button we can fulfil our production quota for the next three years.'

The reforms of the 1950s reintroduced prices into the planning system but the prices used were not market prices in the sense that they did not reflect scarcity. That is, they did not reflect consumers' evaluation of the desirability or otherwise of the products, so that there was no incentive for producers to improve the quality of the goods produced. In the West goods which are perceived to be of higher quality command a higher price. In the Soviet system prices were administered centrally. The system therefore had an in-built inflexibility which did not readily permit price differentials between high-quality and low-quality goods. Moreover, innovation and technical change were extremely slow to occur in the Soviet system. Both in terms of techniques used to produce a given output and in terms of the range of outputs produced, the Soviet system was ossified. One of the strengths of a free enterprise system is its ability to exploit market opportunities, to fill gaps which entrepreneurs spot in the market and to create entirely new markets. The essential point is that the dynamic of the free enterprise system is based on the rewarding of success and the punishing of failure. This in turn is based on profitability. Profits flow from producing things which people are prepared to buy. The deficiencies of the Soviet system stemmed from the lack of any feedback mechanism from consumers to producers, a mechanism we referred to earlier as consumer sovereignty. In a market economy, as we noted in Chapter 14, consumers influence (and, arguably, determine) what is produced. They do this by the purchasing decisions they make. Prices are the link between the wishes of consumers and the actions of producers. In the Soviet system planners decided what would be produced. There was no need for prices.

Prices of course did exist in the Soviet Union, both for producer goods and for consumer goods, but they did not necessarily reflect relative scarcity. Since prices were officially controlled rather than market determined, excess demand gave rise to shortages. These were choked off not by a rise in price but by queuing which then became merely an unofficial form of rationing. To get the goods in question you had to be prepared to wait. Goods had a time price as well as a money price. Similarly, excess supply resulted in the production of surpluses – products which could not be disposed of at the official prices – just as food surpluses are created under the European Community's Common Agricultural Policy.

The fact that consumer sovereignty did not exist even in a weak form in the Soviet system is not in itself surprising. The concept of the market as an allocative mechanism in which resources are allocated in accordance with consumer preferences – in short, the mechanism described in section 14.1 – is not a concept with which Marx would have been familiar. Marx, whose critique of capitalism inspired the creation of the Soviet system, predates those economists like Marshall, Jevons and Pareto who fully worked out the view of the price mechanism described above.[2] Thus, for Marx, planning must be better than no planning because no planning – that is, the market – was simply chaos. The idea that the function of prices might be to bring order out of chaos is not one that Marx would have heard of. Since the concept of an optimal allocation of resources is Paretian in origin, the concept of a misallocation of resources can only be understood within the framework of welfare economics which Pareto originated. Thus the economic inefficiencies of the Soviet system represent misallocations of resources only if one is first prepared to accept the framework of Paretian welfare economics. In other words, in pointing to the economic inefficiencies of the Soviet system and identifying these as misallocations of resources, we tend to assume implicitly that no such misallocations occur in a free market system. That is, we assume that a properly functioning market allocates resources 'correctly' or optimally. This is far from true, however, for the reasons set out in section 14.2 (and other reasons besides). Many people would question, for example, whether the resources devoted to advertising in a capitalist society really do fulfil a socially necessary or even socially useful function. Moreover, some of the most highly skilled and highly paid members of the work force are engaged as accountants, lawyers and tax experts whose sole function is to minimize the contribution that companies make to the Exchequer through the payment of taxes. Two examples, it could be argued, of resource misallocations.

There is another significant failing of market economies to which planned economies are less susceptible, namely the **cycles in economic activity** which periodically produce deep recessions. In the Great Depression of the 1920s and 1930s, for example, roughly one fifth of the workforce in Britain and America lay idle – surely an extreme form of resource misallocation. However, although one could argue that recessions are endemic to a capitalist society, it could also be argued that they result from the application of incorrect policies at a macro level. In other words, governments could prevent recessions from occurring by boosting the overall level of demand in an economy as and when necessary.

17.3 Leontief planning

We conclude our investigation of Soviet planning with a more detailed look at the techniques involved. It is important to recognize that these techniques are not contained within the writings of Karl Marx. His famous work *Das Kapital* was a critique of capitalist society. It was not a blueprint for a socialist state. Hence when the Bolsheviks came to power in 1917 they had no model on which to base an alternative form of economic organization. Indeed at that time the techniques of central planing had not been invented.

It is one of the ironies of history that some years later an American mathematician and economist with a decidedly Eastern European name, Wassily Leontief, developed a technique known as **input-output analysis** which provided the basis for a comprehensive and systematic system of central planning. To understand how this could have worked, recall the discussion of the production function in section 13.3 and recall particularly the notion of a production function with fixed-factor proportions. For example, suppose that the output of cars requires inputs of certain factors of production, namely steel, glass, rubber and plastic. Assume that the relationship between inputs and output is as follows: 700 kilograms of steel + 90 kilograms of glass + 110 kilograms of rubber + 100 kilograms of plastic etc. will give an output of one car (weighing one tonne).

These numbers would have been arrived at on the basis of information relating to available technologies. Note that both the output (a car) and the inputs of steel, glass, rubber and plastic are measured in physical units.

As we have seen, a Soviet plan started with macro aggregates. Thus the Soviet planners would have decided that in the coming year the national economy was to produce, say, five million pairs of shoes, two million tonnes of potatoes and, say, 10 000 cars. On the basis of the input requirements for one car illustrated above they would then have been able to work out how much steel, glass, rubber, plastic and so on would be required to produce this number of cars. As we can see, the steel requirement would be:

$$10\,000 \times 700 \text{ kg of steel} = 7\,000\,000 \text{ kg of steel (7000 metric tonnes)}.$$

By adding together the steel required to produce the planned output of cars, that required to produce refrigerators, to produce tanks and so on the total requirement for steel output for the whole economy could have been determined.

In the same way that there were fixed input-output coefficients for the production of cars, there were also fixed input-output coefficients for the output of steel. For example, 5 tonnes of iron ore + 3 tonnes of coal etc. gives one tonne of steel. That is, one tonne of steel output required 5 tonnes of iron ore plus 3 tonnes of coal. Again these coefficients (5, 3) would have been arrived at on the basis of existing technologies. Thus one could determine the coal required to produce the target output of steel, and by adding together the coal required to produce steel plus that required to heat houses, generate electricity and so on, the total requirement for coal could be arrived at.

There is an additional complexity, however, namely that to produce an output of coal there was also a requirement for an *input* of steel. Steel is an *input* into a raw material industry (coal) but in turn coal is itself an input into the steel industry. For example, the input-output coefficients for the coal industry might take the form: 60 kilograms of steel + 40 kilograms of timber + 20 units of electricity etc. gives one tonne of coal.

It was the mathematical technique of input-output analysis, devised by Leontief, which provided a means of solving mathematically a complex set of interrelated equations where the output of one industry could be the input of another. He developed a technique which could solve the set of equations so as to work out the required quantities of all the factors in the economy.

One cannot fail to notice, however, the huge **informational and computational requirement** necessary to plan the output for a whole economy – and remember that the Russian planners did not have access to the yet-to-be-invented computers. Almost inevitably therefore, central planning produced huge inefficiencies with shortages of some goods and overproduction of others.

Moreover, it is instructive to note that even if the informational and computational requirement could have been met – which arguably it could be with modern information technology – the system would still have produced inefficiencies. There are four main reasons for this.

First, the system was not capable of responding to changes in technology, let alone initiating them. This was because of the assumption of fixed-factor proportions embodied in the fixed input-output coefficients. Thus technical improvements – producing a given output with fewer inputs – were slow to filter through to the Soviet production system. This was made even worse because the Soviet strategy for development was based on the idea of **autarky** – developing separately and independently from the rest of the capitalist world. By cutting themselves off from the excesses of Western capitalism they also cut themselves off from the technological developments – including, ironically, computers – which would have enabled them to reap the benefits of resource-saving technical progress.

Secondly, because the input-output coefficients were based on physical units, and because originally there were no prices, it was not possible for a change in the relative price of factors of production to result in any change in the choice of factors used. In a capitalist economy if one factor of production becomes cheaper, relative to others, firms will normally use more of that factor and less of the other factors which are now relatively more expensive. The **factor mix** which is **optimal** will change in response to changes in relative factor prices. In the Soviet planning system this could not happen. Firms could not respond to changes in the relative scarcities of factors – as reflected in their prices – by changing their production techniques.

Thirdly, because the planning process was based on outputs measured in physical quantities, the *quality* of that output was neglected and ignored. Thus production targets were specified in terms of the number of cars to be produced regardless of whether the cars were of the design, performance, colour, reliability, and so on that consumers wanted and regardless of whether consumers wanted leather shoes, brown shoes size 8 or trainers size 10. Thus central planning produced goods of poor quality, and of low customer appeal.

Fourthly, the system lacked the **incentives of a market system** to produce as cheaply as possible. Since input quotas were determined by the central plan there was no incentive to economize on their use. Indeed, there was every incentive – as in any organization in the West today – to use all of the resources allocated to a particular use, since to use less would result in next year's quota being reduced.

17.4 Planning in wartime

In the Soviet Union the rationale for central planning was to divert into investment those resources which would otherwise have been used up in consumption. Similarly, in wartime there is a need to divert resources into the production of munitions. Since society's productive potential is limited these resources must be drawn away from the consumption-goods sector. The industries producing consumption goods will only produce what people are able to buy. Thus, people's ability to purchase consumer goods must be reduced. In the Second World War in Britain this was achieved in two ways. First, by raising income taxes so that post-tax incomes were reduced. Second, a system of rationing was introduced which limited demand to the reduced supply then available. In this way the government took command of those productive resources needed to produce munitions without at the same time generating demand inflation in the consumer goods' industries.

The extent to which the government was able to divert resources is shown in Table 17.1 which, interestingly, casts doubt on the popular belief about the German economy being an all-out war machine. Throughout the course of the war, and particularly in the early stages, the British government was relatively more successful in diverting resources away from consumption than the German government.

The operation of the system of rationing and price controls in wartime Britain is something which has been well documented and may even be within the range of personal experience of some readers (rationing was finally brought to an end in 1954). The aspect of economic planning which we want to focus on here is the way in which the output of munitions was planned. The methods used resembled the techniques

Table 17.1 Civilian expenditure on consumption in Germany and the UK, 1938–44 (indices based on constant prices 1938 = 100)

Year	Germany (pre-war area)	UK
1938	100	100
1939	108	100
1940	100	87
1941	97	81
1942	88	79
1943	87	76
1944	79	77

Source: N. Kaldor, 'The German War Economy' in *Essays on Economic Policy*, Vol. II, Duckworth, 1965.

of Soviet planning. They were not in any sense modelled on Soviet experience, since literature documenting the experience of Soviet planning in the pre-war period was sparse. Rather, the techniques of planning evolved as the war progressed, with pragmatism rather than dogma being the guiding principle. There does not seem, moreover, to have been a single coordinated master plan for wartime production. Ely Devons,[3] one of the wartime planners in Britain, writes:

> In the early years of the war there was little attempt at the central direction of production. As far as I am aware no-one worked out, or attempted to work out, what resources would be left after meeting the minimum needs of the civilian population, and how these resources should be divided between the armed forces and the production of aircraft, army and naval supplies. It is true that general decisions were taken about the size of the Army, Air Force and Navy to plan for, but these decisions were by no means clear cut and did not in any case take account of the interrelation between the size of the armed forces and the production of munitions that would be needed for them. Each supply department was left to proceed with its plan for expansion in the light of the requirements that were put to it by the appropriate Service Department. It was only later, as the war proceeded, and these various plans came into conflict that a system of central direction to solve these conflicts was evolved; and by that time the general outlines of the plans of the various departments concerned were already determined, at least for a substantial period of time ahead.
>
> (Devons 1980: 73)

In fact, a system of separate committees was established, each one responsible for different aspects of the war effort. There was at first no central coordination between these various committees. Individuals on these committees, Devons writes, 'were often out of touch with what individuals on the other coordinating committees were doing.' Central direction emerged, however, through the medium of the production plans of the various departments:

The main link and coordinating mechanism between the various allocating committees was provided by the production programmes of the individual supply departments. It was by the effect on the plans of the individual departments of the decisions of any one of these allocating committees, and the further reaction of these altered plans on the decisions of the other committees, that the whole planning process was kept in motion. Thus, if the manpower committee cut the allocation of labour to the Ministry of Aircraft Production, as a result MAP would reduce its aircraft programme; this would, in turn, reduce MAP's requirements for steel, timber, building capacity etc., and these reduced requirements would be taken into account by the appropriate allocating committee at the next quarterly review. It might be that at such a review MAP's steel allocation was cut even further, and this would involve a further re-adjustment in its programme, which would again have its effects in MAP's demand for other factors.

(Devons 1980: 74)

In today's terminology we would describe this as an iterative process. Of course, given the speed at which committees worked, the process of iteration had not been completed before action pertinent to the prior decisions of committees had already been taken. Often, however, some of the more cumbersome aspects of the formal planning procedures were overcome by *ad hoc* and informal consultative arrangements between individuals on related committees. Individual initiative made the system workable.

The wartime planners did not, of course, have access to the high-speed data processing capabilities of modern computers, but it is difficult to see that they would have been assisted in their task had such computers been available. As we noted earlier, in the post-war years mathematical techniques were developed to cope with complex resource-allocation problems involving interrelations between inputs and outputs, such as the situation described by Devons above. These were the techniques of input-output analysis developed by Wassily Leontief[4] in the 1940s. The technique in effect speeds up the process of iteration by solving simultaneously a set of equations showing the interrelationships between all of the major inputs and outputs in an economic system. Had this technique been available to the wartime planners, however, the outcome would probably have been little different. The system of planning evolved as the war progressed and became more efficient as a result of human initiative and ingenuity. As Devons says, 'It would be quite mistaken to conclude that the process by which government economic planning operated in wartime in any way resembled the theoretical structures of the overall planners.'

While the divergence between practice and theory is undoubtedly a feature of all planning systems – using the term 'planning' in its widest sense – the reader should not take away the impression of British wartime planning as consisting of Whitehall civil servants muddling through in the face of an ultra-efficient German war effort organized from the centre and characterized by utter ruthlessness and superb organizing ability. In reality very little central planning took place in Germany until the Speer administration took control of the production of munitions in 1942. The success of the Speer administration in increasing the output of munitions occurred rather late in the war and too late to affect the outcome. Table 17.2 gives some illustrative figures of British and German armaments production.

Table 17.2 Comparison of output of particular classes of armaments in Germany and the UK, 1940–44

	1940 Germany	1940 UK	1941 Germany	1941 UK	1942 Germany	1942 UK	1943 Germany	1943 UK	1944 Germany	1944 UK
Military aircraft										
Fighters	3100	4300	3700	7000	5200	9800	11 700	10 700	28 900	10 500
Bombers	4000	3700	4300	4700	6500	6300	8600	7700	6500	8100
Other types	1800	1900	2100	1800	1800	1600	2800	3000	1100	5000
Trainers	1300	5100	900	6600	1200	5900	2100	4800	3100	2900
Total (numbers)	10 200	15 000	11 000	20 100	14 200	23 600	25 200	26 200	39 600	26 500
Bombs (filled weight '000 tons)	n.a.	48	245	143	262	241	273	309	231	370
Tanks	1600	1400	3800	4800	6300	8600	12 100	7500	19 000	4600
Heavy guns (75 mm and over)	6300	1900	7800	5300	13 600	6600	38 000	12 200	62 300	12 400
Light guns (over 20 mm and under 75 mm)	n.a.	2800	3400	11 400	9600	36 400	8100	25 800	8400	3600
Small arms:										
Infantry rifles ('000)	1350	81	1358	78	1370	594	2244	910	2585	547
Infantry machine guns ('000)	170	30	320	46	320	1510	440	1650	790	730

Note: United Kingdom figures refer to UK production only. German figures include all deliveries to the Wehrmacht.
Source: N. Kaldor, 'The German war economy', in *Essays on Economic Policy*, Vol.II, Duckworth, 1965.

Probably the most important of the munitions production programmes was that concerned with aircraft. In Britain this was the responsibility of the MAP (Ministry of Aircraft Production). The MAP's responsibilities covered not just those factories assembling the airframe itself but also those factories manufacturing the principal component parts – the engines, undercarriages, propellers, turrets, etc. Obviously, components had to be manufactured in the correct quantities for the number of completed aircraft coming off the production line. In addition, the requirements for spare parts had to be satisfied. The problem of coordination between the component manufacturers and the airframe manufacturers was solved via the MAP using the medium of the production plan referred to earlier. Each of the individual representatives on the coordinating committee knew the planned output of Spitfires, Hurricanes etc., and the likely demand for spare parts for the next quarter. From this the component manufacturers could estimate the requirement for components. In the event that the planned output of, say, propellers was insufficient to meet the planned requirements for them, then a combination of two things would happen. Either planned requirements for propellers would be reduced by scaling down the planned output of aircraft or more resources would be diverted away from other areas and into propeller production.

The MAP was actively instrumental in the resource allocation programme at all levels. It would have been possible of course to leave it to the market as is done in peacetime, but there were considerable drawbacks with such a system. Consider how such a system would have worked. The MAP would have issued contracts to aircraft manufacturers to purchase given numbers of aircraft at prices which the MAP determined. The manufacturers themselves would then have been free to enter into contracts with the component suppliers to purchase components that would do the job as cheaply as possible.

The drawbacks of such a system are twofold. First, the speed of adjustment of the output of components in response to changes in the output of final aircraft, and *vice versa*, would almost certainly have been slower if it had relied upon price signals to indicate relative scarcities. Certainly there was a widespread belief that this was the case and a widespread acceptance therefore that the MAP should intervene. The MAP, that is, had to be seen to be doing something actively to promote the war effort rather than just leaving it to the market. The second drawback of leaving the aircraft manufacturers to purchase the components they required at the best prices they could obtain was that the contract price of the aircraft (paid by the MAP to the aircraft manufacturer) would determine the quality of the components fitted to it. In effect, the price would determine the specification of the aircraft. The higher the price the better the specification.

> For example, an extra £1000 for a Spitfire would enable the Spitfire manufacturers to command the best Merlin engines, and a reduction of the price for the Hurricane would have forced manufacturers of the Hurricane to engine their aircraft with second best Merlins.
>
> (Devons 1980: 68)

Now it might have been possible for the MAP to set the relative price of Spitfires and Hurricanes in such a way that this outcome was achieved (assuming this was what the MAP desired). But it was much easier to achieve this outcome if the MAP *directed* the output of the engine manufacturers in the way that it saw fit. The desired allocation of resources (in this case engines) was achieved more quickly and with a greater degree of certainty through a system based on the physical direction of resources rather than through a mechanism in which producers responded to prices.

We began this chapter by defining planning as being a system of resource allocation which stands in contrast to a market allocation. The reader may by now be aware, however, that to present the situation as a choice between two stark alternatives – planning or the market – is misleadingly simplistic. In producing a complex manufactured product such as an aircraft, coordination of the various aspects of production (in other words, planning) is a technological necessity. The problems of coordination in aircraft production in peacetime are no less acute than in wartime. They are simply less urgent. Companies like British Aerospace are the modern-day equivalent of the MAP. They have production plans, extending several years into the future, for the various types of aircraft they produce. These plans must be coordinated with the planned production of components, whether these components are produced in-house (within BAe itself) or by independent suppliers. The process of planning is no different from that carried out in wartime except that it is carried out by different people – BAe employees rather than Whitehall civil servants. The only substantive difference is that the resource cost of this indispensable planning – the salaries of the planners – is incorporated in the price of the aircraft rather than paid out of general taxation.

17.5 Planning versus the market: the Conservative Government 1979–97

In Britain during the period of the Conservative Government from 1979 to 1997 a gradual but fundamental shift occurred in public attitudes towards the planning-versus-the-market debate. Certain services such as education and health care had for many decades been provided publicly and paid for out of general taxation. The debate was not so much as to whether such services should be provided publicly as to how the provision of such services should be organized – what role should market forces play in the provision of such services?

Historically, the provision of services such as education had been organized by planning agencies such as Local Education Authorities under the overall control of a central government department called the Department of Education. Similarly, health care was organized by Area Health Authorities under the overall control of the Department of Health. There had always been widespread public acceptance that some inefficiencies occurred in the organization of these services – as there is under any planning system, or indeed under any system. However, the Conservative Government's view – and this view was imposed on the electorate – was that the introduction of 'market forces' would improve the overall efficiency of the provision of such services.

Thus it was, for example, that in education each school was given its own budget with much greater freedom than before to spend this income in the way that it saw fit. The proportion of the school's income devoted to staffing, to the purchase of books, to the upkeep of buildings and so on was to be decided by the Board of Governors of the school (in effect strongly guided by the head teacher) rather than by the Local Education Authority. The school would purchase these goods and services paying market prices for them (though the price of teaching labour was set by government) endeavouring to get the best value-for-money from its expenditures in the same way as a household or firm. Moreover, the school's income would be determined by its 'output' – the number of children on its roll. This in turn would depend upon the extent to which consumers (children and parents) endorsed the product being offered by enrolling at the school rather than at some alternative school in the neighbourhood. In short, schools would become more responsive to consumer wishes and would utilize the resources at their disposal in a more efficient manner.

In health care too hospitals could opt to become self-governing trusts with much more autonomy than had been the case when they were under the control of the Area Health Authority. Their success in generating income would depend upon the extent to which consumers of health care – patients and general practitioners acting as agents for the patients themselves – wished to purchase the services the hospital was offering. These services would be 'bought' and 'sold' in a competitive environment, each hospital being in competition with others for custom. The competitive environment would promote increased efficiency in the use of resources.

In areas such as refuse collection and street cleaning the local authority who was responsible for this had historically carried out the work necessary using its own directly employed labour. Henceforth, the local authority would contract out this work to private firms, issuing contracts which would specify the standard to which the work should be performed and the penalties which would be invoked if the work was not performed satisfactorily. Such contracts would be competed for and would normally be awarded to the firm quoting the lowest price. The contracts were for a fixed term and would normally not be renewed if the firm failed to fulfil its contractual obligations. Other local authority services were contracted out in a similar way – the provision and maintenance of football pitches, swimming pools, parks and gardens and so on.

The most fundamental change which took place in the 1980s was perhaps not directly in the way that these services were provided. In the case of refuse collection, for example, the work which was contracted out may well have been performed by the same individuals and the same vehicles (in different livery) as those previously employed. The fundamental change was in terms of the public's attitude. Increasingly it came to be accepted not just that non-market systems were inefficient and unresponsive to consumer demands but that 'market' systems were *more* efficient and *more* responsive to consumer demands. There was a presupposition that market allocation was better than non-market allocation.

This was the fundamental shift of emphasis. In effect, non-market systems were guilty unless proved innocent. Having followed the arguments in this chapter, readers can judge for themselves whether such a presupposition seems reasonable. Certainly it would not have seemed reasonable to the wartime planners for whom central direction of resources seemed self-evidently to be a preferred option for getting the job done.

17.6 Planning versus the market: Eastern Europe

We saw in section 17.2 that Soviet planning began after the Russian Revolution in 1917 and became entrenched in the interwar era. After the Second World War the Soviet Union imposed her preferred system on those neighbouring countries which she had 'liberated', forming them into a protective buffer between herself and Western Europe. These countries – Poland, Czechoslovakia, Hungary, Rumania, Albania, Yugoslavia... and East Germany – formed CMEA (the Council for Mutual Economic Assistance), otherwise known as the COMECON countries. All of these countries instigated a form of state planning, though there were significant differences between individual cases. In essence, however, they were all command economies to a lesser or greater extent.

By the late 1980s the Soviet Unions's grip on her satellites was loosening and there was talk in the Soviet Union itself of reform and the re-introduction of market forces. In the event the dismantling of the command systems in Poland, Czechoslovakia, East Germany and Rumania occurred suddenly, swept along by political reform. CMEA was officially brought to an end on 1 January 1991 – a fact which went unnoticed and unremarked.

The countries of Eastern Europe which opened up their economies to market forces have begun to experience an economic renaissance. Birth pangs are distinctly unpleasant, however. Unemployment in the former East Germany rose from approximately zero to over 40 per cent in 1991 as uncompetitive firms closed down. The market must indeed seem harsh particularly to those insulated for so long from its realities. The market as we have seen rewards success and punishes failure. You cannot have one without the other.

Summary

In the Soviet planning system the decision about what to produce, how to produce it and who should receive it was taken centrally. The system did not use prices as a means of indicating relative scarcity but rather inputs and outputs were measured in physical units. Typically this led to inefficiencies in the allocation of resources. Moreover, the system could not respond to changes in relative factor scarcities which in a market system are signalled by changes in relative prices.

In wartime Britain the rationale for the central coordination of munitions production was the belief that planning was a quicker and more effective means of procurement than purchasing the arms from the manufacturers. The planning system evolved as the War progressed with some of the more cumbersome aspects of the formal planning procedures being overcome by *ad hoc* consultative arrangements.

Notes

1 Dalton, G. (1974) *Economic Systems and Society*, Penguin.
2 Alfred Marshall 1842–1924 (his famous *Principles of Economics* was published in 1890); William Jevons 1835–82; Vilfredo Pareto 1848–1923; Marx's *Das Kapital* was first published in 1867.
3 Devons, E. (1980) 'Economic planning in war and peace' in *Essays in Economics*, Greenwood Press.
4 Leontief, W.W. (1951) *The Structure of the American Economy 1919–1939* (2nd ed.), Fairlawn, NJ: OUP.

Key terms

centrally planned economies	220	autarky	226
command economies	220	optimal factor mix	227
cycles in economic activity	225	incentives of a market system	227
input-output analysis	225		
informational and computational requirement	226		

Review questions

17.1 'What's in a name?' The words we use to describe economic systems are not value-free. They reflect, to a lesser or greater extent, approval or disapproval of that system. Study the following two lists of names:

price system	central planning
capitalism	socialism
free enterprise	state planning
market mechanism	communism
private enterprise	planned economy
free-market system	command economy

Now re-arrange each list so that it starts with terms which reflect approval of the system and finishes with terms which reflect disapproval of the system.

17.2 In Bogravia, an Eastern European satellite of the USSR, consumers wishing to buy a car must put down their names on a waiting list and pay a deposit. The most sought-after model is the Lada 1200, for which there is a four-year waiting list. There are no demonstration models in the showroom, only photographs. Which of the following statements are correct?

(a) The size of the waiting list is evidence that the price charged is too low. The price should rise to choke off the excess demand.

(b) By keeping the price down the authorities ensure that everyone who wants a car can buy one.

(c) The price of the Lada in Bogravia reflects what the Bogravian consumer thinks about the desirability of the product.

(d) At least it's better than just giving cars to members of the Communist Party.

(e) The Lada is a technically advanced car so everyone wants it.

(f) The Lada is a copy of a model that Fiat stopped making in Italy years ago.

(g) There are no waiting lists for cars in Britain.

What could you predict about the price of second-hand (nearly new) Ladas in Bogravia?

17.3 The Soviet system suffered from both static and dynamic inefficiencies. Explain what this means.

17.4 What is meant by autarky?

18 State intervention in market economies: public spending

18.1 A welfare economics framework?
18.2 Public spending: transfer payments
18.3 Non-excludability and non-rivalness
18.4 Public spending: goods and services

Preview

This chapter examines the rationale for the public provision of certain goods and services. The concepts of non-excludability and non-rivalness are used to explain why some such goods are provided by the state, but other reasons such as the merit good argument are also important.

18.1 A welfare economics framework?

In Chapter 14 we looked at a theoretical model of the way in which resources are allocated by the market, and in Chapter 17 we looked at planning both in the context of Soviet-type economies and in the context of wartime capitalist economies. A **mixed economy** such as that of the UK is fundamentally a market economy but with a significant amount of state intervention. This intervention takes a number of broad forms, namely:

- spending on goods and services;
- spending on income maintenance programmes such as unemployment benefit;
- state ownership and control of certain industrial resources, for example the nationalized industries;
- legal controls on the behaviour of firms.

Within a Paretian welfare economics framework these forms of intervention can be seen as ways of tackling various forms of market failure. Thus the framework of welfare economics sketched out in Chapter 14 forms a sort of overarching theory which can be used to explain and justify these various forms of state intervention. The modern tendency, however, is to place less emphasis on the overarching theory of welfare economics and to adopt a more piecemeal approach to the analysis of intervention. The reason for this may be a suspicion that the all-encompassing nature of welfare theory explains everything, but in such broad generalities as to explain nothing. A second reason, possibly, is the acknowledgement that the all-pervasive existence of market failure in the real world makes a Pareto optimal allocation of resources impossible to attain no matter how much one tries to patch up the system with bits of intervention here and there. Here the piecemeal approach is adopted though we recognize that all forms of state intervention do have a welfare-theoretic base.

This chapter looks at public spending – both spending on goods and services and on income maintenance programmes (the latter was also discussed earlier in Chapter 16). Later, in Chapter 19, we consider the third form of intervention mentioned above – the nationalized industries. The final form of intervention listed above is mostly concerned with policy towards monopolies and mergers, which we considered earlier in Chapter 9.

18.2 Public spending: transfer payments

Table 18.1 presents an analysis of public spending in the UK broken down into broad categories. As can be seen, almost one third of government spending is on **transfer payments**. The major expenditure in this category is on retirement pensions, unemployment benefit (now known euphemistically as 'Jobseeker's Allowance') and supplementary benefit, but also included are things like maternity benefit, child allowances, family income supplement and death grant. From the cradle, as you might say, to the grave. Such transfer payments constitute the cash part of the **income maintenance programme** which all market economies provide to a greater or lesser extent for their citizens. The non-cash part of the income-maintenance programme is the income-in-kind provided by free health care, education, and so on. The objective is to redistribute income in favour of those on low incomes and to prevent their standard of living slipping below some 'acceptable' level.

Table 18.1 Analysis of UK public spending 1997–98
(£ billion and percentage of total)

	£bn	%
Social Security (transfer payments)	100	32
Health and personal social services	53	17
Education	38	12
Defence	22	7
Law and order	17	5
Housing heritage and environment	15	5
Industry, agriculture and employment	13	4
Transport	9	3
Other expenditure	23	7
Debt interest	25	8
	315	100

Source: Financial Statement and Budget Report (The Red Book), 1997–98.

Most of the remaining two-thirds of government spending – that is, the part that is not spent on transfer payments – goes on goods and services. The rationale for the public provision of certain goods and services is related to the **public good characteristics** of certain goods. These characteristics, which were mentioned in section 14.2, are **non-excludability** and **non-rivalness**. The meaning of these terms is explained in the following section and we then consider, in section 18.4, the extent to which this provides a rationale for public provision.

18.3 Non-excludability and non-rivalness

'Non-excludability' means that those who do not pay cannot be excluded from consuming the good in question. Thus defence-of-the-realm is a non-excludable public good. Even if you pay no taxes at all, and thus make no contribution towards the cost of provision, you cannot be excluded from enjoying the benefits of being defended. Neither of course can you choose *not* to consume the good in question. Whether you pay for it or not – and whether you like it or not – you consume the benefits of living under the nuclear umbrella. Declaring your house and garden a nuclear-free zone does not alter this basic fact.

'Non-rivalness' is the second characteristic of public goods. It means that if a good or service is provided for one person then it can be provided for everyone at no extra cost. In other words, the goods are not rivals in consumption. Radio and television broadcasts are an example of a non-rival public good. By tuning to a particular broadcast I do not reduce the signal strength in any way. My consumption in no way diminishes the supply available to my neighbours.

Radio and television broadcasts are also intrinsically non-excludable, of course, though attempts are made through the legal system to render them excludable. In other words, in Britain at least, the law requires you to purchase a television licence in order to use a television set. The enforcement of the law is difficult, however, since broadcasts are in a purely technical sense non-excludable – television sets work just as well whether you have paid your licence fee or not. Thus, in order to catch and prosecute the 'free riders' – those who do not pay their television licence fee – the authorities are forced to incur substantial administrative costs: the cost of advertising campaigns designed to persuade people to buy a licence and the cost of TV detector vans to catch those who do not. When attempts are made to render excludable those goods which are intrinsically non-excludable, the administrative and other costs of so doing are often large. Roads, for example, are by their nature more or less non-excludable. In Britain, however, cars used on public roads must be licensed but, as with the television licence fee, evasion is widespread. However, it is certainly possible – as with continental motorway tolls – to devise systems for making some kinds of roads excludable.

18.4 Public spending: goods and services

The market will fail to provide an adequate supply of public goods – those goods which possess to some degree the characteristics of non-excludability and non-rivalness. It can be seen from Table 18.1 that some of the areas of public spending can be explained in terms of the 'public good' argument. Defence, for example, which even in this post-Cold War period consumes about 7 per cent of total public spending, is a pure public good. If the government did not provide it, no-one else would because no private-sector company is capable of 'selling' £22bn worth of defence to the 57 million consumers in the UK. Defence is either provided for everyone or for no-one. It cannot be divided up into 57 million separate lots and sold to individual consumers, because each consumer would choose to be a **free rider**. If there was a choice, no rational consumer would pay.

Although the public-good argument explains why defence is not provided by the market, it cannot, of course, be used to justify so much – or so little – public expenditure in this area. The decision to devote 7 per cent of public spending to defence is essentially a political decision. It does not result from a set of consumer preferences expressed in the market in the same way that the quantity of washing machines produced ultimately depends on the purchasing decisions of consumers to buy washing machines. Hence, where the market fails because of the existence of public goods there is no mechanism whereby consumers can express their preferences, that is, make known their views, except by the very imperfect means of voting for a political party in an election.

Some of the other areas of public spending shown in Table 18.1 are goods or services which possess the characteristics of non-excludability and/or non-rivalness to a greater or lesser extent. For example, most of the expenditure on environmental services – roads, parks, coastal protection – comes under this heading. No private company could have 'sold' the Thames Flood Barrier to the millions of consumers who could potentially have benefited from it. Thus if it were not provided by the government and financed out of general taxation it would not have been provided at all.

However, it is clear that two of the largest spending areas – health care and education – are not really public goods at all. Between them these two areas comprise almost one-third of total public spending, yet they are neither non-excludable nor non-rival. A hospital bed occupied by a psychiatric patient cannot simultaneously be occupied by a heart transplant patient. They are rival goods. Resources devoted to screening for cervical cancer cannot simultaneously be employed in finding a cure for AIDS. Similarly, because health care and education are essentially personal services they are excludable by their nature. Schools and colleges can decide which students to admit and which to exclude. Doctors decide which patient is to receive a corneal graft or a liver transplant. There are exceptions of course. For example, some of the output of the Open University (the broadcasts) is a pure public good and fluoridation of the water supply (to prevent dental decay) constitutes a non-excludable good. However, the bulk of the output of the education and health-care sectors is both excludable and rival. The implication of this is that there is no reason in principle why both education and health care could not be provided by the market. The existence of private health care and private schools in Britain bears witness to this fact. Moreover, some countries have a much smaller state provision of education and health care than we do in the UK (though some have much larger).

Since the provision of health care and education cannot be justified in terms of the public-good argument, some other justification is required. This is provided by the

merit good argument. Certain goods and services are so important, it is argued, that every individual should be able to consume an adequate amount of them no matter what their income. In effect, by subsidizing certain goods, or by providing them at a zero price to the consumer, the state attempts to persuade individuals to consume a larger quantity than they would do if they were forced to pay the full cost of production. This argument extends to a range of goods like school meals, libraries, museums and the arts, as the following conversation between two high-ranking civil servants illustrates. (Bernard, a naive young personal assistant, has been questioning the rationale for public subsidy of the opera, which only the rich seem to benefit from. He suggests that football should be subsidised too ...)

> *Sir Humphrey Appleby*: ... and what about greyhound racing? Should dog tracks be subsidized as well as football clubs for instance?
> *Bernard*: Well, why not if that's what the people want?
> *Sir Humphrey*: Bernard, subsidy is for art. For culture. It is not to be given to what the people want. It is to what the people don't want but ought to have. If they want something they'll pay for it themselves. No, we subsidize education, enlightenment, spiritual uplift – not the vulgar pastimes of ordinary people.
>
> (Extract from *Yes Minister – the Middle Class Rip off*)

In addition, certain goods and services provided by the state give benefit not just to the direct recipient of the good in question but to society at large. For example, inoculation against communicable diseases benefits not only the patient but also all those with whom he or she is likely to come into contact. In this case **positive external benefits** are said to exist and their existence can be used to justify the provision of treatment below cost or at zero price.

Finally, some areas of public spending, particularly that on education and health care, can be considered as *investment spending* – in this case investment in human capital. The return yielded by this investment is in the form of a more productive workforce. It is argued that through ignorance or myopia individuals will tend to underinvest, preferring immediate consumption benefits. The state, taking a longer view, channels resources away from immediate consumption (by taxing people's incomes) and towards investment in those areas which increase the productive capacity of the economy in the longer term.

Summary

State intervention in market economies takes a variety of forms. This chapter has been principally concerned with public spending on goods and services, the rationale for which can be understood partly in terms of the 'public good' characteristics of non-excludability and non-rivalness associated with some areas of public spending. However, many goods and services provided publicly are both excludable and rival and here the merit good argument must be used to justify their provision by the state.

Key terms

Review questions

18.1 State which of the following constitute expenditure on goods and services, and which are transfer payments:

unemployment benefit (Jobseeker's Allowance)

supplementary benefit payments

student grants

teachers' salaries

salaries of social workers

spending on the school dental service

spending on education (such as the subsidy paid to the Student Loans Company).

18.2 Consider the extent to which the following are either non-excludable or non-rival or both:

television broadcasts   McDonald's hamburgers

the M1 motorway   the pavement outside McDonald's

the River Thames   navigation buoys.

18.3 The Arts Council receives considerable amounts of public money. How can this be justified?

18.4 The Department of Transport is particularly keen to present a favourable public image. To this end when carrying out road improvement schemes it erects large notices bearing the legend 'Investing in roads' and informing drivers how much is being spent on the scheme in question. Drivers have plenty of time to ponder on this as they sit in the traffic jam caused by the road scheme.

Why do you think the Department of Transport uses the word *investment* here?

18.5 In 1997 unemployment benefit was renamed 'the Jobseeker's Allowance' and the rules governing eligibility for payment were tightened. Explain the rationale for this.

18.6 In 1994 the Government launched a campaign to persuade parents to have their babies vaccinated against measles. Explain:

(a) why it is sensible to subsidize this service;

(b) in what circumstances it might be sensible to provide it at zero cost or to provide a cash incentive to persuade parents to have their babies vaccinated;

(c) why it might be rational for an individual parent to persuade others to have their children vaccinated but not to have their own vaccinated.

19 Public corporations

Preview

Various acts of nationalization enacted by the post-war Labour Government brought into public ownership substantial sectors of the UK economy. The Conservative Government of 1979–97 reversed this policy and a new word entered the language – privatization. This chapter considers the rationale for public ownership and appraises the merits of privatization. Some evidence on the efficiency of nationalized industries is reviewed.

19.1 Public corporations and nationalized industries

In Section 18.1 we identified a number of broad areas of state intervention in market economies. One of these was the ownership and control of certain industrial resources – the nationalized industries. It is to this form of state intervention that we now turn.

The term **public corporation** is the official designation given to bodies that are publicly owned (that is, state owned) yet are outside the sectors controlled directly by central government or by local authorities. Most public corporations engage in commercial activities but are independent of the government and Parliament in the day-to-day management of their commercial and financial affairs, though they are subject to constraints on their borrowing. Table 19.1 gives a list of some of the more important public corporations in existence at 31 December 1995, together with the so-called 'vesting date' (the date when they were created).

Table 19.1 Public corporations in existence at 31 December 1995[1]

	Commencing or vesting date
Audit Commission	1983
British Broadcasting Corporation	1927
British Coal[2]	1947
British Nuclear Fuels plc (reclassified to the public sector since 1994)	1971
British Railways Board[3]	1963
British Waterways Board	1963
Caledonian Macbrayne	1990
Channel Four Television Company (formerly part of the ITC)	1980
Civil Aviation Authority	1972
Commonwealth Development Corporation	1948
Covent Garden Market Authority	1961
Crown Agents & Crown Agents Holding & Realisation Board	1980
Highlands and Islands Enterprise (formerly H&I Development Board)	1965
Her Majesty's Stationery Office (HMSO)	1980
Independent Broadcasting Authority	1972
Land Authority for Wales	1976
Local authority airports	1987
Local authority bus companies	1986
London Regional Transport	1970
National Health Service Trusts	1991
New Town Development Corporations and Commission	1946 and various later dates
Northern Ireland Housing Executive	1971
Northern Ireland Transport Holding Company	1968
Nuclear Electric (formerly part of the CEGB)	1989
Passenger Transport Executives	1969 and various later dates
Oil and Pipelines Agency	1985
Post Office	1961
Royal Mint	1975
Scottish Enterprise (formerly Scottish Developemnt Agency)	1975
Scottish Nuclear plc (part of the former South of Scotland Electricity Board)	1989
Trust Ports in Northern Ireland	1974
United Kingdom Atomic Energy Authority	1986
Urban Development Corporations	1981,1987,1988

Notes:
1 Only the more important of the Public Corporations are shown here. For a complete listing see the source quoted.
2 British Coal (formerly the National Coal Board) was privatized in 1996.
3 Renamed as British Rail and privatized in 1996.
Source: *National Income and Expenditure*, 1996, explanatory notes.

As can be seen, the public corporations form a heterogeneous group whose only common feature is their status as commercially independent but publicly owned corporations. The histories of these corporations, and the reasons for their existence, are as varied as their trading activities. Many were set up by the post-war Labour Government – corporations such as British Coal (formerly the National Coal Board, now once again back in the private sector after its privatization in 1996). Others – such as London Regional Transport – were set up to administer functions previously carried out by local authorities. Some were set up as regulatory bodies to cope with newly emerging needs – for example, the Independent Broadcasting Authority and the Civil Aviation Authority. Others, such as the Post Office, had been in existence as government departments for many years before being officially reclassified as public corporations.

As a group, the public corporations at one time formed a significant sector of the national economy. In 1983 they accounted for 10.7 per cent of GDP and 16 per cent of Fixed Capital Formation (Investment). They employed about 1.7 million people (about 7 per cent of the labour force). However, the size of this sector shrank as the Conservative Government of 1979-97 proceeded with its plans to privatize large parts

Table 19.2 Major privatizations

British Petroleum	1979/83/87
British Aerospace	1981
Enterprise Oil	1984
British Telecom	1984
British Shipbuilders	from 1984
Trust Ports in Great Britain	1985
British Gas	1986
British Airways	1987
Royal Ordnance	1987
BAA	1987
National Bus Company	1988
27 Local Authority Bus Companies	1988–94
British Steel	1988
General Practice Finance	1989
Regional Water Authorities, Welsh Water Authority and Water Authorities Association	1989
Liverpool Airport	1990
Girobank	1990
Regional Electricity Companies and National Grid Company	1990
National Power, PowerGen (formerly the CEGB)	1991
British Technology Group	1992
Belfast International Airport	1994
British Coal (coal mines)	1994
Railtrack	1994

Source: derived from *UK National Accounts*, 1996, explanatory notes.

of the public sector and by 1997 few significant public corporations remained. Table 19.2 shows some of the major privatizations.

Some of the more newsworthy privatizations are missing from this list. The reason for this is to do with the activities of the British Technology Group (itself a public corporation). Formerly known as the National Enterprise Board, this had acted as a sort of state holding company for shares bought from the private sector or acquired in some other way. Thus, for example, British Technology Group had held shares in Rolls Royce, ICL (computers), Jaguar and Rover. When these shares were returned to the private sector the resulting transaction did not, strictly speaking, result in a change in the legal status of the company, since these companies had never had a legal existence as public corporations. Nevertheless, transactions such as the sale of Rolls Royce to the public in 1987 are normally regarded as part of the privatization programme even though for the reason outlined above they do not appear in the official list of reclassifications.

19.2 Reasons for nationalization

This chapter is principally concerned with various aspects of the privatization debate. It is first necessary, however, to consider the reasons why the former nationalized industries were originally taken into public ownership. As we have already indicated, these reasons vary from case to case. On a general level, however, it is well known that Clause 4 of the Labour Party's Constitution talked of 'the public ownership of the means of production, distribution and exchange' as a specific political objective. Taken literally, this would have meant nationalizing everything and, while some members of the Labour Party would still support this objective, most did not. More usually, the clause was interpreted to refer to the nationalization of certain key industrial and commercial sectors – the **commanding heights of the economy**. This provided the justification, if not the rationale, for the post-war acts of nationalization.

The economic case for the public ownership of certain industries rests on a number of general principles. Keynes, the acknowledged founder of modern macroeconomics, talks in his *General Theory*[1] of the **stabilizing influence** that a sizeable public sector would have on the economy. It is well known that a market economy without a significant public sector is prone to suffer cycles in economic activity which periodically produce booms and slumps. This is principally because the investment behaviour of private-sector firms is very volatile. In periods when the growth of sales appears to falter, firms cut or delay their investment in new productive capacity. This reduction in investment spending induces a further decline in demand. The economy enters a recession from which it will not automatically extricate itself. The investment spending of the public sector would be less volatile, Keynes argued, and this would tend to reduce the oscillations in economic activity. Moreover, the ability to control large public-sector enterprises would give the government a useful additional instrument of macroeconomic management which could be used as part of an active countercyclical demand management policy. That is, investment spending in the public sector could be boosted to take up the slack in private-sector demand when necessary, and conversely spending by the public-sector corporations could be held back when the economy showed signs of overheating. This then was the macroeconomic case for a public sector in general and, by extension, the case for the public ownership of key industrial sectors.

In addition, certain of these key industrial sectors are what are known as **natural monopolies**. That is, they are industries which can only be run efficiently if one firm supplies the whole market. To allow competition between rival firms would result in wasteful duplication of services. Examples of natural monopolies are electricity distribution (it would not be sensible to allow rival companies to erect transmission lines for electricity), gas distribution, postal deliveries, the railways, water supply and sewage disposal. If such a monopoly were in private hands, it is argued, it could operate against the public interest. A monopolist who pursues the objective of profit maximization will use his market power to raise prices and restrict supply. Since, by definition, barriers to the entry of new firms exist, super-normal profits will continue to accrue to those private individuals who own the monopoly firm. Therefore, it is argued, the private-sector monopolist should be taken into public ownership so that prices can be controlled and output expanded.

Moreover, many of the natural monopolies are thought to have some strategic significance, in the sense that they were important to the defence and security of the state – for example, energy supplies and communications. This reinforced the case for state control of such industries. Ownership, through nationalization, ensures this overall control. In addition to their strategic significance, these industries also form an important part of the infrastructure of the economy – transport, communications, energy supplies, and so on. Since infrastructure is an important prerequisite for the growth and development of the economy, the state may wish to direct investment resources into those areas as a means of promoting economic growth in the economy as a whole.

The foregoing arguments apply to many of the industries which were taken into public ownership. However, the specific circumstances of each individual case are as important as the general case for public ownership. For example, in 1948 the railways were nationalized because they were then in poor condition and would not have been able, in private hands, to attract the necessary investment capital for modernization. Many of the nationalized industries had an equally inauspicious start in life. In 1967, for example, the British Steel Corporation was formed from thirteen separate steel companies which were 'already in a difficult and deteriorating position. In 1957–58 they had earned a net profit of over £400m; by 1962–63 this had fallen to around £200m, and during 1967–68, which was the Corporation's first year, the figure was less than £60m. This represented a return of only 0.5 per cent on net assets at replacement cost.'[2]

The British Steel Corporation came into existence because the government of the day wished to increase concentration in the industry as a means of promoting efficiency. The government of the day was instrumental in the mergers which gave birth to BSC. Similarly, the government was instrumental in promoting the merger activity in the motor industry which eventually produced British Leyland in 1968. BL was taken into public ownership in 1975. In 1988, renamed the Rover Group, it was sold back to the private sector, its shares being sold at a knockdown price to British Aerospace plc. British Aerospace itself had been formed in 1977 as a result of a government-sponsored merger between Hawker Siddley and the British Aircraft Corporation, firms which had both received substantial amounts of government money in the past. In 1979 the incoming Conservative Government began divesting itself of the BAe shares which it owned, the final tranche being sold in 1985.

19.3 Reasons for privatization

It is probably true to say that, following the acts of nationalization, the Labour Party never really knew what to do with the nationalized industries – how they should be regulated, what pricing and investment policies they should pursue, and so on. Mrs Thatcher, however, when she came to power in 1979, knew exactly what to do with them. The Conservative Government's plans for the nationalized industries became increasingly clear in the early 1980s, as the following three quotations show.

> *It remains our purpose, wherever possible, to transfer to the private sector assets which can be better managed there.*
>   (Sir Geoffrey Howe, Chancellor of the Exchequer, Budget speech, 9 March 1982)

> *Privatisation represents by far the most effective means of extending market forces, and in turn of improving efficiency and the allocation of resources.*
>   (Lord Cockfield, then Minister of State, Treasury, 19 November 1981)

> *It must be right to press ahead with the transfer of ownership from the state to private enterprise of as many public sector businesses as possible… The introduction of competition must, whenever possible, be linked to a transfer of ownership to private citizens and away from the state. Real public ownership – that is, ownership by the people – must be and is our ultimate goal.*
>   (Mr Nicholas Ridley, Financial Secretary to the Treasury, 12 February 1982)

From these statements, one is left in no doubt that the intention was to privatize large parts of the public sector, particularly public corporations, and the rationale for so doing rests on the following two propositions. First, privatization ensures competition and, secondly, competition ensures efficiency.

Privatization ensures competition?

The first of these two propositions is clearly wrong, or at least is correct only in a restricted context. A nationalized industry that monopolizes the market which it serves and is returned intact to the private sector is still a monopoly. A state monopoly has merely been replaced by a private-sector one. In the market for its product there has been no increase in competition as a result of privatization. The term **liberalization** has been coined to refer to the introduction of competition into an erstwhile protected monopolistic industry. Clearly, privatization does not ensure liberalization. The two things are quite distinct. Moreover, while it is relatively easy to privatize an industry, it may be much more difficult to liberalize it. Many of the former nationalized industries were natural monopolies, as we have already noted. Moreover, it would be absurd to suggest that such industries could be split up into atomistically competitive firms – indeed, any sort of competition is wasteful in industries such as water supply and electricity distribution where scale economies are such an important feature. Thus for example the privatization of British Telecom did not in itself increase competition in the industry since it was sold off as a single entity. BT's statutory monopoly had been rescinded some years earlier and this did more to liberalize the industry than was achieved by privatization *per se*. Similarly, British Gas was sold off as a single entity, since it was argued at the time that to split it up would have been neither economically desirable nor feasible.

Although it is clearly wrong to equate privatization with an increase in competition in the market for its product, a privatized industry is in a sense exposed to competition on the Stock Market. That is, its shares are in competition with the shares of all other companies and the value of those shares reflects the profitability of the company. Nationalized industries, on the other hand, are not subject to the discipline of the market. They can never suffer the ultimate sanction – liquidation – since their losses will always be made good by the government. It is in this sense, and in this sense only, that privatization *per se* exposes the industry to competition: what may be termed competition in the capital market.

A privatized firm will face competition in the capital market regardless of the market structure in which it finds itself. However, if the firm is indeed a monopolist the argument about the benefits of stock-market competition then loses much of its force, since the absence of competition in the market for its product means that the firm can make profits, not by increasing efficiency and cutting costs, but by simply raising prices. A firm's Stock Market valuation (that is, the price of its shares on the Stock Exchange) reflects not its efficiency but its profitability. Efficiency and profitability are two different things.

Competition ensures efficiency?

The second proposition on which the justification for privatization rests – that competition ensures efficiency – is also open to question. Even if we assume that the industry can be liberalized, such liberalization will clearly not result in a market structure which is anything like a perfectly competitive one. Rather, it will be an oligopolistic market. As we saw in Chapter 9, the behaviour of firms in oligopolistic markets may be competitive, but it may also be collusive. If competition does emerge, it is unlikely to be price competition: non-price competition is much more usual.

We cannot, however, make any general statements on the basis of our analysis about the efficiency of firms in oligopolistic industries. A crucial problem is that we have not yet defined what efficiency is. The debate about the efficiency of nationalized industries relative to private-sector firms is, however, a debate which predates the current spate of privatizations. Nor is the debate confined to the UK, since all market economies have some state-owned industries. What we shall do in section 19.5 is to summarize the evidence that has been collected on this issue. Before we can do this, however, we need to say something about the pricing strategies adopted by nationalized industries and the objectives they pursue.

19.4 Pricing strategies in nationalized industries

The pricing strategies pursued by nationalized industries and the objectives they pursue are clearly related issues. If a private-sector company pursues profit maximization, this has clear implications for the prices it will charge. They will be profit-maximizing prices, not necessarily in the sense that the firm consciously equates marginal cost to marginal revenue, but in the sense that the firm feels its way by a process of trial and error towards prices that maximize the firm's profits. For a nationalized industry, however, particularly a monopolistic one, the pursuit of maximum profit is not necessarily an appropriate objective.

With the growth of the nationalized industry sector in the post-war period it was recognized that guidelines needed to be laid down governing the pricing and investment strategies pursued by nationalized industries. Economists at the time were closely wedded to the idea of **marginal cost pricing** for nationalized industries. Prices, they argued, should be set equal to the marginal production cost of the good or service in question. The reason for the advocacy of marginal cost pricing stemmed from a rather literal interpretation of the Pareto welfare analysis set out in section 14.1. Recall that, according to this analysis, if all goods were sold on markets where prices were set equal to marginal cost, then a Pareto optimal allocation of society's resources would result. Therefore, the economists argued, nationalized industries should set their prices equal to marginal costs, since this would lead society as a whole to gain the maximum benefit from the operation of such industries.

Limitations of marginal cost pricing

The guidelines for pricing and investment were set down in a series of government White Papers in 1961, 1967 and 1978. (A White Paper is a document which lays down in general terms the policy to be followed.) For a number of reasons, however, it came to be realized that a strict adherence to the marginal cost pricing principle was neither desirable nor feasible. These reasons stemmed both from developments in the theory of welfare economics itself and from an increasing realization of the impracticality of applying the policy prescriptions which emanated from it.

On the theory side, economists recognized that nationalized industries operated in an environment where most firms' prices were *not* equal to marginal cost. If nationalized industries were to set price equal to marginal cost when prices were above marginal cost in the private sector generally, this would lead to a misallocation of society's resources. Consider the following hypothetical example of an economy in which there are only two sources of energy, both indigenous. The oil industry is in private hands and the gas industry is state owned. Prices are set equal to marginal cost for gas, but are above marginal cost for oil. Table 19.3 summarizes this.

Consider the choice facing the consumer who is considering how to heat his or her home in winter. The decision will be based on the set of relative prices – in this case the price of oil relative to the price of gas – but in this instance relative prices do not reflect relative scarcities. The price of gas is too low relative to the price of oil so that the price

Table 19.3 Example: energy pricing

Private sector	Public sector
Oil	Gas
P > MC	P = MC

ratio between the two does not reflect the relative cost of producing gas in comparison with the cost of producing oil. Because prices for gas are 'too low', demand for gas will be higher than it would otherwise have been. Too large a proportion of society's resources will flow into gas production, and too small a proportion into oil production. Recognizing this, economists developed the **general theory of the second best**. In a first-best world (in which all other prices are equal to marginal cost) nationalized industries should also set price equal to marginal cost. But in a second-best world, where in the private sector price exceeds marginal cost, nationalized industries should emulate the behaviour of private-sector firms. In other words, if prices in the private sector exceed marginal cost by 10 per cent then nationalized industries should set their prices on the same basis. In this way, a Pareto optimal allocation of resources is still assured, even in this second-best world.

Although the general theory of the second best clears up a problem in welfare theory, it leaves untouched the thorny problem of how marginal cost is to be measured. It is not at all clear what 'marginal cost' means in practice. Economists know what it means in theory. It is the first derivative of the total cost function. Less mathematically, it is the increase in total costs which results from the production of one extra unit of output. In the real world, however, there are **indivisibilities**. For example, on the railways the marginal cost of carrying an extra passenger when there are still empty seats on the trains that are running is virtually zero. When the train is full, however, the marginal cost of carrying an extra passenger is the cost of putting an extra coach on the train, or of running an extra train. To adhere strictly to marginal cost pricing would result in most passengers paying almost nothing, and one extremely unfortunate passenger paying a very high price indeed. In addition, in calculating marginal costs some account must be taken of capital costs. In electricity generation, for example, the short-run marginal cost of power generation is the fuel cost alone. But if prices to the consumer took into account only fuel costs, then the industry would not be raising sufficient revenue to cover the depreciation of its generating capacity, nor to pay for new capacity. A related point is that firms which are subject to substantial scale economies cannot hope to cover all their operating costs if they set price equal to marginal cost. To see why this should be so, consider Fig. 19.1, which shows a typical declining cost firm (or industry). The downward-sloping long-run average cost (LRAC) curve indicates that unit costs fall as the level of output rises. Such cost conditions are typical in capital-intensive industries such as electricity generation and telecommunications. It can be demonstrated (see section 5.3) that if average costs are declining then marginal cost must be less than average cost, as in Fig. 19.1. If the firm sets price equal to marginal cost and charges a price of P_1, then losses

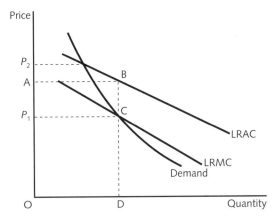

Figure 19.1 In declining cost industries marginal cost is less than average cost

will result. This is because the firm's total revenue which is equal to the rectangle OP_1CD is less than its total costs represented by the rectangle OABD. (Remember that total revenue is equal to the revenue per unit, OP_1, multiplied by the number of units sold, OD. Similarly, total costs are the costs per unit, OA, multiplied by the number of units produced OD.) The firm therefore makes losses equal to the rectangle P_1ABC.

In order to 'break even', the firm must set price equal to average cost rather than marginal cost and charge a price of P_2 (Figs 19.1 and 19.2). At this price and with output restricted to OZ, both total revenue and total cost can be represented by the rectangle OP_2YZ. This seems to mean that the firm is making zero profits. If we remember, however, that our definition of cost includes a normal return to capital, what this really means is that the firm is making zero *super-normal* profits.

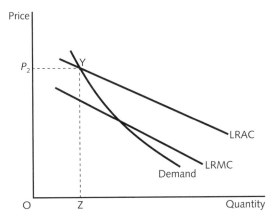

Figure 19.2 The industry breaks even if price is set equal to average cost

Controls on pricing and investment

For the reasons set out above, successive White Papers on the nationalized industries tended to move away from an advocacy of marginal cost pricing. In its place they substituted the requirement that nationalized industries should set their prices in such a way that the industry met the financial target imposed upon it. This financial target was in the form of a prescribed rate of return on the value of the assets employed in the industry. This rate of return could obviously be varied from time to time by the government. A problem existed, however, in that the valuation of the assets employed in the industry was by no means straightforward. Different approaches produced different estimates of the value of assets and it was not possible to say objectively which is 'correct'. The major area of disagreement centres around whether assets should be valued at their historical cost (minus an allowance for depreciation) or at their replacement value. The latter would normally have given a much higher value.

In addition to financial targets, nationalized industries were also subject to two additional controls. Both of these controls affected the industry's investment and, therefore, indirectly the prices it could charge. The first requirement was that an investment project could only be undertaken if it would yield the **required rate of return (RRR)**. This RRR was normally 5 per cent in real terms (that is, after allowing for inflation and using standard discounted cash flow techniques). Additionally, the borrowing which the industry undertook to finance its investment was subject to an **external financing limit (EFL)**. This effectively put a ceiling on the amount of capital that the industry could raise on the capital market in any one financial year. The implication of this may have been to deprive the industry of the investment funds needed to purchase new capital equipment.

19.5 The efficiency of public-sector industries

We saw in section 19.3 that the advocates of privatization argued that the efficiency of the nationalized industries would be increased if they were transferred to the private sector. Implicit in this view is the belief that nationalized industries are inherently less efficient than similar industries in private hands. It also implies, in particular, that the record of the nationalized industries in Britain shows evidence of inefficiency.

In this section we review some of the evidence on the relative efficiency of public- and private-sector firms. We have already noted that profitability is a poor measure of efficiency. Profits depend, among other things, on the prices charged and these were often held artificially low in nationalized industries as part of the anti-inflation policy of the government of the day. An alternative measure of efficiency therefore needs to be found, and several writers have used 'productivity' indices as yardsticks. Labour productivity can be calculated by dividing output by labour input. That is:

$$\text{output per employee} = \text{labour productivity} = \frac{\text{value of output}}{\text{labour input}} \qquad [19.1]$$

The denominator in the expression 'labour input' can be measured by the number of employees. The numerator, however, is measured in value terms, rather than in volume terms. (It would be possible to measure output in volume terms if it were homogeneous – for example, tons of coal – but comparisons of labour productivity in different industries would not then be possible). This immediately casts doubt on the validity of the index as a true measure of efficiency since variations in prices will affect the value of output and hence the value of labour productivity.

A more serious objection is that other factors of production in addition to labour are involved in the production process. The most important of these, of course, is capital. Capital-intensive industries, like telecommunications and electricity generation, therefore have high levels of labour productivity in comparison with labour-intensive industries like postal services, but this says nothing about their relative efficiency.

A better measure of efficiency would take account of both the labour and capital used in production. These factor inputs would perforce have to be measured in value terms. Although the value of labour input can be measured quite simply by the wages bill, the value of capital input is much more difficult to determine. Usually some arbitrary assumption is made. For example, the value of capital input is equal to 10 per cent of the value of the industry's capital stock. In this way a (somewhat questionable) measure of the value of total factor inputs is obtained and from this a measure of **total factor productivity**, so called, can be derived. Thus:

$$\text{total factor productivity} = \frac{\text{value of output}}{\text{value of labour input} + \text{value of capital input}}$$

Alternatively, the *rate of growth* of either labour productivity or total factor productivity can be used. This overcomes – or sidesteps – many of the practical difficulties involved in making efficiency comparisons on the basis of observed productivity levels. Table 19.4 shows the rate of growth of productivity of certain selected nationalized industries in comparison with UK manufacturing industry generally.

No definitive conclusions can be drawn from this table. In general, it appears that industries that did badly in the earlier period fared rather better in the latter. However, the performance of industries such as telecoms, gas and electricity showed little change.

Some authors are critical of the use of the sort of 'productivity' measures used in Table 19.4. Such measures, they argue, are meaningless because they are influenced by the price movements of both inputs and outputs. This argument has particular force in the case of industries that have some monopolistic power and are therefore able to influence these prices.

A further difficulty is apparent from Table 19.4, namely that the nationalized industries do not form a homogeneous group. British Telecom, British Airways and British Gas apparently secured large increases in 'productivity'. These three industries were in a particularly favoured position, however. They were capital-intensive industries and during this period improvements in technology enabled large increases in productivity to be secured. British Airways, for example, benefited from the introduction of wide-bodied jets; British Gas benefited from the exploitation of North Sea gas; and British Telecom from the general advances in electronics. Moreover, the demand for the

Table 19.4 Rate of change of productivity in selected nationalized industries
(% per annum)

	Output per head		Total factor productivity	
	1968–78	1978–85	1968–78	1978–85
British Rail	0.8	3.9	n.a.	2.8
British Steel	–0.2	12.6	–2.5	2.9
Post Office	–1.3	2.3	n.a.	1.9
British Telecom	8.2	5.8	5.2	0.5
British Coal	–0.7	4.4	–1.4	0.0
Electricity	5.3	3.9	0.7	1.4
British Gas	8.5	3.8	n.a.	1.2
National Bus	–0.5	2.1	–1.4	0.1
British Airways	6.4	6.6	5.5	4.8
UK Manufacturing	2.7	3.0	1.7	n.a.

Source: quoted in J. Vickers and G. Yarrow, *Privatization: an economic analysis*, 1988. The studies on which this is based are those by Pryke (1981) and Molyneux and Thompson (1987).

output of these industries was increasing. The electricity industry was similarly favoured, though not to the same extent, as demand was not increasing as fast and unit costs were rising. In contrast, most of the other nationalized industries were suffering a decline in the demand for their output. Costs were, in most cases, rising, necessitating price increases which further depressed demand.

The only conclusion that emerges from Table 19.4 is that some nationalized industries did better than the average for manufacturing industry generally, and others did worse. Those that did better were the industries with generally favourable demand and cost conditions. Those that did worse had unfavourable demand and cost conditions. No general conclusion can therefore be reached about the relative efficiencies of public ownership versus private ownership, even if we accept the view that 'productivity' indexes do in fact measure efficiency.

Some writers argue that a more satisfactory approach to the general question of whether public ownership affects efficiency is to compare the performance of public- and private-sector firms operating in the same industry. Opportunities for doing this are relatively rare, but Millward[3] reported the results of a number of such studies. In Canada there were two main railway companies, the publicly owned Canadian National and the privately owned Canadian Pacific, operating in competition with each other over many routes. The major conclusion Millward drew was that there was no significant evidence that productivity was lower in Canadian National than in Canadian Pacific. A study of Australian airlines where a public firm (Trans-Australian Airways) coexisted with a private firm (Ansett Transport Industries) produced broadly similar conclusions. Millward's third case study was that of electricity supply in the United States, where a large number of firms, some public and some private, supplied the nation's power. Because of its relevance to the general issue of whether public ownership affects efficiency, this industry has been subject to scrutiny by a number of authors. In reviewing these studies, Millward concludes that 'none of the cost studies support the proposition that public electricity firms have lower productivity or higher unit costs than private firms', allowing for differences in factor prices and the size of plant. Similar conclusions emerge from studies of unit costs in areas such as water supply and refuse collection. (Economists, as Millward once remarked, always end up talking rubbish.)

19.6 Privatization and the PSBR

The academic studies cited in the previous section were all addressed to the central question of whether public as opposed to private ownership materially affected the managerial efficiency of firms. In the event, in the 1980s the Conservative Government's view that nationalization was synonymous with inefficiency came to be generally accepted and the privatization programme in Britain went ahead and gathered momentum. In addition to being spurred on by the desire to 'roll back the frontiers of the state' it was also prompted by the desire to reduce government borrowing, known as the Public Sector Borrowing Requirement or **PSBR**.

A full analysis of the PSBR takes us into the realm of macroeconomics and hence is outside the scope of this book. Broadly speaking, however, the PSBR is equal to the financial deficit of the public sector, which is composed of central government, local authorities and public corporations. The financial deficit of the public corporations sector is the excess of its expenditure over its income in any one year. This excess is met by borrowing from the public, that is, from private individuals and financial institutions, by the issue of bonds and other debt instruments.

The Public Sector Borrowing Requirement, of which the Public Corporations Borrowing Requirement forms a part, was a key target of government policy. The objective was to reduce it to as low a level as possible, because it was seen as a burden on the economy. Whether or not this is a sensible interpretation of the PSBR will not be considered here. However, given that the government was pursuing the objective of reducing the PSBR, privatization was an excellent way of so doing.

This follows for three reasons. First, any public corporation which is incurring a deficit adds an equivalent amount to the government's spending and hence to its borrowing requirement. Secondly, and more importantly, borrowing by public corporations to finance future investment is treated as part of the PSBR even though this borrowing is really little different from the borrowing which private-sector firms undertake to finance investment. Because the public-sector firm is treated differently from the private-sector firm, however, any borrowing by a nationalized BT would have increased the PSBR (and was therefore a 'burden' on the economy) whereas borrowing by a privatized BT would not have increased the PSBR (and by definition would therefore not be a burden on the economy). This seems nonsensical but, like all sophistry, there is a grain, but only a grain, of truth in it. Private-sector companies, the argument runs, are ultimately subject to the discipline of the Stock Market. Investments must produce a return which in the long term is no less than the average return in the company sector generally. If not, the company's shares will fall in value and it will eventually be taken over or go into liquidation. Public-sector companies, on the other hand, are not subject to such discipline. Although their investments are required to earn a specified return, nationalized industries do not suffer a fall in their Stock Market valuation if the investments are unsuccessful. Their investments are, in a sense, underwritten by the government. They cannot go bankrupt. This therefore is the argument which is used to justify the inclusion of public corporations' borrowing as part of the PSBR and to view it as 'a burden on the economy'.

19.7 Regulating the newly privatized monopolies

Many of the former public corporations which were privatized by the Conservative Government were natural monopolies. Companies like BT and British Gas were sold off intact to become private-sector monopolies. In contrast, before it was sold off, the Central Electricity Generating Board was split up into National Power (with roughly 70 per cent of the assets) and PowerGen (with 30 per cent), the objective being to introduce some sort of competition into the industry. When the Area Electricity Boards were sold off, however, they retained for all practical purposes a local monopoly, as did the Regional Water Companies when they were privatized.

Because of the monopoly or near-monopoly position of some of these newly privatized companies, and the threat that this posed, the government established regulatory bodies whose job was to oversee the activities – and particularly the pricing behaviour – of such companies. The first of these was OFTEL (the Office of Telecommunications). BT, who had a near-monopoly position in the market for telecoms, was compelled to fulfil certain obligations such as the maintenance of the 999 emergency service, and to keep its price increases below the rate of inflation according to some **RPI-minus-x formula** (where x was set at 3 per cent). Notwithstanding this, however, BT made large profits in the period following privatization, as did British Gas and the Electricity and Water companies, which led some to argue that these companies were abusing their market power. Moreover, the efficacy of the regulators like OFTEL, OFGAS and OFWAT was questioned and they were accused of succumbing to **regulatory capture** – that is the regulators themselves were unduly influenced by the firms they were supposed to be regulating. It came to be realized that the regulation of private-sector monopolies was just as difficult as ensuring the efficiency of such industries when they were in the public sector.

Where possible, structural changes were proposed which would have the effect of introducing a greater degree of effective competition. In telecoms for example the Government sought to encourage other firms to enter the industry by licensing other operators, and by the mid-1990s a number a new entrants such as Mercury, Ionica and cable companies were offering customers alternatives to the BT service. Competition was also introduced into the supply of gas (though not into its distribution since this is a natural monopoly) and from 1996 customers in the South-West of England had a choice of suppliers from whom to purchase the gas that was delivered through Transco's pipes.

In 1997 the incoming Labour Government imposed a windfall tax on the profits of the newly privatized utilities. Their justification for this was twofold. First, they argued that the shares in the utilities had been sold off too cheaply when they were originally privatized, therefore enabling the companies to make a return on capital employed which was excessive when compared with the average return in industry generally. Secondly, it was an implicit recognition that the regulatory mechanism had not worked effectively and that the newly privatized utilities had indeed been abusing their monopoly positions.

Summary

The public corporations (or nationalized industries) formed a heterogeneous grouping which had been brought into public ownership at various times and for a variety of reasons. They constituted a significant sector of the economy (contributing over 10 per cent of GDP). The Conservative Government of 1979–97 sold many of these industries to the private sector because it believed that the assets could be better managed there, the argument being that exposure to market forces would increase efficiency. However, privatization does not necessarily ensure a more competitive environment for the firm. The introduction of competition (liberalization) may be more difficult to achieve since some of the newly privatized companies are still natural monopolies.

There had been a widespread belief that state-owned firms had been inefficient but the evidence on this is difficult to assess both because of the heterogeneous nature of the firms and because they often occupied a monopolistic position.

Notes

1 Keynes, J.M. (1939) *The General Theory of Employment, Interest and Money*.
2 Pryke, R. (1981) *The Nationalised Industries: Policies and Performance since 1968*, Martin Robertson, p.183.
3 Pryke, R. *Public Enterprise in Practice*, MacGibbon and Kee (1971); Pryke (1981) *op.cit.*; Millward, R. *et al.* (1983) *Public Sector Economics*, Harlow: Longman.

Key terms

public corporation	242	indivisibilities	250
commanding heights of the economy	245	required rate of return (RRR)	252
stabilizing influence of public sector	245	external financing limit (EFL)	252
natural monopolies	246	total factor productivity	253
privatization	247	PSBR	255
liberalization	247	RPI-minus-x formula	256
marginal cost pricing	249	regulatory capture	256
general theory of the second best	250		

Review questions

19.1 In 1983 the public corporations accounted for 16 per cent of total investment but only 10.7 per cent of output. Suggest reasons for the difference.

19.2 Consider the extent to which the former nationalized industries (listed in Table 19.2) constitute 'natural monopolies'.

19.3 Which of the following necessarily results from the privatization of a nationalized industry?
   (a) Selling off assets brings a windfall gain to the Treasury.
   (b) Privatization increases competition in the industry.
   (c) Privatization increases efficiency in the industry.

19.4 How might one best measure 'efficiency' in the operation of a nationalized industry which monopolizes the market which it serves? An 'efficient' industry is one which:
   (a) achieves a specified output level at least cost;
   (b) uses the minimum amount of resources to produce a particular output;
   (c) charges low prices;
   (d) achieves the highest profits;
   (e) has the greatest return on assets employed;
   (f) none of the above is a satisfactory definition of efficiency.

19.5 Suppose state-owned industries compete with private-sector companies whose prices exceed marginal cost. What does the theory of the second best advocate about prices in the state-owned industries?
   (a) The nationalized industries should still set price equal to marginal cost.
   (b) The state-owned industries should merely try to cover their total costs.
   (c) Prices in the state-owned industries should be above marginal cost.
   (d) The ratio of price to marginal cost should be the same in the nationalized industries as it is in the private sector.
   (e) Nationalized industries should behave commercially and try to maximize profits.

The producer, the consumer and the state

This is a concluding chapter only in the sense that it comes at the end of the book. It does not purport to come to any conclusions. The issues are too complex, the questions are too large and an introductory textbook is not the appropriate forum within which to state any conclusions, definitive or otherwise. It is not an indictment to say, as George Bernard Shaw did, that if all the economists in the world were laid end to end they still would not reach a conclusion. Rather it is a reflection of the complexity of the issues involved.

Nor does this short chapter attempt to summarize what has gone before, since any summary would be overly superficial. What it does is to restate and highlight some of the issues raised in this book. The readers can if they wish form their own conclusions. Be warned, however. If you think you know the answer it is probably because you do not fully understand the question.

An undercurrent in this book, implicit up to now, has been the relationship between the three *dramatis personae* in the economic system – the producer, the consumer and the state. The form of the relationship between these three characterizes the mixed economy. On the one hand, we have presented a model – that of Pareto welfare theory – which portrays the individual consumer as being sovereign. Producers – that is, firms – merely respond passively to consumers' wishes. There is no need for the state to intervene except in those few areas of market failure, principally those areas concerned with pure public goods like defence. Clearly, this view is untenable, however. Producers do not passively respond to consumers' wishes. Rather, they shape and manipulate those wishes through advertising and through the exercise of market power. Typically, markets in the real world are not atomistically competitive. They are oligopolistic, and much of Chapter 9 was devoted to the study of cases in which producers attempted to use and abuse their market power. The pursuit of self-interest by such firms does not, as Pareto claimed, lead to an allocation of resources which is optimal in any sense. It does not lead to the greatest happiness of the greatest number. There is a need for state intervention to curb the power of large firms when that power is abused.

Market failure – in the sense of externalities and public goods – is characterized in a Pareto model as a minor blemish on an otherwise perfect system. In fact, market failure runs through that system, touching every part. Externalities are all-pervasive in an industrialized, urbanized society. The public-good area is of major significance, shaping as it does the physical and social environment within which individuals live out their lives. The market mechanism cannot by definition provide an adequate supply of those public goods like universal health care and education and environmental services which become more important as society becomes more affluent. Again, there is need for state intervention in the provision of public goods and to address the problem of externalities.

There is, I would guess, an overwhelming consensus that some state intervention in these areas is both appropriate and desirable. There never can be any consensus, however, in deciding exactly how much state intervention is desirable. To what extent should private producers be free to pursue their self-interested – and indeed selfish – ends? To what extent should society's productive resources be in the untrammelled hands of private individuals, free to pursue those ends? And to what extent should the state intervene to correct for market failure? These questions are of course – as if you had not already realized it – political. Economics is political economy. It can never divorce itself from that no matter how much it pretends to be an objective, value-free science.

There is of course a political tide in Britain. That tide, which has been running in Britain for several years, has been referred to as 'rolling back the frontiers of the state'. It is about shifting the emphasis of our mixed economy away from increasing reliance on state intervention and towards greater reliance on market forces. Supply-side economics, it is sometimes called. What characterizes this policy is the view that an economy actually functions better – that is, is more productive – if individuals both as consumers and producers are motivated by the rewards and punishments that are an essential feature of the market mechanism. This view is, of course, based on a particular interpretation of how the market mechanism works and is open to challenge. In this book we have tried to give an analysis of how that market mechanism works. The reader should by now be aware that our analysis is not characterized by a world of competitive markets where price is determined by demand and supply (whatever that is), where producers passively respond to consumers' wishes and in which market failure is only a minor defect.

We have not set out in our analysis to persuade the reader into accepting any particular view about the appropriate role of the state. We shall not have failed, however, if the reader has been brought to a more informed agnosticism.

If you have found this chapter – and parts of this book – somewhat abstract and difficult to follow then relax for a moment and consider the view from the terraces…

OK, so here's the big picture. The most important item on the agenda in the latter half of the twentieth century has been the single issue of how society should organize its resources to produce the things that make life better. Should these things be organized by the market or should economic activity be planned centrally? The market mechanism versus state planning. And we now know the result. The market mechanism won. Or rather: market mechanism, one – state planning, nil, and the game didn't even have to go to extra time. The market mechanism simply proved itself to be the superior team and after 90 minutes they had, quite literally, delivered the goods. The goods and the services that people wanted because those things made their lives more comfortable, more enjoyable, more fulfilling. At least, on balance when compared with the alternative.

Many economists, like other observers, were quite surprised by the result. To some it seemed to be against the run of play – particularly in the 1960s when a superior Soviet technology had put the first man in space. It seemed as though the market mechanism team would be overrun – 'we will bury you', as team manager Kruschev had said.

But as the 1970s and 1980s wore on it became apparent that, although state planning was good at directing resources into a few specific production areas – it was good at producing armaments, space vehicles and very good at producing diminutive female gymnasts – these were not the things from which people derived utility. And even if they had wanted to, the managers of the State Planning team would not have been able to supply their supporters with those things they really wanted, because the things they really wanted kept changing and people's wants sometimes settled on new things which hadn't even been thought of before like digital watches, combined shampoo and conditioner, and heavy-metal music.

So State Planning lost the game, and its supporters trooped away disconsolately. This was a pity really, because although State Planning had been pretty useless, they hadn't been totally useless. They had shown some nice touches – a respect for art, for scholarship, for job security and stability. They had established priorities for basic health care and education which were not necessarily market driven.

But the worst part was that, in the wake of State Planning's defeat, the Market Mechanism team didn't have any opposition at all. And they were not really particularly good at producing some of the things from which people derived utility. OK, they were extremely good at producing what economists call private goods – the digital watches, combined shampoo and conditioner and heavy-metal music – but they were not very good when it came to what economists call public goods. You couldn't package up a sense of community and civic pride and sell it in small packets to individual consumers. For that you needed a social sense as well as a private one.

You remember Maggie Thatcher? Yeah, best thing that ever happened to this country, or so the *Sun* says. Well, she used to say, 'There is no such thing as society, only individuals and families,' and she was right too. Only trouble is there was some bloke in the paper the other day taking the mickey. Some article saying we shouldn't be building more roads. It said, 'There is no such thing as a traffic jam – only individual men and women in their cars.'

Answers to review questions

Chapter 2

2.1   (a) demand is inelastic
     (b) demand is elastic
     (c) unit elasticity.

2.2   Responses (c) and (d) are correct.

2.3   The *availability of substitutes* is the most important factor, but things such as the proportion of income spent on the good in question will also affect the elasticity of demand.

2.4   The demand for one particular brand of chocolate will be more elastic than the demand for chocolate generally. There are lots of close substitutes for Cadbury's Fruit 'n Nut but no substitutes for chocolate generally, as chocoholics know only too well.

2.5   There are more opportunities for substitution in the long run than there are in the short run. In the short run consumers are 'locked in' to a particular lifestyle. But in the longer run they can buy a more fuel-efficient car, they can get a job nearer home, or they can move nearer their work. Producers too will produce more economical cars but their development takes several years.

2.6   (a) margarine and butter – substitutes
     (b) petrol and motor vehicles – complementary goods
     (c) coffee and cocoa – substitutes
     (d) motor cycles and motor cycle helmets – complements
     (e) CD players and CDs – complements
     (f) coal and gas – substitutes
     (g) holidays in Ireland and holidays in Scotland – substitutes.
       If goods are substitutes the cross-price elasticity of demand is positive – if the price of one good goes up the demand for the other goes up.
       If goods are complementary to one another the cross-price elasticity of demand is negative.

2.7   An inferior good is one which has a negative income elasticity of demand.
     standard white loaves – inferior
     croissants – normal
     remould tyres – inferior
     Earl Grey tea – normal

colour television – normal

coffee – normal (though it depends what type of coffee you are talking about. Cheap powder coffee is inferior, freeze-dried granules are normal, ground coffee – as distinct from instant coffee – is normal)

rice – inferior

monochrome television – inferior

package holidays to Spain – inferior

Armani suits – normal.

2.8 Statement (d) is correct. So too, in a less technical way, is statement (a). Inferior goods are often of low quality (statement (c)) but this is not how they are defined.

2.9 The price of substitutes such as electricity, oil and coal has also increased, in some case by more than the increase in gas prices. Incomes have also risen and since gas is non-inferior this would also lead to an increase in demand.

2.10 Percentage change in price = 5%

Percentage change in demand = 20%.

So the price elasticity of demand would appear to be 4 (that is, demand is very elastic).

However, one would want to know what the other filling stations in the vicinity are doing. Are they matching price cuts or are they allowing this filling station to poach all their customers? And is Friday a typical day, or is demand always higher on Fridays than on other days?

2.11 Unlike other 'Easter Eggs' these eggs are eaten all the year round, though they are promoted more in the run-up to Easter. They are not perceived as a 'luxury' in the same way as other chocolate eggs – simply as a sweet snack.

2.12 Shops will tell you that it is because they are trying to make room for their Spring merchandise. In fact, it has got more to do with the elasticity of demand. In the run-up to Christmas consumers are gripped by a spending frenzy (which is a more colourful way of saying that demand is quite inelastic, and they are prepared to pay quite high prices). They are more price sensitive after Christmas, so shops have to lower prices to tempt them to buy.

2.13 (a) A tax on petrol will not have much effect on consumption. True.

(b) A tax on petrol will raise lots of revenue because demand is inelastic. Also true.

(c) A rise in incomes of 10 per cent will lead to an increase in the amount of petrol bought of more than 10 per cent. True. The rise will be 12 per cent.

(d) The price and quality of public transport, and the presence or absence of cycleways, will affect the elasticity of demand for petrol. True.

2.14 The price that Eurotunnel can charge is governed by the price and availability of substitutes – the ferries and the airlines. The fact that the Tunnel cost £10 billion to build, and that Eurotunnel has such a huge debt is irrelevant.

2.15 There are no close substitutes for milk (what else can you put on you cornflakes or in your tea?) but there are lots of substitutes for fruit juice – such as mineral water, cola, milk and fresh fruit.

2.16 A negative income elasticity of demand implies that the goods are inferior – people with higher incomes will tend to buy less of these goods.

Chapter 3

3.1 (a) The products being sold by different firms are more or less the same, i.e., they are homogeneous. Perfect competition.
   (b) There are barriers to the entry of new firms. Monopoly and oligopoly.
   (c) A few firms supply the whole market. Oligopoly.
   (d) There is extensive non-price competition. Oligopoly (possibly also imperfect competition).
   (e) Firms are price takers. Perfect competition.
   (f) Firms are price makers. All other market structures.
   (g) There are lots of suppliers with similar products which are only differentiated by branding. Imperfect competition.
   (h) It is easy for new firms to enter the market (and to leave it). Perfect competition and imperfect competition.
   (i) Existing firms enjoy cost advantages over new firms by virtue of their size. Oligopoly.
   (j) There are lots of traders and none can affect the price. Perfect competition.

3.2 minicabs in London – imperfect competition
   instant coffee – oligopoly (two firms supply most of the market)
   painters and decorators – imperfect competition
   potatoes – perfect competition
   confectionery (e.g., chocolate bars) – oligopoly (three firms)
   water and sewerage services in London – monopoly
   food retailing – oligopoly (the major multiples like Tesco, Sainsbury, Safeway and Asda have most of the market. There are also a large number of very small corner stores.)
   the foreign exchange market for sterling – perfect competition
   the 'rag trade' – imperfect competition
   tobacco and tobacco products – oligopoly (two main firms)
   postal deliveries – monopoly
   mobile phone services (i.e., not the handsets themselves) – oligopoly (two major suppliers)
   the domestic supply of mains gas – monopoly (though consumers in the South-West of England can now choose from about six rival suppliers. Competition is to be extended to the rest of the UK so it will become an oligopolistic market.)
   hairdressers – imperfect competition
   milk production – perfect competition
   motor cycles – oligopoly ('Big Four' Japanese producers have about 80 poer cent of the market)
   home delivery pizza restaurants – imperfect competition
   household detergents – duopoly.

3.3 (a) A perfectly competitive firm can sell as much as it likes at the prevailing market price. So there is no need – and no point – in advertising.
   (b) Only large firms (oligopolists and monopolists) are likely to use this form of advertising.

(c) Small firms in imperfectly competitive markets, such as hairdressers, local removal firms, painters and decorators, plumbers.

3.4 Only the perfectly competitive firm is a price taker. All of the others face a downward-sloping demand curve and hence have some discretion in setting prices.

3.5 The elasticity of demand depends on the availability of substitutes (or the perceived availability of substitutes). The message of Coca Cola's advertising is not that its product is superior to other colas but that these substitutes simply do not exist. Coke is it.

The production of flavoured carbonated water is not subject to large-scale economies. Transport costs per can are higher than the costs of the contents of the can. Therefore small local firms would be able to undercut the majors if the majors were to engage in price competition. To prevent this happening the majors spend huge amounts on promotion (direct advertising and sports sponsorship). Surveys have shown that the most recognized brand in the world is... Coca Cola.

3.6 Perfectly competitive markets, are characterized by *homogeneity* of the product. Such homogeneity enables consumers to check prices more easily, since they can compare like with like. Perhaps the EU's desire for standardization can be explained in terms of the desire to promote competition. Consumer protection is sometimes cited as the rationale though it is unclear why consumers need protecting from non-standard cauliflowers.

3.6 If rivals follow suit the increase in demand will not be as great as it would otherwise be, so demand is less responsive (less elastic) than it would have been. The correct response is (b).

3.7 The C_5 concentration ratio shows the proportion of the market (in this case the European market) supplied by the five largest firms. In clothing manufacture there are thousands of small firms, each with just a few employees. In motor vehicle manufacture there are only a few dozen firms in total and, as the estimates show, the top five firms supply more than half the market.

Chapter 4

4.1 (a) The demand curve for the raw material (cocoa) will shift to the right, causing both the price and the quantity traded to increase.

(b) This will cause the supply curve to shift to the left – less will be offered for sale at each price than previously. Hence equilibrium price rises and the quantity trade falls.

(c) The increase in the price of coffee will cause the demand curve for cocoa to shift to the right, causing an increase in equilibrium price and quantity.

The effect of the new bean will be to cause the supply curve to shift to the right causing price to fall and output to expand.

Thus the net effect on price is indeterminate. We can definitely say that equilibrium output will expand however.

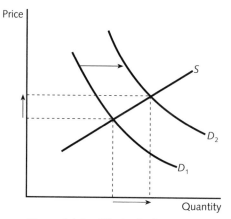

Figure A4.1a Effect of advertising campaign

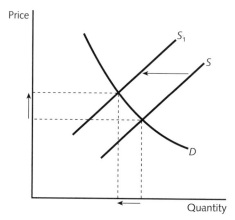

Figure A4.1b Effect of drought

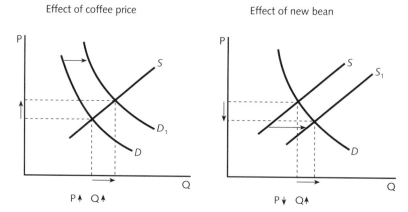

Figure A4.1c Combined effect of increase in the price of coffee and high yielding cocoa bean

4.3 (a) Over the period the percentage increase in output was much more than the percentage increase in price. Therefore the supply of this commodity is shown to be very *elastic*.

(b) The easier it is to switch from growing one crop to growing another, the more elastic will be the supply.

(c) Any estimate of the elasticity of supply is valid only if we are prepared to accept the assumption of *ceteris paribus*. In practice, other things may not remain the same. For example, the price of cereals and vegetable crops may also have increased.

(d) Switching from wheat production to rape production depends on relative prices – that is, the price of rape relative to the price of wheat.

4.4 (a) This will increase the demand for housing generally and hence push up house prices everywhere including Ealing.

(b) In effect, loans for house purchase become more expensive. Thus people will become more reluctant to borrow money for house purchase. This will reduce demand, depressing prices.

(c) Improved transport links will make Ealing more attractive, increasing the demand for houses there.

(d) This will expand the supply of new houses which will tend to reduce house prices *ceteris paribus*.

(e) These are substitutes. A rise in the price of a substitute will cause consumers to switch to a (cheaper) alternative so house prices in Ealing will receive a further boost.

(f) This is a supply-side effect which will tend to increase house prices.

(g) A demand-side effect which tends to increase house prices.

4.5 De Beers restricts the supply of diamonds on to the market ensuring that diamonds remain scarce and therefore command a high price. The price is not a 'market price'. Rather it is administered by de Beers.

4.6 Statements (b) and (c) are correct.

4.7 (a) An increase in recycling will reduce the demand for the virgin material. The demand curve shifts to the left. Price and output fall.

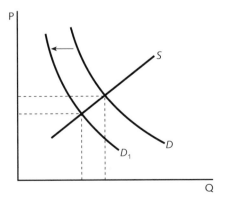

Figure A4.7a Reduced demand for aluminium

Coca Cola stops using aluminium

Increased productivity in bauxite production

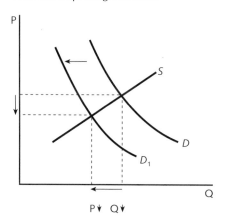

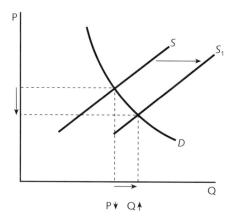

Figure A4.7b Coca Cola stops using aluminium and there is increased productivity in bauxite production

(b) The decision by the Coca Cola company will reduce the demand for aluminium. Price and output will fall. Increased productivity in bauxite production will shift the supply curve to the right. Price will fall, output will rise. In combination therefore price will definitely fall but output may rise or fall or stay the same.

Chapter 5

5.1 £5.

5.2 The marginal cost is zero.

5.3 All the diagrams are incorrect with the exception of diagram 3) showing that if AC is constant it must also be equal to MC.

5.4 Technical scale economies: large oil tankers. By doubling the external dimensions you more than double the carrying capacity.
Financial: large firms can borrow money more cheaply.
Managerial: large ships again. A ship needs more or less the same complement of crew regardless of size.
Marketing and R&D: motor vehicle manufacture, all sorts of consumer durables.
Risk bearing: running a fleet of buses: you need to keep vehicles in reserve to cover the possibility of breakdowns. The larger the fleet the smaller the proportion you need to keep in reserve.
   All of the above represent real savings of society's resources with the exception of financial scale economies.

5.5 Its revenues of £5100 cover all it variable costs and make some contribution to its fixed costs. If it closed in the winter its losses would be £1000 per month whereas

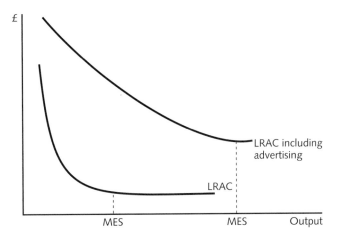

Figure A5.8 Advertising increases the minimum efficient scale

if it stays open its losses are only £900 per month. Hence it is better to stay open *provided* of course that its revenue in the summer is such that on a year round basis it makes a profit.

5.6 If the aircraft did not fly you could obviously save the cost of fuel (£11 882); landing fees and navigation charges ((£9920); passenger services (£15 870); and ground service (£17 200). Seemingly you should also count the salaries of the flight crew as a variable cost but you would probably have to pay them anyway whether the aircraft flew or not unless they are paid on a piece-rate basis, which is unlikely. The only truly fixed cost is the contribution to airline overheads (£68 350). Note, however, that these fixed costs exceed all the variable costs put together (which sum to £64 122). Since the airline will have to pay these costs regardless, it will be anxious to use its aircraft to the fullest extent to spread these huge fixed costs as thinly as possible.

5.7 There are large technical scale economies in refining and distribution, as well as some scale economies in marketing and R&D. Hence they can achieve lower unit costs by merging their activities.

5.8 Advertising acts as an artificial barrier to the entry of smaller firms. It raises the Minimum Efficient Scale. Small firms cannot enter the market because without heavy expenditure on advertising their products are unacceptable to the image-conscious consumer. But such advertising needs to be spread over a large number of units of output in order that the cost per unit can be kept down. Figure A5.8 illustrates this.

These companies spend huge amounts on advertising, and more importantly sponsorship. When sporting superstars such as golfers and motor-racing drivers are photographed they are often to be seen wearing a baseball cap bearing the logo of their sponsor. They are not wearing it to keep their head warm.

5.9 In effect, Fig. 5.15 is a long-run average-cost curve for the supply of gas. It has the 'classic' shape that we would expect from an LRAC curve.

Chapter 6

6.1 If demand is elastic it should lower the price to increase revenue.

6.2 Response (c) is correct.

6.3 The effect of a cut in fares would depend on the elasticity of demand for their services. Experience and empirical evidence suggest that demand is rather inelastic, so that a 10 per cent cut in fares increases demand by less than 10 per cent.

If they have spare capacity then costs will not rise by very much, if at all (their marginal cost is very low). But at peak times demand may run up against a capacity constraint so substantial additional costs may be incurred in providing extra trains and buses.

6.4 This depends on the extent to which the amount of other work the skilled workers can perform is reduced by the time they spend training apprentices. If all of their time is taken up as instructors then the real cost to the company of such a training scheme would be the value of the output these workers would have produced had they not been engaged in training.

6.5 Had they not been rescuing Mr Bullimore the Australian navy would have been tied up in port getting bored or otherwise engaged on training exercises. The salaries for the crew, the insurance for the ship and so on are all fixed costs which would have been paid regardless. The extra cost involved in rescuing the yachtsman would have consisted only of the fuel cost of the rescue.

6.6

	Price (£/p)	Marginal revenue (£/p)	Output	Total revenue (£)	Total cost (£)	Profit	Average costs (£/p)	Marginal cost (£/p)
A	1.00	0.80	3000	3000	2500	500	83	0.75
B	1.50	1.20	5000	7500	7500	0	1.50	1.20
C	1.00	0.90	5000	5000	5000	Zero SNP	1.00	0.90
D	1.20	1.50	4000					1.50
E	1.00	<£1	4000	4000	2500	1500	62.5	1.00
F	0.90	0.75	4000	3600	2000	1600	50p	50p

Firm A should reduce price and expand output.
Firm B should remain at present position.
Firm C should remain at present position.
Firm D – these figures are impossible. MR cannot be greater than P.
Firm E should increase price and reduce output.
Firm F should lower price and increase output.

Chapter 7

7.1 British Gas can store its output. The other utilities cannot.

7.2 This is an example of price discrimination. The demand by business users will be more inelastic, hence the rail operators charge higher prices from Monday to Friday and particularly at peak times. Outside these times, especially at weekends, the demand will be coming from private individuals who are more price sensitive. Lower prices tempt them to travel.

7.3 Most passengers on the ferries are individuals and families going on holiday. Certainly they are travelling for pleasure, in contrast to the business user who will choose the plane because it is quicker. For holidaymakers the peak time is the weekend – particularly Friday and Saturday – because most holidays tend to run from Saturday to Saturday. The ferry company therefore charges higher prices on Friday and Saturday – an example of price discrimination. On the airlines and on the trains most of the demand comes from business users and the peak demand is during the week with the weekend being a period of low demand – hence lower prices at that time.

Chapter 8

8.1 See definitions in text – these key words are in bold.

8.2 (a) Their salaries and their long-term prospects may be more dependent upon the growth of the firm – now and in the future – than on its current level of profitability.

(b) Growth may involving 'ploughing back' profits into investment, rather than paying these profits out to shareholders as dividends. If the dividends distributed to shareholders are low this will tend to depress the value of the company's shares, and if this happens the firm may fall victim to a take-over by another company which feels it can get a larger return on the capital employed. If the company is taken over the managers may lose their jobs.

(c) They may lack the necessary information about the elasticity of demand for their product, and of the various market segments.

8.3 The statement is false. The 'full cost' model of pricing behaviour (also known as the *mark-up* or *cost plus* model) is not incompatible with profit maximization.

8.4 Profit-maximizing models have a high *predictive* ability – that is, they can be used to analyse and predict how the firm will respond to a variety of situations. They do not describe the *process* used by firms in coming to their decisions.

8.5 The additional insight which this report may give you is that individual shareholders can have very little influence over the way a company is run, particularly if a large proportion of the company's shares are held by the so-called **institutional investors** – the life assurance and pension funds. The people who control these institutional investments are likely to support the status quo, even if it means siding with the likes of Mr Brown.

Chapter 9

9.1 (a) Prices in the industry will inevitably rise. FALSE

(b) The monopolist may choose not to maximize profits, so prices may not rise. This may be TRUE.

(c) The monopolist will have lower costs by virtue of his size so prices will fall. If you replace 'will' by 'may' this statement is OK.

(d) The monopolist may have lower costs by virtue of his size, but prices will rise if the monopolist exploits his market power. It depends on the extent of the cost reductions. The statement may or may not be true.

(e) The MES in the industry may be quite small so that further concentration does not lead to significant cost reductions. Possibly.

(f) Increased concentration at firm level will result in increased concentration at plant level. Unit costs will therefore fall. This does not follow.

9.2 The correct definition is (c).

9.3 The ease with which new firms can enter the market (and existing firms can leave it).

9.4 This is backwards (vertical) integration.

9.5 Diversification, and possibly (c) as well.

9.6 Neither of these two statements is necessarily true.

9.7 If an industry is characterized by substantial technical scale economies, small firms may be unable to operate plants of sufficient size to get the full benefit of these scale economies. If they were to merge their activities and close down smaller and less efficient plant then unit costs would fall and this may well be 'in the public interest'.

9.8 Companies selling a homogeneous product would like to differentiate their product from that of rivals so that they can then support the brand by advertising, charge a higher price and get bigger profits.

The star-octane rating system was brought in (by the government) as a form of consumer protection. Hence drivers would know what they were getting when they filled their tanks with a particular grade of petrol.

9.9 Responses (a) and (b) will increase the incentive to collude. Responses (c) and (d) will increase the incentive to compete.

9.10 The large supermarkets enjoy technical and managerial scale economies, enabling them to spread their fixed costs over a larger volume of output, which means they can sell more cheaply. These are *real* economies from which society as a whole benefits. However, they can also take advantage of their market power in their dealings with suppliers. While some of these suppliers may themselves be large powerful oligopolists like Heinz and Nestlé, others may be small local farmers who are forced to accept the terms and the prices which the large multiple offers, or go out of business. These economies resulting from the exploitation of market power are known as *financial* or *pecuniary* economies of scale – one firm benefits at the expense of others.

9.11 (a) The acquisition by British Airways of the package-tour operator, Airtours. Forwards vertical integration.

(b) The ownership of pubs ('tied houses') by the major brewers. Forwards vertical integration.

(c) The expansion by Sainsbury into the DIY market (Homebase). Diversification (into a related area).

(d) The ownership by the major ferry operators (P&O and Stena) of harbour facilities at Dover. Vertical integration (backwards).

(e) Expansion by Richard Branson's Virgin Group into the financial services industry. Diversification (into an unrelated area).

9.12 (a) A's minimax strategy is S_2 (leave prices unchanged). This minimizes the maximum loss the firm could suffer.

(b) S_3 will never be pursued since it is dominated by S_2. Whatever Firm B does, it would have been better to have played S_2 than S_3.

(c) Looking at the main diagonal one can see that demand for the industry as a whole is inelastic. If both firms raise prices then revenues increase and if both firms cut prices revenue falls.

Chapter 10

10.1 Renaissance Man: a person who typifies the renaissance ideal of *wide-ranging* culture and learning. Sadly, the Industrial Revolution brought an end to the renaissance ideal, since it required individuals to become *specialized*.

10.2 Producers in the Far East have a comparative advantage, mainly because cycle manufacture is rather labour intensive and labour costs are somewhat lower in the Far East. Costs are also lower there as a result of an acquired expertise in this specialist area. See 'learning by doing' and 'learning effect' in Chapter 5.

10.3 The table shows the number of units of labour input required to produce one unit of output in the clothing and domestic appliance industries in two hypothetical countries Alphaland and Betaland.

	Alphaland	Betaland
Clothing	5	7
Domestic appliances	50	63

(a) Does either country have an absolute advantage in both clothing and domestic appliances? Answer = yes, Alphaland.

(b) In Alphaland what is the opportunity cost of one domestic appliance? Answer = ten units of clothing. What is it in Betaland? Answer = nine units of clothing.

(c) Which country has a comparative advantage in appliance production? Answer = Betaland, because what you have to give up in Betaland (nine units of clothing) is less than what you have to give up in Alphaland (ten units of clothing).

(d) Which country has a comparative advantage in the production of clothing? Answer = Alphaland.

(e) What should Alphaland specialize in? Answer = clothing.

(f) Suppose a multinational conglomerate owns clothing factories and appliance factories in both countries. Assume that redundant appliance workers are always redeployed in the conglomerate's clothing factories, and *vice versa*. How much extra output could the conglomerate produce if it closed down its 1000 unit appliance factory in Alphaland and transferred appliance production to Betaland?

Answer = Closing down the Alphaland appliance factory would free $50 \times 1000 = 50\,000$ man-hours. If these man hours were transferred to clothing they would produce $50\,000/5 = 10\,000$ extra units of clothing.

Clothing production could therefore be cut by this amount in Betaland, freeing $10\,000 \times 7 = 70\,000$ man-hours. By transferring this labour to appliance production output could be increased by $70\,000/63 = 1111$ (approx).

This gives a net increase in appliance production of 1111 minus 1000 = 111 appliances.

(g) The ULRs shown in the table above are in physical units (man-hours or whatever). We could also show them in *value* terms (i.e., money terms) but we could only compare them if both countries used the same currency, or if we converted them into a common currency. Suppose we do the latter and choose the ECU to be that common currency.

If one man-hour costs one ECU the figures would remain unchanged. Suppose now, however, that wage rates in Alphaland increase by 50 per cent. The input requirements *measured in money terms* (in this case ECUs) would become

	Alphaland	Betaland
Clothing	7.5	7
Appliances	75	63

Which country now has a comparative advantage in the production of appliances? Answer = It's still Betaland.

(h) What would a profit-seeking multinational company do as a result of the wage rise described above? Answer = If it were 'footloose and fancy free' and it didn't worry about making people redundant in Alphaland then it would close down all its Alphaland factories.

(i) Suppose now the value of the alpha falls by 20 per cent on foreign exchange markets (the value of the beta remaining unchanged). What then would the multinational company do? (Construct a table similar to those above.)

Answer = The costs in Betaland remain the same at 7, 63. In Alphaland, however, the figures become 6, 60 (i.e., they fall by 20 per cent because they are measured in a common currency. One alpha now buys 20 per cent fewer ECUs on foreign exchange markets). The new input requirements thus become:

	Alphaland	Betaland
Clothing	6	7
Appliances	60	63

Note that the fall in the exchange rate has succeeded in re-establishing the competitiveness of Alphaland (which had been lost by the rise in wage costs). The multinational company will now close down all its factories in Betaland and transfer production to Alphaland. The point of this question is to show how the exchange rate affects competitiveness.

Chapter 11

11.3 There was a relatively cheap and compliant labour force in the UK. Transport costs were reduced. The fact that these Nissans now became 'British built' cars meant that they could be sold on the UK and continental European markets without restrictions – that is, they were not subject to import quotas.

11.4 Alphaland is a high tax country so the multinational would like to minimize the profits made (and therefore the tax paid) in Alphaland. Therefore they should charge a high price for gearboxes bought in from Betaland (300) and a low price for cars transferred from Alphaland for sale by the Betaland subsidiary (4000).

Chapter 12

12.1 utility = 'the power to satisfy the wants of people in general'

12.2 (b) and (e) (but if the jokes have to be explained then they're not funny).

12.3 Statement (a) illustrates it best.

12.4 *Crisps*   *Seven-up*
    MU = 12   MU = 14
     P = 20   P = 28
    12/20 = 0.6 > 14/28 = 0.5

So the consumer should buy more crisps, driving down the utility of the marginal packet. Statement (c) is correct (and so is (d)).

12.5 The price of colour sets stayed the same whereas the price of B&W sets fell. Since B&W sets became relatively cheaper the substitution effect would lead consumers to switch to this cheaper substitute and buy more B&W. However, B&W televisions are an inferior good. With rising incomes they will buy less of this inferior good. Since overall sales of B&W declined this is an example of the (negative) income effect outweighing the substitution effect.

Chapter 13

13.1 Continuous factor substitutability means that you can always use a little bit less fertiliser and a little bit more irrigation, or *vice versa*, while keeping output unchanged.

    The isoquants are convex to the origin. This means that, when only a small amount of fertiliser is being used, a little additional fertiliser can compensate for a large reduction in irrigation. Similarly, when a large amount of fertiliser is currently being used (and a small amount of irrigation) a little additional irrigation could offset the effect of a large drop in fertiliser application. Figure A13.1a shows the optimal factor mix at the point of tangency.

    When water prices rise the effect is to make the budget line steeper (the dotted line in Fig. A13.1b). If he keeps his spending at the old level he can no longer produce the same amount as before. If he wishes to keep output at I_0, he will have to

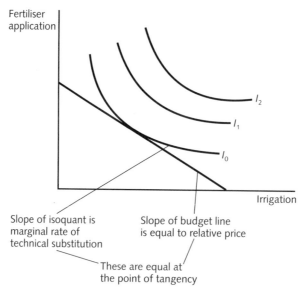

Slope of isoquant is
marginal rate of
technical substitution

Slope of budget line
is equal to relative price

These are equal at
the point of tangency

Figure A13.1a The optimal factor mix

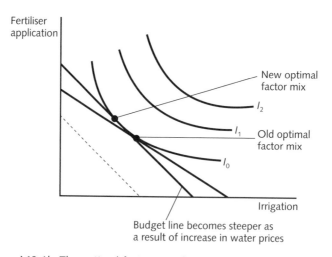

Budget line becomes steeper as
a result of increase in water prices

Figure A13.1b The optimal factor mix changes when water prices rise

spend more, but at the new set of relative prices, so the budget line must be moved
out, giving a new point of tangency.

13.2 It is difficult to substitute capital for labour in osteopathy, but all of the other activities provide opportunities for labour/capital substitution.

13.3 (a) All graduates earn more than non-graduates. Untrue.

(b) The higher the level of educational attainment the higher the lifetime earnings, *ceteris paribus*. This is true.

(c) Earnings and educational attainment are positively correlated but so are earnings and age. Also true.

(d) Earnings and gender are related. Also true.

(e) IQ influences educational attainment which in turn influences earnings. Therefore IQ determines earnings. Untrue because the word 'determines' is too strong. 'IQ influences earnings' would be a true statement.

Chapter 14

14.1 A Pareto optimal allocation of resources:
   (a) cannot be achieved under a planned system. Untrue, though the allocation of resources would have to mirror what would have been achieved under a market system.
   (b) is automatically achieved in a market system. Untrue, because of market failure.
   (c) is never achieved in reality. Probably true, for the same reason (market failure).
   (d) could be achieved if prices conveyed information about relative scarcities. Probably true.

14.2 Statements (b) and (c) are correct. The rest are incorrect.

14.3 Statement (c) is correct. People have to be free to choose whether to do business or not.

14.4 Statement (c) is correct. Although statement (b) may be factually correct it has got nothing to do with market failure.

14.5 *Guns*   *Butter*

    $MU = 20$ $MU = 17$

    $MC = 40$ $MC = 30$

    $MU/MC = 0.5 < MU/MC = 0.57$

Therefore resources should be transferred from guns to butter, increasing the utility of the last gun produced and reducing the utility of the last unit of butter. Response (a) is correct.

14.6 Statement (c) is correct. If statement (d) said '…which *may* not reflect social cost…' it would be correct. There is an important grain of truth in statement (e) too.

Chapter 15

15.1 'The nuclear power industry discharges a certain amount of radioactivity into the environment on a daily basis, particularly from its reprocessing plant at Sellafield. This can be called *operational pollution*. Occasionally, as a result of human error or machine breakdown there are accidents which result in the discharge of large amounts of radioactivity. This is *accidental pollution*.

15.2 raw sewage discharged into the sea – flow pollutant (biodegrades)
   discarded dry-cell batteries – stock pollutant

emissions from cars with catalytic converters – flow

noise from aircraft at Heathrow – flow

low level radioactive waste, e.g., clothing – flow, since it degrades, but only after a very long time and should therefore probably be treated as a stock.

Magnox power stations that have been closed down – similar to above.

15.3 Acid rain is caused by the burning of fossil fuels, particularly coal. The pollution is carried along by air currents in the upper atmosphere, falling to earth again in the form of weak acid, often many hundreds perhaps thousands of miles from the source.

The Rhine passes through a number of countries. Pollution discharged into the river upstream causes problems for other countries downstream.

15.4 Farmers around York have dug drainage ditches to allow water to flow off their fields more rapidly. This prevents their fields becoming waterlogged and helps the crops grow. But because the rainwater finds its way into the river more quickly, the carrying capacity of the river is now often exceeded and the river bursts its banks.

15.5 Two-stroke outboard motors are highly polluted and can damage sensitive inland lakes. CAC (outright banning) is a more straightforward policy and easier to administer and enforce than an MBI.

15.6 This was a 'green tax' because it would have helped to reduce CO_2 emissions (inasmuch as people reduced their use of fuel). But it was regressive because the poor – and particularly the elderly poor – spend a larger proportion of their income on heating than other households do.

Chapter 16

16.1 (a) The system of cash benefits has a marked equalizing effect on the distribution of incomes. The direct tax system is mildly progressive and the indirect tax system mildly regressive. Benefits in-kind have an equalizing effect.

16.2 The distribution of earnings is skewed to the right, which means that a small proportion of the population receives very high earnings, and the bulk of the population receives quite low earnings. The distribution of incomes is similarly skewed. The distribution of wealth is more unequal than the distribution of incomes, and more skewed to the right – remember Pen's *Parade of dwarfs … and a few giants.*

Chapter 17

17.1 free enterprise

free-market system

market mechanism

private enterprise

price system

capitalism

(you may not agree with this ordering)

planned economy
central planning
state planning
socialism
communism
command economy
(similarly, you may not agree with this)

17.2 Statement (a) is correct. All the rest are incorrect, apart from (f).
You could predict that the price of a nearly new Lada would exceed the price of a new one.

17.3 Static inefficiencies: resources were not allocated in a Pareto optimal way. Least-cost methods of production were not used because resources (factor inputs) did not command any price and were not purchased – rather they were allocated to enterprises on the basis of last year's allocations.
Dynamic inefficiencies: the system could not respond to changes in relative factor scarcities because there were no prices to act as signals of such scarcity.

17.4 Autarky: self-sufficiency.

Chapter 18

18.1 Unemployment benefit and supplementary benefit payments are transfers. The salaries of teachers, however, represent expenditure on goods and services. These would be included when calculating GDP whereas transfer payments would not. Similarly, one wishes to include the output of the social work 'industry' as part of the output of the economy (GDP). Since one cannot measure this directly, government statisticians take *inputs* to this industry to represent outputs – so the salaries of social workers would be included in GDP.

18.2 Television broadcasts are non-rival. If you tune in to watch *Neighbours* the signal strength is not diminished. The supply of *Neighbours* available to everyone else is not reduced.

Broadcasts are also non-excludable. In the UK you are supposed to purchase a receiving licence (costing £89.50 in 1997) if you have a TV. But in fact the TV works just as well if you don't have a licence. Legally, TV broadcasts are excludable, but they are intrinsically non-excludable. It is technically possible to make them excludable, by scrambling them, and forcing would-be consumers to purchase or rent a decoder.

The M1 motorway, like any public road, is non-excludable. You do not have to pay directly to use the road. Like any non-excludable good the M1 tends to suffer from over-use (congestion) since prices are not used to choke off excess demand. The M1 is non-rival when uncongested, but rival when congested. The presence of other road users reduces the utility that I get from the road, because it reduces my average speed.

The River Thames is non-excludable and rival and hence suffers from pollution since some users (upstream) are imposing costs on users downstream by using the river to discharge effluent etc. In recent years the legal system has been used to render it excludable (by prohibiting the discharge of certain wastes) and the level of pollution has fallen.

Incidentally, the Thames Barrier (a flood prevention scheme for London) is a classic non-excludable, non-rival public good. The tramps in Cardboard City are protected from flooding even though they pay no tax. How lucky they are.

McDonald's hamburgers are a pure, private good. If you don't pay, you don't get. And you cannot have mine because I've eaten it.

The pavement outside McDonald's is non-excludable and covered with hamburger wrappers.

Navigation buoys are non-excludable and non-rival. Like lighthouses, a classic public good. We all pay for them through our taxes.

18.4 It stresses the word *investment* merely because it is keen to present a favourable image. It used to use the term *spending on roads*, which was a more honest description. The distinction between consumption spending and investment spending is often difficult to make objectively.

Chapter 19

19.1 They were relatively capital-intensive industries who invested rather more than industry generally.

19.2 British Gas, the Regional Water Authorities, the Regional Electricity Companies, the National Grid, and Railtrack were (and remain) natural monopolies.

19.3 Only statement (a) is correct.

19.4 Statement (f), I'm afraid.

19.5 Statement (d) is correct.

Index